PROPERTIUS
ELEGIES
BOOK IV

PROPERTIUS
ELEGIES

BOOK IV

EDITED BY

W. A. CAMPS

*Fellow of Pembroke College and
Lecturer in Classics in the University of
Cambridge*

CAMBRIDGE
AT THE UNIVERSITY PRESS
1965

PUBLISHED BY

THE SYNDICS OF THE CAMBRIDGE UNIVERSITY PRESS

Bentley House, 200 Euston Road, London, N.W.1
American Branch: 32 East 57th Street, New York 22, N.Y.
West African Office: P.O. Box 33, Ibadan, Nigeria

©

CAMBRIDGE UNIVERSITY PRESS

1965

*Printed in Great Britain by Richard Clay and Company Ltd.,
Bungay, Suffolk*

PREFACE

This edition of Book IV of Propertius was conceived as a complement to my edition of Book I (C.U.P. 1961). Book IV represents, as does Book I, a distinct and interesting phase of the poet's activity. Between them, the two books span his career and exhibit the working of a remarkable poetic talent on contrasted subjects and in widely different emotional contexts.

In making this edition I have had indispensable help from books and friends. The books[1] principally used (apart from standard works of reference) have been the commentaries of Rothstein (1924) and Butler and Barber (1933), D. R. Shackleton Bailey's *Propertiana* (1956), and the Teubner edition with its useful ancillary material (Hosius–Schuster–Dornseiff 1958). The friends are the same who helped me with my edition of Book I, Mr Sandbach, Mr Wilkinson, Mr Lee and Sir Roger Mynors; with the addition this time of Professor Brink, who escaped my importunity earlier through his absence overseas. I must emphasize that their help has not been confined to the removal of errors: they have placed generously at my disposal learning which was beyond my own reach, and which is exploited in the notes below without separate acknowledgement.[2] For any misuse of their help, and for what else may be found wrong in this book, they are not responsible at all; nor is Mr R. D. Milns, to whose judgement and kindness I have become much indebted in the final stages of the work.

[1] I should like also here to mention with appreciation P. Grimal, *Les Intentions de Properce et la composition du livre 4 des Élégies* (1952), and Laura Celentano, *Significato e valore del 4 libro di Properzio* (1956).

[2] Except conjectures, which are attributed to their authors. The remarks of a friend quoted verbatim on p. 93 of my edition of Book I, in the introductory note to Elegy i, 20, have been commended by several reviewers; they will like to know that the friend was Mr A. G. Lee.

The text here printed is based on E. A. Barber's Oxford text of 1960; divergences from this are listed on pp. 7–8. The *apparatus criticus*, apart from a few details, has been excerpted bodily from the same edition, with the permission, here gratefully acknowledged, of the Delegates of the Clarendon Press. In accordance with the limited scope of the present work, the abridged *apparatus* records very few conjectures other than those adopted in the text or discussed in the notes; and where the text printed agrees with the reading of the Neapolitanus, the readings of other manuscripts are only occasionally shown: e.g. because possibly significant, or to illustrate a relationship between manuscripts. The result is without scientific value, but it may offer practical convenience to a reader who wishes, as he goes along, to be informed of the readings of the Neapolitanus (shown in the text if not in the *apparatus*) and to get some impression of the other branch of the tradition.

The text of Book IV is not in such bad condition that anyone need be discouraged from approaching it on that account. Only in one place is there any doubt about the division between elegies; only in two is there apparently extensive corruption; and only in three or four is there reason to think that a couplet needs to be transposed. But there are many problems of detail, affecting both text and interpretation, and due partly to the poet's idiosyncrasies of thought and language, partly to our imperfect knowledge of the background of daily life and speech which he shared with his readers, and partly to the fact that at least one manuscript in the succession through which the text has passed must have been notably hard for later copyists to decipher. Hence it often occurs that several reasonably founded possibilities are available, but no decisive probability; and in such cases full annotation may bewilder, while summary annotation may mislead. The present work is a compromise, with all the disadvantages which that involves. It is also a compromise in that it attempts to have regard to the conjectured needs or interests of a fairly wide range of readers, from the enterprising sixth-form boy to the classical schoolmaster or don whose special expertise lies in another field. It is designed as a reader's edition; and the purpose of the introduction and notes is to supply a minimum of information about the literary context of the elegies, and to try to elucidate (at the intellectual level) the sequence of the poet's ideas and the meaning of his language, as one condition of the enjoyment of the poetry. The poetry will be found in the poems themselves; and the reader must in fairness be warned not to look for it in my part of the book, which is dry stuff.

Professor Luck's new text of Propertius, with a highly readable translation and short but useful notes, appeared (Zurich, Artemis Verlag, 1964) when substantial changes in the present book were no longer economically possible; and so I have not, except in a few details, attempted to revise my text or interpretation in the light of Luck's, as I should else have wished to do. The area of agreement between us is very extensive, and I believe that it will be enlarged by further reflexion on my part. In a few places Luck has adopted conjectures which I had not recorded as available; a list of these will be found on p. 8, and should be regarded as addenda to the *apparatus criticus*.

I am equally sorry that Dr Tovar's Edition was not available to me in time for this book to profit from it.

CAMBRIDGE   W. A. C.

CONTENTS

INTRODUCTION

Book IV is the last known work of Propertius. The latest datable references in it are to events of 16 B.C., notably the submission of the Sygambri (IV, vi, 77) and the consulship of P. Cornelius Scipio (IV, xi, 66); and in both contexts it is implied that these events are recent. The latest event mentioned in the preceding Book III is the death of Marcellus in 23 or 22 B.C. If, as is probable, Propertius was born between 57 and 50 B.C.,[1] he will have been in his thirties when most of the elegies of Book IV were written. Whether any of them belongs to a date appreciably later than 16 B.C. we cannot know, though we may doubt it. We only know that by 2 A.D. Propertius was dead, since Ovid then (*Rem. Am.* 763) refers to him in the past tense.

The contents of the three previous books consist (with a few exceptions) of examples of personal love elegy. There is indeed observable within them a marked change of tone,[2] from the emotional glow which pervades Book I, written when the poet was in a state of chronically excited sensibility, to the more professional manner of Book III, in which much space is occupied by discourses on general topics (women's avarice, women's passions, the power of women, etc.) and discussion of the poet's achievement and intentions as an artist in love

[1] From I, xxii it appears that in 40 B.C. he was old enough to experience acute and lasting personal distress at the death (not witnessed) of a relative (remoter than father or brother) in the Perusine war. On the other hand from IV, i, 129-32 it appears that in the same year, 40 B.C., he was young enough to have only just (or not yet) assumed the *toga uirilis*, which he would do at an age most unlikely to be later than seventeen.

[2] There is also a marked change in the treatment of the ending of the pentameter. In Book I there are 127 pentameters which end in a word of more than two syllables; in Book III, which is rather longer, there are 11. (In Book IV, about as long as Book III, there are 6.)

poetry. But it is precisely on the status of love poet that he still insists in Book III, though in his insistence he makes it plain that he has been asked to attempt and has contemplated attempting other kinds of poetry, and at the end he professes to dismiss for good the woman, Cynthia, who had been his inspiration. Book IV marks a new departure. It begins with the announcement of a new subject: his talent is to be at the service of his country, and he will write on Roman themes. This promise is fulfilled in about half of the elegies which follow. Of the remainder, several have still some reference to the love theme and two of them refer specifically to Propertius' relations with Cynthia: but the treatment (see below) is now altogether different from that of the earlier books. Lastly, the relation between the poet and his material is also new; it has become objective. Whereas in the previous books the poet tells in his own person of his own feelings or opinions, the elegies of Book IV consist almost entirely of narrative, or of speeches put into the mouth of some character other than the poet. One influence on these character speeches has been that of the *prosopopoea*, an exercise in characterization that was practised in the schools of rhetoric.

Of the eleven elegies that compose the book three stand apart from the rest. The first, really a pair of separate but related poems, is introductory and imparts information about the poet's literary intentions and personal history. The eleventh (last in the book) is a funeral elegy for a lady of the Roman nobility,[1] the form of which is largely based on that of a forensic apologia, with *exordium, narratio, probatio, peroratio* as prescribed in the textbooks. The sixth elegy, which occupies the central place in the book, is in honour of Augustus, com-

[1] She was a Cornelia married to an Aemilius Paullus. Propertius must have enjoyed the patronage or friendship of people of high consequence at this time. It is notable however that he does not mention Maecenas at all in Book IV, after addressing him as patron in II, i and III, ix. Maecenas fell from Augustus' favour in 22 B.C.

memorating his victory at Actium.[1] This and the eleventh elegy are in a grander manner than the rest.

The remaining eight elegies fall into two groups of four apiece. Those of one group (iii, v, vii, viii) are a miscellany, but all in varying degrees related to the love theme which was the poet's earlier preoccupation. Those of the other group (ii, iv, ix, x) are 'aetiological' poems, purporting to relate the origins of some existing object or name or institution. The poems of the first group have contemporary subjects, and their treatment is realistic, recalling Greek mime or Roman satire. One of them is a genre anecdote (viii), the others are person-sketches, one of Cynthia (vii), the other two of types,[2] the Anxious Wife (iii) and the *Lena* (Go-Between) (v). This group is foreshadowed by the second half (i B) of the book's intro-ductory elegy, a study of a genre figure, the Astrologer, who prophesies the poet's continued subjection to love. The aetiological poems of the other group are introduced by the first half (i A) of the same introductory elegy, in which the poet imagines the site of Rome in pre-Roman days and the condi-tions of life in the city's infancy, and promises to serve his country by telling of *sacra diesque...et cognomina prisca loco-rum*. These aetiological elegies (partly inspired by Tib. II, v and Virg. *Aen.* VIII, 306ff.) are intended to be a Latin counter-part to the celebrated *Aitia* of Callimachus, which was, like them, a collection, and in elegiac metre. Here Propertius is 'serving his country' in more ways than one: he honours Rome both by writing about Roman antiquities, and also by providing Latin literature with an equivalent, in this new department, to

---

[1] Elegy vi is also, formally, an aetiological poem, and can be classified with the poems of that group; for it presents the story of Actium as 'origin' of the temple of Apollo on the Palatine (cf. lines 11 and 67). I have treated it separately here because it plainly differs from the other aetiological poems in the collection as being a court poem, on a contemporary subject, and in a grander manner.

[2] The status of Elegy iii is conjectural. Some may prefer to regard it as a portrait of a real person under a fictitious name.

3

one of the masterpieces of Greek literature. He is the ' Roman Callimachus ' (IV, i, 64) in the same way as Virgil is the Roman Theocritus and Hesiod and Homer, Horace the Roman Archilochus and Alcaeus, etc.

Aetiology was a characteristically Hellenistic interest. So was genre. These broad resemblances apart, Hellenistic example is also apparent in a number of motives in the settings of the elegies of this book. Such are: the poet as guide to a visitor (IV, i, 1 and cf. Catull. IV, 1, no doubt after a Hellenistic precedent); the mentor who warns the poet against attempting a certain kind of poetry (IV, i, 71 ff. and cf. Callimachus' Prologue to his *Aitia*); the statue of the god that imparts information about itself (IV, ii, 1 ff. and cf. Callimachus *Iambi* 7 and 9); the curse poem (IV, v, 1 ff. and cf. Callimachus' lost *Ibis* and its Ovidian descendant); the poet as officiant in a ceremony (IV, vi, 1 and cf. Callimachus' *Hymn to Apollo*); the dead person who speaks from the tomb (cf. IV, i, 1 ff. and many Hellenistic grave epigrams such as—again Callimachus—*Anth. Pal.* VII, 525).

There is also apparent in this book a relationship with certain passages of Virgil and Tibullus, who died in or about 19 B.C., after (probably) the completion of Book III[1] and before the completion of this one. Thus in Elegy v we have a curse pronounced on a *lena*, described as commanding a witch's power and as advising on the arts of love. Here we have a combination of motives which occur separately in Tibullus, e.g. at 1, v, 49 ff., 1, ii, 42 ff. and 1, iv, 23 ff. In Elegy i A the poet imagines the pastoral scene that once was where Rome now stands and refers to a Sibylline prophecy of Rome's foundation. This combination of motives shows that Tibullus II, v, 19 ff. has suggested part of the background of this elegy, as perhaps it has also the references to the former state of the Velabrum in IV, ii, 8 ff. and IV, ix, 5. The conception of

---

[1] See introductory note to elegy iii below.

Elegy iA has also been influenced by the account of Aeneas at the site of Rome in Virgil *Aen*. VIII, 306ff., where again the pastoral scene is described (*Aen*. VIII, 360), and the contrast between past and present is conveyed through a review of Roman landmarks with notable associations. It is important to note that these affinities with Tibullus and Virgil consist only in the adoption of certain general motives; in the application of these to their contexts, and in the detailed development of them, Propertius is completely and no doubt deliberately independent. Likewise, when in Elegy ix he touches on the story of Hercules and Cacus he seems deliberately to avoid any coincidence with *Aeneid* VIII, 185ff.; and when in Elegy vi he describes the battle of Actium he succeeds, despite the coincidence of subject, in avoiding repetition of any feature of the Virgilian treatment in *Aeneid* VIII, 675ff. except a couple of purely aural echoes in lines 23 and 29 (see notes on the elegy below).

When Propertius was writing this book, Ovid (born 43 B.C.) was in his twenties. The correspondence between some of its contents and some works of Ovid is obvious: the letter in verse from woman to absent man (IV, iii) brings to mind Ovid's *Heroides*, and the aetiological poems on Roman antiquities bring to mind Ovid's *Fasti*. As far as concerns the aetiological poems, there is no doubt that Propertius here set the example for Ovid, for the *Fasti* came relatively late (cf. *Trist*. II, 549 ff.) in the series of Ovid's works. The other relationship could in theory be accounted for by Ovidian influence on Propertius; but considering the relative ages of the two, and Propertius' insistence (e.g. in III, i, 12 ff. and IV, i, 64 and 136) on his status as an innovator and example to others, it is more natural to suppose that here too Ovid is the pupil and Propertius the originator. This is not incompatible with Ovid's claim, made with reference to the *Heroides*, that (A.A. III, 346) *ignotum hoc aliis ille nouauit opus*; for the idea of a letter in verse is in itself a less distinctive innovation than the idea of attributing such letters to a collection of the heroines of legend.

Because the elegies composing it differ so widely in subject and emotional content, Book IV illustrates very well the range of the poet's talent. It also illustrates well the tendency of his thought to shape itself in emphatically visible or audible images: e.g. in the soliloquy of Tarpeia (IV, iv, 31–66), or the speech of the dead Cynthia (IV, vii, 13–94). The diction is characterized by strongly significant single words (e.g. IV, i, 22 *macrae*; IV, vii, 15 *uigilacis*; IV, viii, 55 *fulminat*; IV, xi, 86 *cauta*), and comprehensively significant phrases (e.g. IV, iv, 67 *incerto permisit bracchia somno*; IV, v, 67 *uidi ego rugoso tussim concrescere collo*; IV, xi, 3 *cum semel infernas intrarunt funera leges*). The co-operation of sound with meaning is perfectly exemplified in the lines evocative of ruined Veii (IV, x, 27–30), which contrast strangely, and no doubt designedly, with the manner of the rest of the elegy in which they are set. But to attempt an assessment of Propertius' poetic gift is outside my present purpose. I have had moreover to leave the reader to construct for himself the context of elegy vii, since I have not so far been able to find a construction of my own in which I could feel confidence.

In the arrangement of the elegies within the book a concern for order is apparent, and this will be found to be true also of the disposition of the matter in the individual elegies themselves, though the fact in a few places has been obscured by accidental dislocation of the text in transmission and in others by temporarily disconcerting features such as the parenthesis in IV, i, 38–54, the postscript in the last four lines of IV, ix, and the shift of conception that takes place in IV, xi between lines 1 and 19.

VARIANTS FROM THE
OXFORD TEXT (1960)

i, 4 concubuere   9 quot...sustulit!   18 *semicolon at end of line*   19 celebrata   33 paruae   36 hinc ubi   38 pudet   45 hinc...*and semicolon at end of line*   57 conor *after* 68 *insert* 87–8   93 Lupercus eques, dum   101 'Iunoni facito: uotum impetrabile' dixi   125 Asisi   134 *colon at end of line*   135 'at tu...   138...hostis eris.'   141 discusseris   142...suo

ii, 3 Tuscus ego: Tuscis orior: 10–11 *no lacuna*   12 credis id esse sacrum?   28 corbis in   35 specie   37 sub petaso   49 haec tu

iii, 10 tunsus et...discolor   11 pactae tum mihi   34 in chlamydas uellera lecta tuas   48 astricto in   51 nunc purpura   56 toro

iv, 1 Tarpeium scelus et   7 hunc Tatius contra...*and remove comma at end of line*   13 Curia, saepta.   34 conspicer esse Tati   55 sic hospes patria metuar regina sub aula: 59 soluere nupta: 83 *remove daggers and put colon at end of line*   88 petit, quem uelit ipse, diem.   93 Tarpeium...cognomen

v, 55–6 *quote-marks instead of square brackets*   58 aere   64 ossa mihi   65–6 *no transposition, and no brackets; colon at end of 66*

vi, 28 non tulit   36 deae   45 Latinos   72 blanditaeque   74 perque

vii, 34 cado?   36 bibi;   37 ut Nomas arcanas tollat uersuta saliuas,   57 una...uehit, aut ea Cressae   69 sanamus   79 pone hederam   80 mollis...alliget

viii, 2 *semicolon at end of line*   3 *before this line insert* 19–20; *at its end, change comma to semicolon*   4 sicubi, tam rarae non perit hora morae;   39 crotalistria Phyllis,   40 et facilis   41 Magnus   45 secundam   50 Lares   78 sudet   84 suffiit, ac

ix, 35 fontis egens erro, circaque   42 *lacuna*   65–6 *trans-*

pose to precede 43   67 *insert single quote mark at beginning of line*   72 Sance   74 sanctum

x, 23–4 *no transposition*   42 euectis

xi, 8 euersos   19 uindex   20 iudicet   21 assideant fratres, iuxta Minoia sella, et   39† . . . proaui stimulantem pectus Achilli   48 ne possis   53 uel cui, iusta suos cum   70 fata   102   aquis

ADDENDA TO THE APPARATUS CRITICUS

Readings not shown in text or otherwise which are recommended by G. Luck in his edition of 1964

i, 81–2 (et fallitur auro Iuppiter) *dist. Luck*   117 delige *Bailey*

iv, 48 tum *Rossberg*   55 sin *Phillimore*

v, 19–20 exornabat (ς) opus uerbis ceu blanda pererrat (*Wakker*) saxosamque forat (*Rossberg*) sedula gutta (*Jacob*) uiam   40 dentibus alterius *Heinsius*

vii, 2 exstinctos *Passerat*

viii, 4 huc, ubi *Haupt-Vahlen edn.*   10 raditur Cornelissen

ix, 11 manifestaque *Luck*   21 torret (ς)   35 circa antra *Burmann*

x, 41 Brenno ς   42 e Raetis *Alton*   43 illi . . . iaculanti ante agmina *Kraffert*

xi, 93 lenire *Schrader*

SIGLA

N=codex Neapolitanus, nunc Guelferbytanus Gudianus 224.
      circa annum 1200 scriptus
F=codex Laurentianus plut. 36. 49. circa annum 1380 scriptus
L=codex Holkhamicus 333. anno 1421 scriptus
P=codex Parisinus 7989. anno 1423 scriptus
D=codex Dauentriensis 1. 82 (olim 1792). saec. XV
V=codex Ottoboniano-Vaticanus 1514. saec. XV
$Vo.$=codex Leidensis Vossianus 117. saec. XV
Δ=consensus codd. $D\ V\ Vo.$
μ=codex Parisinus 8233, siue Memmianus. anno 1465 scrip-
      tus
π=codex Parisinus 8458. saec. XV
υ=codex Vaticanus Vrbinas 641. saec. XV
O=codicum consensus $NFLPDVVo.$
ς=codices deteriores

scito, lector, ex multis quae exstant codicum lectionibus et
uirorum doctorum coniecturis paucas admodum in apparatu
ostendi.

SEXTI PROPERTI ELEGIARVM
LIBER QVARTVS

I A

'Hoc quodcumque uides, hospes, qua maxima Roma est,
    ante Phrygem Aenean collis et herba fuit;
atque ubi Nauali stant sacra Palatia Phoebo,
    Euandri profugae concubuere boues.

fictilibus creuere deis haec aurea templa,   5
    nec fuit opprobrio facta sine arte casa;
Tarpeiusque pater nuda de rupe tonabat,
    et Tiberis nostris aduena bubus erat.

quot gradibus domus ista Remi se sustulit! olim
    unus erat fratrum maxima regna focus.   10

Curia, praetexto quae nunc nitet alta senatu,
    pellitos habuit, rustica corda, Patres.

bucina cogebat priscos ad uerba Quiritis:
    centum illi in prato saepe senatus erat.

nec sinuosa cauo pendebant uela theatro,   15
    pulpita sollemnis non oluere crocos.

nulli cura fuit externos quaerere diuos,
    cum tremeret patrio pendula turba sacro;

annuaque accenso celebrata Parilia faeno,
    qualia nunc curto lustra nouantur equo.   20

Vesta coronatis pauper gaudebat asellis,
    ducebant macrae uilia sacra boues.

parua saginati lustrabant compita porci,
    pastor et ad calamos exta litabat ouis.

---

1 qua *Scioppius*: quam *O*   8 bubus *NF4V2Vo*.: tutus *F1L*, *P primo*,
DV1   9 quot (quo *Ries*). . . . sustulit! *Dieterich*: Quo *FLP* Δ: Quod *N*:
Qua *5δ*   14 prati saepe (= *saepto*) *Heinsius*   19 celebrata *Phillimore*:
celebrate *D*: celebrare *cett*.: celebrante *Housman*   palilia Δ   21 Vesta
F?, *P corr*., Δ: Vestra *NF1L*, *P primo*

uerbera pellitus saetosa mouebat arator,   25
    unde licens Fabius sacra Lupercus habet.
nec rudis infestis miles radiabat in armis:
    miscebant usta proelia nuda sude.
prima galeritus posuit praetoria Lycmon,
    magnaque pars Tatio rerum erat inter ouis.   30
hinc Tities Ramnesque uiri Luceresque Soloni,
    quattuor hinc albos Romulus egit equos.
quippe suburbanae paruae minus urbe Bouillae
    et, qui nunc nulli, maxima turba Gabi.
et stetit Alba potens, albae suis omine nata,   35
    hinc ubi Fidenas longa erat isse uia.
nil patrium nisi nomen habet Romanus alumnus:
    sanguinis altricem non pudet esse lupam.
huc melius profugos misisti, Troia, Penatis;
    heu quali uecta est Dardana puppis aue!   40
iam bene spondebant tunc omina, quod nihil illam
    laeserat abiegni uenter apertus equi,
cum pater in nati trepidus ceruice pependit,
    et uerita est umeros urere flamma pios.
hinc animi uenere Deci Brutique secures;   45
    uexit et ipsa sui Caesaris arma Venus,
arma resurgentis portans uictricia Troiae:
    felix terra tuos cepit, Iule, deos;
si modo Auernalis tremulae cortina Sibyllae
    dixit Auentino rura pianda Remo,   50
aut si Pergameae sero rata carmina uatis
    longaeuum ad Priami uera fuere caput:
"uertite equum, Danai! male uincitis! Ilia tellus
    uiuet, et huic cineri Iuppiter arma dabit."

28 nuda N: facta plerique   29 lygmon N: ligmon plerique   30 tacito N
31 titiens et sim. O: corr. ς   soloni N: coloni plerique   33 paruae ς,
Passerat: parua O   Bouillae Itali: uiol(a)e O   36 hinc ubi Ritschl: Hac
ubi O   longa . . . via ς: longe . . . uias O   isse N: ire FLPDV1
38 pudet P: putet codd. plerique   45 hinc Heinsius: tunc codd.

optima nutricum nostris lupa Martia rebus,   55
    qualia creuerunt moenia lacte tuo!
moenia namque pio conor disponere uersu:
    ei mihi, quod nostro est paruus in ore sonus!
sed tamen exiguo quodcumque e pectore riui
    fluxerit, hoc patriae seruiet omne meae.   60
Ennius hirsuta cingat sua dicta corona:
    mi folia ex hedera porrige, Bacche, tua,
ut nostris tumefacta superbiat Vmbria libris,
    Vmbria Romani patria Callimachi!
scandentis quisquis cernit de uallibus arces,   65
    ingenio muros aestimet ille meo!
Roma, faue, tibi surgit opus, date candida ciues
    omina, et inceptis dextera cantet auis!   68
dicam: "Troia, cades, et Troica Roma resurges;"   87
    et maris et terrae longa sepulcra canam;   88
sacra diesque canam et cognomina prisca locorum: 69
    has meus ad metas sudet oportet equus.'   70

I B

'QVO ruis imprudens, uage, dicere fata, Properti?
    non sunt a dextro condita fila colo.
accersis lacrimas cantans, auersus Apollo:
    poscis ab inuita uerba pigenda lyra.
certa feram certis auctoribus, aut ego uates   75
    nescius aerata signa mouere pila.
me creat Archytae suboles Babylonius Orops
    Horon, et a proauo ducta Conone domus.
di mihi sunt testes non degenerasse propinquos,

57 conor ⊊: coner O   60 seruiat ⊊   65 quisquis N (? ex corr.), DV1:
quasuis F1L: siquis P in ras., V2Vo.: asis in mg. F4, µv   66 (a)estimet
NLVo.: extimet FPDV   87–8 huc post 68 transposuit Marcilius, post 70
Scaliger   88 longa pericla ⊊   71 sqq. separabant iam Itali, continuant
codd.   71 caue Schippers   discere ⊊   73 cantans Baehrens: cantas O
75 haud ⊊   79 Dic N

inque meis libris nil prius esse fide.   80

nunc pretium fecere deos et (fallitur auro
   Iuppiter) obliquae signa iterata rotae,
felicesque Iouis stellas Martisque rapaces
   et graue Saturni sidus in omne caput;
quid moueant Pisces animosaque signa Leonis,   85
   lotus et Hesperia quid Capricornus aqua.   86
dixi ego, cum geminos produceret Arria natos   89
   (illa dabat natis arma uetante deo):   90
non posse ad patrios sua pila referre Penatis:
   nempe meam firmant nunc duo busta fidem.

quippe Lupercus eques, dum saucia protegit ora,
   heu sibi prolapso non bene cauit equo;
Gallus at, in castris dum credita signa tuetur,   95
   concidit ante aquilae rostra cruenta suae:
fatales pueri, duo funera matris auarae!
   uera, sed inuito, contigit ista fides.

idem ego, cum Cinarae traheret Lucina dolores,
   et facerent uteri pondera lenta moram,   100
"Iunoni facito: uotum impetrabile" dixi:
   illa parit: libris est data palma meis!

hoc neque harenosum Libyae Iouis explicat antrum,
   aut sibi commissos fibra locuta deos,
aut si quis motas cornicis senserit alas,   105
   umbraue quae magicis mortua prodit aquis:
aspicienda uia est caeli uerusque per astra
   trames, et ab zonis quinque petenda fides.

exemplum graue erit Calchas: namque Aulide soluit
   ille bene haerentis ad pia saxa ratis;   110

81–2 *dist. Schippers, Tyrrell*   81 In *F1LPDV1*   deos et fallimus a.
(Iuppiter!) obl. *Housman*   83 rapacis (cap–*F*) *O corr.* ͻ   85 moneant
LDV1   86 qui *N*   87–8 *post* 68 *Marcilius, post* 70 *Scaliger*   93 eques
Heinsius: equi *codd.*   101 Iunoni ͻ: Iunonis *O*   facito *Lachmann* (uotum
facito *iam Burman*): facite *O*   dist. *Reitzenstein*   103 libyci ͻ   104 At
FLP1DV1   106 Vmbrane quę *N*: Vmbraque ne *FLPDV*: corr. *Turnebus*
107 uarusque *Palmer*

14

idem Agamemnoniae ferrum ceruice puellae
    tinxit, et Atrides uela cruenta dedit;
nec rediere tamen Danai: tu diruta fletum
    supprime et Euboicos respice, Troia, sinus!
Nauplius ultores sub noctem porrigit ignis,   115
    et natat exuuiis Graecia pressa suis.
uictor Oiliade, rape nunc et dilige uatem,
    quam uetat auelli ueste Minerua sua!
hactenus historiae: nunc ad tua deuehar astra;
    incipe tu lacrimis aequus adesse nouis.   120
Vmbria te notis antiqua Penatibus edit—
    mentior? an patriae tangitur ora tuae?—
qua nebulosa cauo rorat Meuania campo,
    et lacus aestiuis intepet Vmber aquis,
scandentisque Asisi consurgit uertice murus,   125
    murus ab ingenio notior ille tuo.
ossaque legisti non illa aetate legenda
    patris et in tenuis cogeris ipse lares:
nam tua cum multi uersarent rura iuuenci,
    abstulit excultas pertica tristis opes.   130
mox ubi bulla rudi dimissa est aurea collo,
    matris et ante deos libera sumpta toga,
tum tibi pauca suo de carmine dictat Apollo
    et uetat insano uerba tonare Foro:
"at tu finge elegos, fallax opus: haec tua castra!— 135
    scribat ut exemplo cetera turba tuo.
militiam Veneris blandis patiere sub armis,
    et Veneris pueris utilis hostis eris."
nam tibi uictrices quascumque labore parasti,
    eludit palmas una puella tuas: 140
et bene cum fixum mento discusseris uncum,

---

123 Quam *O, corr.* ⛿   125 Asisi *Lachmann*: asis *NF* (Asis *in mg. F?*),
LP1: axis *in mg. pro u.l. P2*, Δ   133 tibi *om. N*   135–8 *Apollini dat*
Luetjohann, astrologo alii edd.   140 Eludet ⛿   141 confixum *O*,
corr. ⛿   discusseris ⛿: discusserit *O*: decusseris *Broekhuyzen*

nil erit hoc: rostro te premet ansa suo.
illius arbitrio noctem lucemque uidebis:
　　gutta quoque ex oculis non nisi iussa cadet.
nec mille excubiae nec te signata iuuabunt　　145
　　limina: persuasae fallere rima sat est.
nunc tua uel mediis puppis luctetur in undis,
　　uel licet armatis hostis inermis eas,
uel tremefacta cauo tellus diducat hiatum:
　　octipedis Cancri terga sinistra time!'　　150

II

QVI mirare meas tot in uno corpore formas,
　　accipe Vertumni signa paterna dei.
Tuscus ego: Tuscis orior: nec paenitet inter
　　proelia Volsinios deseruisse focos.
haec me turba iuuat, nec templo laetor eburno:　　5
　　Romanum satis est posse uidere Forum.
hac quondam Tiberinus iter faciebat, et aiunt
　　remorum auditos per uada pulsa sonos:
at postquam ille suis tantum concessit alumnis,
　　Vertumnus uerso dicor ab amne deus.　　10
seu, quia uertentis fructum praecepimus anni,
　　Vertumni rursus credis id esse sacrum?
prima mihi uariat liuentibus uua racemis,
　　et coma lactenti spicea fruge tumet;
hic dulcis cerasos, hic autumnalia pruna　　15
　　cernis et aestiuo mora rubere die;

142 rostro π, *Calderinus*: nostro *O*　　premat *NLP*Δ: premit *F*: *corr.* ς　　ausa
O, *corr. Calderinus*　　suo *plerique*: tuo *N*　　144 quoque *N*: quidem
plerique　　non] nunc *N*　　146 Limina *P corr.*, *V2Vo.*: Lumina *cett.*
rima *Beroaldus*: prima *NF4LP*Δ: *om. F1*
II　　1 Qui ς: Quid *O*　　2 paterna *NF4V2Vo.*: petenda *cett.*　　regna paterna
Housman　　3 et *post* ego *add.* ς　　5 me *P*Δ: mea *NFL*　　10 *post* hunc *u.*
duo uu. excidisse putat Barber　　11 uertentes *N* praecerpimus *Fea*　　12 credis
id *Postgate*: credidit *O*: creditur ς: creditis *Merkel*

insitor hic soluit pomosa uota corona,
    cum pirus inuito stipite mala tulit.
mendax fama, noces: alius mihi nominis index:
    de se narranti tu modo crede deo.   20
opportuna mea est cunctis natura figuris:
    in quamcumque uoles uerte, decorus ero.
indue me Cois, fiam non dura puella:
    meque uirum sumpta quis neget esse toga?
da falcem et torto frontem mihi comprime faeno: 25
    iurabis nostra gramina secta manu.
arma tuli quondam et, memini, laudabar in illis:
    corbis in imposito pondere messor eram.
sobrius ad lites: at cum est imposta corona,
    clamabis capiti uina subisse meo.   30
cinge caput mitra, speciem furabor Iacchi;
    furabor Phoebi, si modo plectra dabis.
cassibus impositis uenor: sed harundine sumpta
    fautor plumoso sum deus aucupio.
est etiam aurigae specie Vertumnus, et eius   35
    traicit alterno qui leue pondus equo.
sub petaso piscis calamo praedabor, et ibo
    mundus demissis institor in tunicis.
pastor me ad baculum possum curuare, uel idem
    sirpiculis medio puluere ferre rosam.   40
nam quid ego adiciam, de quo mihi maxima fama est,
    hortorum in manibus dona probata meis?
caeruleus cucumis tumidoque cucurbita uentre
    me notat et iunco brassica uincta leui;

---

19 noces *NF4V2*: uoces *F1LPVo.*: uaces *DV1*   26 secta *NVo.*: facta
cett.   28 Corbis in *NV2Vo.*: Corbis *FLP*: Corbis ab *DV1*: Corbis et *ϛ*
31 achei(y) *O, corr. ϛ*   34 fautor *Rossberg*: Fauor *N*: Fauuor *F1*:
Faunor *F4L*: Faunus *F4 Δ*: Fauon (?) *in ras. P*   35 specie *Heinsius*: species
codd.   et elus *O, corr. ϛ*   37 sub petaso *uid. W. R. Smyth in C.R.* 1948,
p. 14: Suppat hoc *N*: Suppetat hoc *cett.*   hic *Heinsius*   39 pastor me
Ayrmann: Pastorem *O*   curare *O, corr. ϛ*   44 necat *F1LPDV1*   iunco
LPΔ: uinco *NF4*: uinci *F1*   iuncta *FLPVo.*

nec flos ullus hiat pratis, quin ille decenter   45
  impositus fronti langueat ante meae.
at mihi, quod formas unus uertebar in omnis,
  nomen ab euentu patria lingua dedit;
haec tu, Roma, meis tribuisti praemia Tuscis,
  (unde hodie Vicus nomina Tuscus habet),   50
tempore quo sociis uenit Lycomedius armis
  atque Sabina feri contudit arma Tati.
uidi ego labentis acies et tela caduca,
  atque hostis turpi terga dedisse fugae.
sed facias, diuum Sator, ut Romana per aeuum   55
  transeat ante meos turba togata pedes.
sex superant uersus: te, qui ad uadimonia curris,
  non moror: haec spatiis ultima creta meis.
stipes acernus eram, properanti falce dolatus,
  ante Numam grata pauper in urbe deus.   60
at tibi, Mamurri, formae caelator aenae,
  tellus artifices ne terat Osca manus,
qui me tam docilis potuisti fundere in usus.
  unum opus est, operi non datur unus honos.

III

Haec Arethusa suo mittit mandata Lycotae,
  cum totiens absis, si potes esse meus.
si qua tamen tibi lecturo pars oblita derit,
  haec erit e lacrimis facta litura meis:
aut si qua incerto fallet te littera tractu,   5
  signa meae dextrae iam morientis erunt.
te modo uiderunt iteratos Bactra per ortus,

49 haec *scripsi*: Et *NV2*: At *cett.*   52 contudit *N*: contulit *cett.*   59
Stipes *DV1*: Stipis *cett.*   63 Qui *NF*: Quod *LPDV*   tot docilem *Hertz-
berg olim*
III   1 H(a)ec aret(h)usa *PDV*: Haret(h)usa *NFL*   7 blactra *F1L, P primo,
DV1*   bactra per ortus *om. N*

te modo munito Sericus hostis equo,
hibernique Getae, pictoque Britannia curru,
    tunsus et Eoa discolor Indus aqua.   10
haecne marita fides et pactae tum mihi noctes,
    cum rudis urgenti bracchia uicta dedi?
quae mihi deductae fax omen praetulit, illa
    traxit ab euerso lumina nigra rogo;
et Stygio sum sparsa lacu, nec recta capillis   15
    uitta data est: nupsi non comitante deo.
omnibus heu portis pendent mea noxia uota:
    texitur haec castris quarta lacerna tuis.
occidat, immerita qui carpsit ab arbore uallum
    et struxit querulas rauca per ossa tubas,   20
dignior obliquo funem qui torqueat Ocno,
    aeternusque tuam pascat, aselle, famem!
dic mihi, num teneros urit lorica lacertos?
    num grauis imbellis atterit hasta manus?
haec noceant potius, quam dentibus ulla puella   25
    det mihi plorandas per tua colla notas!
diceris et macie uultum tenuasse: sed opto
    e desiderio sit color iste meo.
at mihi cum noctes induxit uesper amaras,
    si qua relicta iacent, osculor arma tua;   30
tum queror in toto non sidere pallia lecto,
    lucis et auctores non dare carmen auis.
noctibus hibernis castrensia pensa laboro
    et Tyria in chlamydas uellera lecta tuas;
et disco, qua parte fluat uincendus Araxes,   35

---

8 munitus *O, corr. Beroaldus*   Sericus *Beroaldus*: hericus *NF1LPV2Vo.*:
Neuricus *Jacob*   9 pictoque]-que *om. F1LP*   Briantia *Postgate*: Hyrcania
Housman   10 tusus (= tunsus) *Housman*: ustus *codd.*   discolor *O*:
decolor *ς, Passerat*   11 pactae tum mihi *Shilleto*: parce auia *N*: pacat(a)e
mihi *FL*: pact(a)e iam mihi *PVo.*   19 quae *N*   23 Num *P corr., V2*:
Dum *cett.*   34 chlamydas . . . tuas *Barber olim*: gladios *O*: clauos *ς,
Passerat*   lecta *Heinsius*: secta *O*   suos *O*: tuos *Passerat*: suo *Rossberg* (*a
suendo*)

quot sine aqua Parthus milia currat equus;
cogor et e tabula pictos ediscere mundos,
　　qualis et haec docti sit positura dei,
quae tellus sit lenta gelu, quae putris ab aestu,
　　uentus in Italiam qui bene uela ferat.　　　　　　　40
assidet una soror, curis et pallida nutrix
　　peierat hiberni temporis esse moras.
felix Hippolyte! nuda tulit arma papilla
　　et texit galea barbara molle caput.
Romanis utinam patuissent castra puellis!　　　　　45
　　essem militiae sarcina fida tuae,
nec me tardarent Scythiae iuga, cum Pater altas
　　astricto in glaciem frigore nectit aquas.
omnis amor magnus, sed aperto in coniuge maior:
　　hanc Venus, ut uiuat, uentilat ipsa facem.　　　　50
nam mihi quo Poenis nunc purpura fulgeat ostris
　　crystallusque meas ornet aquosa manus?
omnia surda tacent, rarisque assueta kalendis
　　uix aperit clausos una puella Lares,
Craugidos et catulae uox est mihi grata querentis:　55
　　illa tui partem uindicat una toro.
flore sacella tego, uerbenis compita uelo,
　　et crepat ad ueteres herba Sabina focos.
siue in finitimo gemuit stans noctua tigno,
　　seu uoluit tangi parca lucerna mero,　　　　　　　60
illa dies hornis caedem denuntiat agnis,
　　succinctique calent ad noua lucra popae.
ne, precor, ascensis tanti sit gloria Bactris,
　　raptaue odorato carbasa lina duci,
plumbea cum tortae sparguntur pondera fundae,　　65

36 Quod *N*　　37 conor *Broekhuyzen*　　41 *post* curis *dist. N*　　42 deierat
Liuineius　　48 astricto *Rothstein*: Affricus *siue* Africus *codd.*: acrius *Postgate*
51 nunc *Housman*: ter *Palmer*: te *N*: tibi *cett.*　　52 meas *N*: tuas *cett.*
55 Craugidos *Bergk*: Graucidos *uel* Grancidos *O*: Glaucidos *Puccius, Scaliger*
56 toro *O*: tori *V2*　　62 Succin(c)t(a)eque *O, corr. Itali*

subdolus et uersis increpat arcus equis!
sed (tua sic domitis Parthae telluris alumnis
   pura triumphantis hasta sequatur equos)
incorrupta mei conserua foedera lecti!
   hac ego te sola lege redisse uelim: 70
armaque cum tulero portae uotiua Capenae,
   subscribam SALVO GRATA PVELLA VIRO.

IV

TARPEIVM scelus et Tarpeiae turpe sepulcrum
   fabor et antiqui limina capta Iouis.
lucus erat felix hederoso conditus antro,
   multaque natiuis obstrepit arbor aquis,
Siluani ramosa domus, quo dulcis ab aestu   5
   fistula poturas ire iubebat ouis.
hunc Tatius contra uallo praecingit acerno
   fidaque suggesta castra coronat humo.
quid tum Roma fuit, tubicen uicina Curetis
   cum quateret lento murmure saxa Iouis?   10
atque ubi nunc terris dicuntur iura subactis,
   stabant Romano pila Sabina Foro.
murus erant montes: ubi nunc est Curia, saepta.
   bellicus ex illo fonte bibebat equus.
hinc Tarpeia deae fontem libauit: at illi   15
   urgebat medium fictilis urna caput.
et satis una malae potuit mors esse puellae,
   quae uoluit flammas fallere, Vesta, tuas?
uidit harenosis Tatium proludere campis
   pictaque per flauas arma leuare iubas: 20
obstipuit regis facie et regalibus armis,
   interque oblitas excidit urna manus.

IV 1 scelus *Krafffert*: nemus *codd.*   7 contra *scripsi*: fontem *codd.*   10
saxa *NF4, P corr. et P2, V2Vo.*: facta *F1L, P primo, DV1*   12 foro *F4, in
mg. P2, V2*: foco *O*   13 Curia, saepta *dist. Castalio*: Curia saepta, *multi*

saepe illa immeritae causata est omina lunae,
　　et sibi tingendas dixit in amne comas:
saepe tulit blandis argentea lilia Nymphis,　　　　　25
　　Romula ne faciem laederet hasta Tati:
dumque subit primo Capitolia nubila fumo,
　　rettulit hirsutis bracchia secta rubis,
et sua Tarpeia residens ita fleuit ab arce
　　uulnera, uicino non patienda Ioui:　　　　　　30
'Ignes castrorum et Tatiae praetoria turmae
　　et formosa oculis arma Sabina meis,
o utinam ad uestros sedeam captiua Penatis,
　　dum captiua mei conspicer esse Tati!
Romani montes, et montibus addita Roma,　　　　　35
　　et ualeat probro Vesta pudenda meo:
ille equus, ille meos in castra reponet amores,
　　cui Tatius dextras collocat ipse iubas!
quid mirum in patrios Scyllam saeuisse capillos,
　　candidaque in saeuos inguina uersa canis?　　　40
prodita quid mirum fraterni cornua monstri,
　　cum patuit lecto stamine torta uia?
quantum ego sum Ausoniis crimen factura puellis,
　　improba uirgineo lecta ministra foco!
Pallados exstinctos si quis mirabitur ignis,　　　45
　　ignoscat: lacrimis spargitur ara meis.
cras, ut rumor ait, tota potabitur urbe:
　　tu cape spinosi rorida terga iugi.
lubrica tota uia est et perfida: quippe tacentis
　　fallaci celat limite semper aquas.　　　　　　50
o utinam magicae nossem cantamina Musae!
　　haec quoque formoso lingua tulisset opem.

30 compatienda *FL*, *P primo*, *DV1*　　32 formosa *Δ*: famosa *cett.*　　34
esse *NFLPDV1*: ora *Gronouius*　　37 reponat *Puccius*　　38 dextra *P2*, *ς*
39 secuisse (*om.* in) *nescioquis*　　40 foedos *Heinsius*　　47 potabitur *Palmer*,
Rossberg: pugnabitur *O*: purgabitur *ς*: pigrabitur *Housman*　　50 semper]
caespes *Palmer*

te toga picta decet, non quem sine matris honore
    nutrit inhumanae dura papilla lupae.
sic hospes patria metuar regina sub aula: 55
    dos tibi non humilis prodita Roma uenit.
si minus, at raptae ne sint impune Sabinae,
    me rape et alterna lege repende uices!
commissas acies ego possum soluere nupta:
    uos medium palla foedus inite mea.   60
adde, Hymenaee, modos: tubicen, fera murmura conde:
    credite, uestra meus molliet arma torus.
et iam quarta canit uenturam bucina lucem,
    ipsaque in Oceanum sidera lapsa cadunt.
experiar somnum, de te mihi somnia quaeram: 65
    fac uenias oculis umbra benigna meis.'
dixit, et incerto permisit bracchia somno,
    nescia se furiis accubuisse nouis.
nam Vesta, Iliacae felix tutela fauillae,
    culpam alit et plures condit in ossa faces.   70
illa ruit, qualis celerem prope Thermodonta
    Strymonis abscisso pectus aperta sinu.
urbi festus erat (dixere Parilia patres),
    hic primus coepit moenibus esse dies,
annua pastorum conuiuia, lusus in urbe,   75
    cum pagana madent fercula diuitiis,
cumque super raros faeni flammantis aceruos
    traicit immundos ebria turba pedes.
Romulus excubias decreuit in otia solui
    atque intermissa castra silere tuba.   80
hoc Tarpeia suum tempus rata conuenit hostem:

55 Sic *O*: hic (*sc. Romae*) *Barber* patria metuar *Weidgen, Phillimore*: patrianue
tua *F1* (n *suppunxit et* -ue *in* -ne *corr. F4?*): patria ue tua *P*: patriã ne (*om.* tua)
Vo.: pariãne tua *N*: patrare tua *L* (*prior* r *in ras.*): patiare tua *DV*   59
nupta *Luetjohann*: nuptae *codd.*   60 media *Baehrens*: mediae *Bailey*
66 uenias oculis *NV2Vo.*: oculis uenias *F4PDV1*: oc. nimias *F1*: oc. minias *L*
68 nefariis *O, corr. ed. Brix.* (1486), *Liuineius*   72 pectus *Hertzberg*: fertur
O   74 Hi p. cępi *N*   75 urbi *N*   78 inmundas . . . dapes *O, corr.* ς

pacta ligat, pactis ipsa futura comes.
mons erat ascensu dubius festoque remissus:
    nec mora, uocalis occupat ense canis.
omnia praebebant somnos: sed Iuppiter unus   85
    decreuit poenis inuigilare suis.
prodiderat portaeque fidem patriamque iacentem,
    nubendique petit, quem uelit ipse, diem.
at Tatius (neque enim sceleri dedit hostis honorem)
    'Nube' ait 'et regni scande cubile mei!'   90
dixit, et ingestis comitum super obruit armis.
    haec, uirgo, officiis dos erat apta tuis.
a duce Tarpeium mons est cognomen adeptus:
    o uigil, iniustae praemia sortis habes.

V

TERRA tuum spinis obducat, lena, sepulcrum,
    et tua, quod non uis, sentiat umbra sitim;
nec sedeant cineri Manes, et Cerberus ultor
    turpia ieiuno terreat ossa sono!
docta uel Hippolytum Veneri mollire negantem,   5
    concordique toro pessima semper auis,
Penelopen quoque neglecto rumore mariti
    nubere lasciuo cogeret Antinoo.
illa uelit, poterit magnes non ducere ferrum,
    et uolucris nidis esse nouerca suis.   10
quippe et, Collinas ad fossam mouerit herbas,
    stantia currenti diluerentur aqua:
audax cantatae leges imponere lunae
    et sua nocturno fallere terga lupo,
posset ut intentos astu caecare maritos,   15

86 tuis *O, corr.* ϛ   88 ipse *V2*: ipsa *cett.*   93 Tarpeium *Palmer*:
tarpeia ϛ: tarpei(y)o *O*   94 iniustę *N*: iniuste *cett.*
V 5 Docta *NF4V2Vo.*: Nocto *F1* Nocte *LPDV1*   9 inducere *F1LP*   15
ut ϛ: et *O*

cornicum immeritas eruit ungue genas
consuluitque striges nostro de sanguine, et in me
   hippomanes fetae semina legit equae.
†exorabat opus uerbis ceu blanda perure
   saxosamque ferat sedula culpa uiam†:   20
'Si te Eoa Dorozantum iuuat aurea ripa,
   et quae sub Tyria concha superbit aqua,
Eurypylique placet Coae textura Mineruae,
   sectaque ab Attalicis putria signa toris,
seu quae palmiferae mittunt uenalia Thebae,   25
   murreaque in Parthis pocula cocta focis;
sperne fidem, prouolue deos, mendacia uincant,
   frange et damnosae iura pudicitiae!
et simulare uirum pretium facit: utere causis!
   maior dilata nocte recurret amor.   30
si tibi forte comas uexauerit, utilis ira:
   post modo mercata pace premendus erit.
denique ubi amplexu Venerem promiseris empto,
   fac simules puros Isidis esse dies.
ingerat Aprilis Iole tibi, tundat Amycle   35
   natalem Mais Idibus esse tuum.
supplex ille sedet—posita tu scribe cathedra
   quidlibet: has artis si pauet ille, tenes!
semper habe morsus circa tua colla recentis,
   litibus alternis quos putet esse datos.   40
nec te Medeae delectent probra sequacis
   (nempe tulit fastus ausa rogare prior),
sed potius mundi Thais pretiosa Menandri,

19–20 *ita NFLD*   peruret *P1*, ?*V1*, *Vo.*: perurens *in mg. P2*: perurat *V2*
culpa] talpa *V2*: turba *ς* exercebat o., u. heu b., perinde saxosam atque forat
(*Rossberg*) s. gutta (*Jacob*) uiam *Housman*   21 dorozantum *N*: derorantum
FL, P primo, Δ   23 Eurypylisque *Heinsius*   24 Sextaque *FLPDV1*
28 Frangent *O, corr. ς*   34 similes *NF4 alii*: *corr. ς*   sideris *O, corr.*
Beroaldus   deos *LPDV1*   35 amycle *V2*: ãmicle *N*: omicle *FLP*: omincle
D: Omichle *Palmer, fort. recte*   36 maiis *DVo.*: malis *cett.*

cum ferit astutos comica moecha Getas.
in mores te uerte uiri: si cantica iactat,   45
  i comes et uoces ebria iunge tuas.
ianitor ad dantis uigilet: si pulset inanis,
  surdus in obductam somniet usque seram.
nec tibi displiceat miles non factus amori,
  nauta nec attrita si ferat aera manu,   50
aut quorum titulus per barbara colla pependit,
  cretati medio cum saluere foro.
aurum spectato, non quae manus afferat aurum!
  uersibus auditis quid nisi uerba feres?
'quid iuuat ornato procedere, uita, capillo   55
  et tenuis Coa ueste mouere sinus?'
qui uersus, Coae dederit nec munera uestis,
  istius tibi sit surda sine aere lyra.
dum uernat sanguis, dum rugis integer annus,
  utere, ne quid cras libet ab ore dies!   60
uidi ego odorati uictura rosaria Paesti
  sub matutino cocta iacere Noto.'
his animum nostrae dum uersat Acanthis amicae,
  per tenuem ossa mihi sunt numerata cutem.
sed cape torquatae, Venus o regina, columbae   65
  ob meritum ante tuos guttura secta focos:
uidi ego rugoso tussim concrescere collo,
  sputaque per dentis ire cruenta cauos,
atque animam in tegetes putrem exspirare paternas:
  horruit algenti pergula curua foco.   70
exsequiae fuerint rari furtiua capilli

44 comis amica *Guyet*   getes *N*   47 ad dantis *inscr. Pomp.* (= *CIL* 4.
1894): dantes *O*   pulset *O*: pulsat *inscr.*   50 (a)era *in mg. pro u.l. F2*,
P corr., Δ: acra *NF1LP primo*   52 Celati *NFLPDV*: Elati *Vo.*: *corr.
Casellius*   55–6 (= 1. ii. 1–2) *delebant Itali*   58 Ipsius (*in ras. P*) *O*,
corr. ς   aere *NV2*: arte *FLPDV*   61 odoratum . . . Paestum *Schippers*
63–4 *post*   66 *Bailey*   63 animum *ς*: animus *NLPVo*: animis *FDV*.
64 *ita Jacob*: per tenues ossa sunt numerata cutes *O*   70 percula
NLPD1V1Vo.: *corr. ς*   curta *ς*   71 fuerint *Graeuius*: fuerant *O*

uincula et immundo pallida mitra situ,
et canis, in nostros nimis experrecta dolores,
   cum fallenda meo pollice clatra forent.
sit tumulus lenae curto uetus amphora collo: 75
   urgeat hunc supra uis, caprifice, tua.
quisquis amas, scabris hoc bustum caedite saxis,
   mixtaque cum saxis addite uerba mala!

VI

SACRA facit uates: sint ora fauentia sacris,
   et cadat ante meos icta iuuenca focos.
serta Philiteis certet Romana corymbis,
   et Cyrenaeas urna ministret aquas.
costum molle date et blandi mihi turis honores,   5
   terque focum circa laneus orbis eat.
spargite me lymphis, carmenque recentibus aris
   tibia Mygdoniis libet eburna cadis.
ite procul fraudes, alio sint aere noxae:
   pura nouum uati laurea mollit iter.   10
Musa, Palatini referemus Apollinis aedem:
   res est, Calliope, digna fauore tuo.
Caesaris in nomen ducuntur carmina: Caesar
   dum canitur, quaeso, Iuppiter ipse uaces.
est Phoebi fugiens Athamana ad litora portus,   15
   qua sinus Ioniae murmura condit aquae,
Actia Iuleae pelagus monumenta carinae,
   nautarum uotis non operosa uia.
huc mundi coiere manus: stetit aequore moles
   pinea, nec remis aequa fauebat auis.   20

---

73 experrecta *F3*?, *DV1*: exporrecta *NF1LPV2Vo*.   74 clatra *Beroaldus*:
caltra *NFLDV1*   77 c(a)edito *O, corr. Liuineius*
VI *priori continuant N1F1LPDV1*   3 Cera *O, corr. Scaliger*   philippeis
O, corr. 5, Volscus, Beroaldus.   11 noua el. *in FLP∆: in mg. tantum dist. N*

altera classis erat Teucro damnata Quirino,
　　pilaque feminea turpiter acta manu:
hinc Augusta ratis plenis Iouis omine uelis,
　　signaque iam patriae uincere docta suae.
tandem aciem geminos Nereus lunarat in arcus,　　25
　　armorum et radiis picta tremebat aqua,
cum Phoebus linquens stantem se uindice Delon
　　(non tulit iratos mobilis una Notos)
astitit Augusti puppim super, et noua flamma
　　luxit in obliquam ter sinuata facem.　　30
non ille attulerat crinis in colla solutos
　　aut testudineae carmen inerme lyrae,
sed quali aspexit Pelopeum Agamemnona uultu,
　　egessitque auidis Dorica castra rogis,
aut qualis flexos soluit Pythona per orbis　　35
　　serpentem, imbelles quem timuere deae.
mox ait 'O Longa mundi seruator ab Alba,
　　Auguste, Hectoreis cognite maior auis,
uince mari: iam terra tua est: tibi militat arcus
　　et fauet ex umeris hoc onus omne meis.　　40
solue metu patriam, quae nunc te uindice freta
　　imposuit prorae publica uota tuae.
quam nisi defendes, murorum Romulus augur
　　ire Palatinas non bene uidit auis.
et nimium remis audent prope: turpe Latinos　　45
　　principe te fluctus regia uela pati.
nec te, quod classis centenis remigat alis,
　　terreat: inuito labitur illa mari:
quodque uehunt prorae Centaurica saxa minantis,

21 tenero $D2V$　　22 femineae . . . apta $Markland$　　acta $F4$, $in mg.$ $P2$, Δ:
apta $NF1LP1V2$　　25 nereus $F4$: neruis O　　lunarat $FP2V2$: limarat
$NP1DV1Vo.$: liniarat $L1$:　　28 non $F2$: nam O: una ς: unda O　　34
Egessitque $V2$: Egissetque O　　35 quali $Rossberg$　　36 deae $ed. Eton.$:
lyrae O　　45 En ς　　nimium $NF4V2Vo.$: numen $LPD1V1$: lumen $F1D2$
prope] proh ς　　Latinos $Markland$: latinis $codd.$　　47 remigat ς: remiget
(-es $F1$)

  tigna caua et pictos experiere metus.   50
frangit et attollit uires in milite causa;
  quae nisi iusta subest, excutit arma pudor.
tempus adest, committe ratis: ego temporis auctor
  ducam laurigera Iulia rostra manu.'
dixerat, et pharetrae pondus consumit in arcus: 55
  proxima post arcus Caesaris hasta fuit.
uincit Roma fide Phoebi: dat femina poenas:
  sceptra per Ionias fracta uehuntur aquas.
at pater Idalio miratur Caesar ab astro:
  'Sum deus; est nostri sanguinis ista fides.'   60
prosequitur cantu Triton, omnesque marinae
  plauserunt circa libera signa deae.
illa petit Nilum cumba male nixa fugaci,
  hoc unum, iusso non moritura die.
di melius! quantus mulier foret una triumphus,   65
  ductus erat per quas ante Iugurtha uias!
Actius hinc traxit Phoebus monumenta, quod eius
  una decem uicit missa sagitta ratis.
bella satis cecini: citharam iam poscit Apollo
  uictor et ad placidos exuit arma choros.   70
candida nunc molli subeant conuiuia luco;
  blanditaeque fluant per mea colla rosae,
uinaque fundantur prelis elisa Falernis,
  perque lauet nostras spica Cilissa comas.
ingenium positis irritet Musa poetis: 75
  Bacche, soles Phoebo fertilis esse tuo.
ille paludosos memoret seruire Sycambros,
  Cepheam hic Meroen fuscaque regna canat,
hic referat sero confessum foedere Parthum:
  'Reddat signa Remi, mox dabit ipse sua: 80

---

56 furit *Heinsius* 59 miratus *Itali* 71 subeam *Perreius* 72 blanditaeque π, *Scaliger*: blanditiae *O* 74 Perque *O*: Terque *V2* 75 potis *DV* 80 reddita *Enk*

siue aliquid pharetris Augustus parcet Eois,
  differat in pueros ista tropaea suos.
gaude, Crasse, nigras si quid sapis inter harenas:
  ire per Euphraten ad tua busta licet.'
sic noctem patera, sic ducam carmine, donec   85
  iniciat radios in mea uina dies.

VII

SVNT aliquid Manes: letum non omnia finit,
  luridaque euictos effugit umbra rogos.
Cynthia namque meo uisa est incumbere fulcro,
  murmur ad extremae nuper humata uiae,
cum mihi somnus ab exsequiis penderet amoris,   5
  et quererer lecti frigida regna mei.
eosdem habuit secum quibus est elata capillos,
  eosdem oculos: lateri uestis adusta fuit,
et solitum digito beryllon adederat ignis,
  summaque Lethaeus triuerat ora liquor.   10
spirantisque animos et uocem misit: at illi
  pollicibus fragiles increpuere manus:
'Perfide, nec cuiquam melior sperande puellae,
  in te iam uires somnus habere potest?
iamne tibi exciderant uigilacis furta Suburae   15
  et mea nocturnis trita fenestra dolis?
per quam demisso quotiens tibi fune pependi,
  alterna ueniens in tua colla manu!
saepe Venus triuio commissa est, pectore mixto
  fecerunt tepidas pallia nostra uias.   20
foederis heu taciti, cuius fallacia uerba

81 aliquis O, corr. ς   82 differet Francius   85 carmina N
VII   2 euictos F1, ς: eiunctos N: euinctos cett. et F2   5 amores N
7 Hosdem O, corr. ς   capillos P Δ: capillis NFL   8 Eosdem N: Hosdem
cett.   15 furta NV2: tecta cett.   19 commissa Vo.: commista F: com-
mixta cett.   20 tepidas NP2: trepidas cett.   pa(l)lia NF4V2Vo.: pectora
F1LPDV1

non audituri diripuere Noti.
at mihi non oculos quisquam inclamauit euntis:
    unum impetrassem te reuocante diem:
nec crepuit fissa me propter harundine custos,   25
    laesit et obiectum tegula curta caput.
denique quis nostro curuum te funere uidit,
    atram quis lacrimis incaluisse togam?
si piguit portas ultra procedere, at illuc
    iussisses lectum lentius ire meum.   30
cur uentos non ipse rogis, ingrate, petisti?
    cur nardo flammae non oluere meae?
hoc etiam graue erat, nulla mercede hyacinthos
    inicere et fracto busta piare cado?
Lygdamus uratur—candescat lamina uernae—   35
    sensi ego, cum insidiis pallida uina bibi;
ut Nomas arcanas tollat uersuta saliuas,
    dicet damnatas ignea testa manus.
quae modo per uilis inspecta est publica noctes,
    haec nunc aurata cyclade signat humum;   40
at grauiora rependit iniquis pensa quasillis,
    garrula de facie si qua locuta mea est;
nostraque quod Petale tulit ad monumenta coronas,
    codicis immundi uincula sentit anus;
caeditur et Lalage tortis suspensa capillis,   45
    per nomen quoniam est ausa rogare meum.
te patiente meae conflauit imaginis aurum,
    ardente e nostro dotem habitura rogo.
non tamen insector, quamuis mereare, Properti:
    longa mea in libris regna fuere tuis.   50
iuro ego Fatorum nulli reuolubile carmen,
    tergeminusque canis sic mihi molle sonet,

23 euntis *O*: eunti *Reland*   33 erat *N*: erit *cett.*   37 ut ς: Aut *O* saliuas
Vo.: salinas *cett., nisi quod* sabinas *P*   41 at *Markland*: Et *O* rependit
NF4V2: fundit *F1LDV1Vo.*: effundit *P*   47–8 *post*   40 *Schrader*
48 Ardent e (e' *N*, ex *V2Vo.*) *O, corr.* ς

me seruasse fidem. si fallo, uipera nostris
    sibilet in tumulis et super ossa cubet.
nam gemina est sedes turpem sortita per amnem,   55
    turbaque diuersa remigat omnis aqua.
una Clytaemestrae stuprum uehit, aut ea Cressae
    portat mentitae lignea monstra bouis:
ecce coronato pars altera rapta phaselo,
    mulcet ubi Elysias aura beata rosas,   60
qua numerosa fides, quaque aera rotunda Cybebes
    mitratisque sonant Lydia plectra choris.
Andromedeque et Hypermestre sine fraude maritae
    narrant historiae tempora nota suae:
haec sua maternis queritur liuere catenis   65
    bracchia nec meritas frigida saxa manus;
narrat Hypermestre magnum ausas esse sorores,
    in scelus hoc animum non ualuisse suum.
sic mortis lacrimis uitae sanamus amores:
    celo ego perfidiae crimina multa tuae.   70
sed tibi nunc mandata damus, si forte moueris,
    si te non totum Chloridos herba tenet:
nutrix in tremulis ne quid desideret annis
    Parthenie: potuit, nec tibi auara fuit.
deliciaeque meae Latris, cui nomen ab usu est,   75
    ne speculum dominae porrigat illa nouae.
et quoscumque meo fecisti nomine uersus,
    ure mihi: laudes desine habere meas.
pone hederam tumulo, mihi quae praegnante corymbo

56 cumbaque *Housman*   57 una *O*: unda *Hertzberg*: cumba *Rossberg*
aut ea *scripsi*: altera *O* Cressam . . . mentitam *Haupt*   58 ratis *Palmer*
59 rapta *Palmer*: parta *O*   61 quaque aera rotunda *in mg. μ, Turnebus*
qua quaerar *NV2*: qua qu(a)erat *LPDV1Vo.*: qu(a)e qu(a)erat *F* ut unda
O, nisi quod nuda *F1* (et unda *F4*) cybeles *N*: ci(y)belles *cett.*   63 marita
Heinsius   64 tempora *Ayrmann*: pectora *O* nota pericla *Heimreich*
historias . . .suas *Markland*   65 sum(m)a (a)eternis (ect-*F1*) *O, corr. in*
mg. μ, ς   69 sanamus *O*: sancimus *Rossberg*   78 me sine *Baehrens*
79 pone *Sandbach*: Pelle *O* pugnante *O, corr. Cornelissen*

mollis contortis alliget ossa comis.   80
ramosis Anio qua pomifer incubat aruis,
   et numquam Herculeo numine pallet ebur,
hic carmen media dignum me scribe columna,
   sed breue, quod currens uector ab urbe legat:
HIC TIBVRTINA IACET AVREA CYNTHIA TERRA: 85
   ACCESSIT RIPAE LAVS, ANIENE, TVAE.
nec tu sperne piis uenientia somnia portis:
   cum pia uenerunt somnia, pondus habent.
nocte uagae ferimur, nox clausas liberat umbras,
   errat et abiecta Cerberus ipse sera.   90
luce iubent leges Lethaea ad stagna reuerti:
   nos uehimur, uectum nauta recenset onus.
nunc te possideant aliae: mox sola tenebo:
   mecum eris, et mixtis ossibus ossa teram.'
haec postquam querula mecum sub lite peregit,   95
   inter complexus excidit umbra meos.

VIII

DISCE, quid Esquilias hac nocte fugarit aquosas,
   cum uicina nouis turba cucurrit agris;   2
turpis in arcana sonuit cum rixa taberna,   19
   si sine me, famae non sine labe meae.   20
Lanuuium annosi uetus est tutela draconis;   3
   sicubi, tam rarae non perit hora morae;
qua sacer abripitur caeco descensus hiatu,   5
   qua penetrat (uirgo, tale iter omne caue!)
ieiuni serpentis honos, cum pabula poscit

80 Mollis *codd. Burmanni*: Molli *O*: mollia � 5⟩   alliget *Bailey*: alligat *O*
81 anio *V2Vo.*: amo *N, F primo*: hamo *F corr., LDV1*: almo *P*   84 uictor
F1LPDV1   85 *ita P corr.* Sed *NFL, P primo, D*   tiburtina *F*:
ti(y)burna *N*: *alii alia*   iacet hic *O*   86 aniane *N* (*uel* amane), *LPDV*
93 Nec *F1LPDV1*
VIII *priori continuat N1*   1 quod *NF1*   19-20 *huc transtulit Luetjohann*   4 sicubi *Lee*: hic ubi *O*   6 *dist. Lachmann, alii*

annua et ex ima sibila torquet humo.
talia demissae pallent ad sacra puellae,
    cum temere anguino creditur ore manus.   10
ille sibi admotas a uirgine corripit escas:
    uirginis in palmis ipsa canistra tremunt.
si fuerint castae, redeunt in colla parentum,
    clamantque agricolae 'Fertilis annus erit.'
huc mea detonsis auecta est Cynthia mannis: 15
    causa fuit Iuno, sed mage causa Venus.
Appia, dic quaeso, quantum te teste triumphum
    egerit effusis per tua saxa rotis!   18
spectaclum ipsa sedens primo temone pependit,   21
    ausa per impuros frena mouere locos.
serica nam taceo uulsi carpenta nepotis
    atque armillatos colla Molossa canis;
qui dabit immundae uenalia fata saginae,   25
    uincet ubi erasas barba pudenda genas.
cum fieret nostro totiens iniuria lecto,
    mutato uolui castra mouere toro.
Phyllis Auentinae quaedam est uicina Dianae,
    sobria grata parum: cum bibit, omne decet.   30
altera Tarpeios est inter Teia lucos,
    candida, sed potae non satis unus erit.
his ego constitui noctem lenire uocatis,
    et Venere ignota furta nouare mea.
unus erat tribus in secreta lectulus herba.   35
    quaeris concubitus? inter utramque fui.
Lygdamus ad cyathos, uitrique aestiua supellex

8 i(y)ma *F4, P corr.*: una *O*   11 colligit *FLPDV1*   15 ab annis *O,*
corr. in mg. μ, *Beroaldus*   19–20 *post* 2 *transtulit Luetjohann*   21
Spectaclum *F4*: Spectaculum *NLPVo.*: Spectandum *F1DV1*   23 Sirica
nam tacto *V1*: Si riganam tacto *et similia cett.*: *corr. Beroaldus*   nepotis *Vo.*:
nepoti *cett.*   28 Mul(c)tato *O, corr.* ς   uoluit *NFPΔ*: noluit *L*: *corr.*
Beroaldus   29 noua el. in *O praeter N1*   31 est om. *N1, post* inter
add. m. rec.   34 notare *F1LPDV1*   36 utramque *L primo,* P Δ: utraque
NF1, L corr.: utrasque *F3*   37 utrique *NF4L2V2Vo.*: uterque *F1,* ?*L1,*
PDV1: *corr. Scaliger*

et Methymnaei Graeca saliua meri.
Nile, tuus tibicen erat, crotalistria Phyllis,
    et facilis spargi munda sine arte rosa,   40
Magnus et ipse suos breuiter concretus in artus
    iactabat truncas ad caua buxa manus.
sed neque suppletis constabat flamma lucernis,
    reccidit inque suos mensa supina pedes.
me quoque per talos Venerem quaerente secundam 45
    semper damnosi subsiluere canes.
cantabant surdo, nudabant pectora caeco:
    Lanuuii ad portas, ei mihi, solus eram;
cum subito rauci sonuerunt cardine postes,
    et leuia ad primos murmura facta Lares.   50
nec mora, cum totas resupinat Cynthia ualuas,
    non operosa comis, sed furibunda decens.
pocula mi digitos inter cecidere remissos,
    palluerantque ipso labra soluta mero.
fulminat illa oculis et quantum femina saeuit,   55
    spectaclum capta nec minus urbe fuit.
Phyllidos iratos in uultum conicit unguis:
    territa uicinas Teia clamat aquas.
lumina sopitos turbant elata Quiritis,
    omnis et insana semita nocte sonat.   60
illas direptisque comis tunicisque solutis
    excipit obscurae prima taberna uiae.
Cynthia gaudet in exuuiis uictrixque recurrit
    et mea peruersa sauciat ora manu,
imponitque notam collo morsuque cruentat,   65
    praecipueque oculos, qui meruere, ferit.
atque ubi iam nostris lassauit bracchia plagis,

---

39 coralistria *F4LPDV1*: colistria *F1*: eboralistria *N*: c(h)oristria *V2Vo.*:
corr. *Turnebus*   phil(l)is *O*: Byblis *Palmer*: *alii alia*   40 haec *Baehrens*
41 Magnus *O*: nanus *in mg.* μ, *Beroaldus*   45 secundam *Palmer*: secundos
DV: secundo *cett.*   56 Spectaclum *F4L*: Spectaculum *NPVo.*: Spectandum *F1DV*

Lygdamus ad plutei fulcra sinistra latens
eruitur, geniumque meum protractus adorat.
Lygdame, nil potui: tecum ego captus eram.   70
supplicibus palmis tum demum ad foedera ueni,
   cum uix tangendos praebuit illa pedes,
atque ait 'Admissae si uis me ignoscere culpae,
   accipe, quae nostrae formula legis erit.
tu neque Pompeia spatiabere cultus in umbra,   75
   nec cum lasciuum sternet harena Forum.
colla caue inflectas ad summum obliqua theatrum,
   aut lectica tuae sudet aperta morae.
Lygdamus in primis, omnis mihi causa querelae,
   ueneat et pedibus uincula bina trahat.'   80
indixit leges: respondi ego 'Legibus utar.'
   riserat imperio facta superba dato.
dein quemcumque locum externae tetigere puellae,
   suffiit, ac pura limina tergit aqua,
imperat et totas iterum mutare lucernas,   85
   terque meum tetigit sulpuris igne caput.
atque ita mutato per singula pallia lecto
   respondi, et toto soluimus arma toro.

IX

AMPHITRYONIADES qua tempestate iuuencos
   egerat a stabulis, o Erythea, tuis,
uenit ad inuictos pecorosa Palatia montis,
   et statuit fessos fessus et ipse boues,
qua Velabra suo stagnabant flumine quoque   5
   nauta per urbanas uelificabat aquas.

68 fusca *O, corr. π, in mg. μ, Beroaldus*   71 uenit *O, corr. ς*   78 sudet *O*:
se det *Gruter*: sidat *Palmer*   82 rato *Heinsius*   84 Suffiit ac *Baehrens*
et *Beroaldus*: Sufficat *NFL2*, ?*P1*: Sufficiat *L1P2V2Vo.*: Suffocat et *DV1*
85 lucernas *NVo.*: lacernas *LP2DV*: laternas *FP1*
IX *priori continuat N1*   2 uenit et aduictos *N*, adiutos *F*, ad iunctos *LP*:
corr. Itali   5 flumine *in mg. F2*, Δ: fulmine *F1LP*: flumina *N*

sed non infido manserunt hospite Caco
  incolumes: furto polluit ille Iouem.
incola Cacus erat, metuendo raptor ab antro,
  per tria partitos qui dabat ora sonos.   10
hic, ne certa forent manifestae signa rapinae,
  auersos cauda traxit in antra boues;
nec sine teste deo: furem sonuere iuuenci,
  furis et implacidas diruit ira fores.
Maenalio iacuit pulsus tria tempora ramo   15
  Cacus, et Alcides sic ait: 'Ite boues,
Herculis ite boues, nostrae labor ultime clauae,
  bis mihi quaesitae, bis mea praeda, boues,
aruaque mugitu sancite Bouaria longo:
  nobile erit Romae pascua uestra Forum.'   20
dixerat, et sicco torquet sitis ora palato,
  terraque non ullas feta ministrat aquas.
sed procul inclusas audit ridere puellas,
  lucus ubi umbroso fecerat orbe nemus,
femineae loca clausa deae fontisque piandos,   25
  impune et nullis sacra retecta uiris.
deuia puniceae uelabant limina uittae,
  putris odorato luxerat igne casa,
populus et longis ornabat frondibus aedem,
  multaque cantantis umbra tegebat auis.   30
huc ruit in siccam congesta puluere barbam,
  et iacit ante fores uerba minora deo:
'Vos precor, o luci sacro quae luditis antro,
  pandite defessis hospita fana uiris.
fontis egens erro, circaque sonantia lymphis;   35
  et caua succepto flumine palma sat est.

8 Incolumis *O, corr.* ς   9 Incola ς: Insula *O*   21 at *Housman*   22
ullas *V2*: nullas *O*   ministrat *V2*: ministret *O*   24 ubi *Heinsius*: ab *O*
29 glaucis *Housman*   32 minore *NL*   33 lucis *O, corr.* ς   34 uana
O, corr. Scaliger   uiis *O, corr.* ς   36 succepto *N*: suscepto *cett.*   38
suscepta *N*

audistisne aliquem, tergo qui sustulit orbem?
   ille ego sum: Alciden terra recepta uocat.
quis facta Herculeae non audit fortia clauae
   et numquam ad uastas irrita tella feras,   40
atque uni Stygias homini luxisse tenebras?

            *   *   *   42

angulus hic mundi nunc me mea fata trahentem   65
   accipit: haec fesso uix mihi terra patet.   66
quodsi Iunoni sacrum faceretis amarae,   43
   non clausisset aquas ipsa nouerca suas.
sin aliquem uultusque meus saetaeque leonis   45
   terrent et Libyco sole perusta coma,
idem ego Sidonia feci seruilia palla
   officia et Lydo pensa diurna colo,
mollis et hirsutum cepit mihi fascia pectus,
   et manibus duris apta puella fui.'   50
talibus Alcides; at talibus alma sacerdos,
   puniceo canas stamine uincta comas:
'Parce oculis, hospes, lucoque abscede uerendo;
   cede agedum et tuta limina linque fuga.
interdicta uiris metuenda lege piatur   55
   quae se summota uindicat ara casa.
magno Tiresias aspexit Pallada uates,
   fortia dum posita Gorgone membra lauat.
di tibi dent alios fontis: haec lympha puellis
   auia secreti limitis unda fluit.'   60
sic anus: ille umeris postis concussit opacos,
   nec tulit iratam ianua clausa sitim.

---

40 uastas *Vo.*: uatas *N*, ?*L1*: natas *FL2PD2*: uacuas *D1V, unde* nocuas *Santen*
42 *in codd. nulla lacuna sed* accipit et (*sive* haec *siue* hic) fesso uix mihi terra
patet *O*   accipite: haec . . . �⟩   65–6 *post* 42 *transtulit Jacob*   45 ali-
quam *P*   47 sidonia *P2Δ*: sinonia *FLP1*: symonia *N*   52 uincta
FPVo.: iuncta *NLDV*   57 Magno *codd. Passeratii et Gebhardi*: Magnam
O   60 una *O, corr. Housman*   fuit *O, corr. Fruter*

at postquam exhausto iam flumine uicerat aestum,
    ponit uix siccis tristia iura labris: 64
'Maxima quae gregibus deuota est Ara repertis,   67
    ara per has' inquit 'maxima facta manus,
haec nullis umquam pateat ueneranda puellis,
    Herculis aeternum ne sit inulta sitis.'   70
hunc, quoniam manibus purgatum sanxerat orbem, 73
    sic sanctum Tatiae composuere Cures.   74
Sancte pater salue, cui iam fauet aspera Iuno: 71
    Sance, uelis libro dexter inesse meo.   72

X

Nvnc Iouis incipiam causas aperire Feretri
    armaque de ducibus trina recepta tribus.
magnum iter ascendo, sed dat mihi gloria uires:
    non iuuat e facili lecta corona iugo.
imbuis exemplum primae tu, Romule, palmae   5
    huius, et exuuio plenus ab hoste redis,
tempore quo portas Caeninum Acrona petentem
    uictor in euersum cuspide fundis equum.
Acron Herculeus Caenina ductor ab arce,
    Roma, tuis quondam finibus horror erat.   10
hic spolia ex umeris ausus sperare Quirini
    ipse dedit, sed non sanguine sicca suo.
hunc uidet ante cauas librantem spicula turris
    Romulus et uotis occupat ante ratis:
'Iuppiter, haec hodie tibi uictima corruet Acron.'   15
    uouerat, et spolium corruit ille Ioui.

65–6 *uide post u.* 42   70 Herculis *PV2*: Hercule (u *erasa L*) *cett.*: Herculea
Housman olim   aeternum *Heinsius*: exterminium *O, nisi quod* extremum *P*:
eximii *V2*   ne sit *PV2*: nescit *cett.*   73–4 *transtulit Schneidewin*   74
Sancum *Heinsius*   Tatii *Scaliger*   72 Sance *Richmond*   Sancte *O*
X *priori continuat N*   1 feretri] fateri *N*   6 exuuio *LPDV1Vo.*: exuiuo
N: eximio *FV2*   7 acronta *O, corr. Itali*   8 in euersum *V2*: nec uersum
O   14 ratis *P2*: rates *O, nisi quod* ratas *P1*

Vrbis uirtutisque parens sic uincere sueuit,
    qui tulit a parco frigida castra lare.
idem eques et frenis, idem fuit aptus aratris,
    et galea hirsuta compta lupina iuba.   20
picta neque inducto fulgebat parma pyropo:
    praebebant caesi baltea lenta boues.
Cossus at insequitur Veientis caede Tolumni,
    uincere cum Veios posse laboris erat,
necdum ultra Tiberim belli sonus, ultima praeda   25
    Nomentum et captae iugera terna Corae.
heu Vei ueteres! et uos tum regna fuistis,
    et uestro posita est aurea sella foro:
nunc intra muros pastoris bucina lenti
    cantat, et in uestris ossibus arua metunt.   30
forte super portae dux Veiens astitit arcem
    colloquiumque sua fretus ab urbe dedit:
dumque aries murum cornu pulsabat aeno,
    uinea qua ductum longa tegebat opus,
Cossus ait 'Forti melius concurrere campo.'   35
    nec mora fit, plano sistit uterque gradum.
di Latias iuuere manus, desecta Tolumni
    ceruix Romanos sanguine lauit equos.
Claudius at Rheno traiectos arcuit hostis,
    Belgica cum uasti parma relata ducis   40
Virdomari. genus hic Rheno iactabat ab ipso,
    mobilis euectis fundere gaesa rotis.

17 uirtutisque *NF4P2V2*: uirtutemque *F1LP1Vo.*: uirtutumque *DV1*
parens *NF4DV1Vo.*: parem *F1LP*: pares *V2*   18 a parco *Jacob*: aporco
NF1V1: a porco *F2?*, *LP1D*   21 pyropo Δ: piroto *cett.*   25–6 *post*
22 *Passerat*   26 captae *DV1Vo.*: capta *cett.*   terra *O, corr.* ϛ   27 heu
Luetjohann: Ẹ *N*: E *F1*: Et *in mg. F2*, *LP1*Δ: 31 Veiens *Dempster*:
uei(y)us *O*: Veius dux *Heraeus*   36 gradu *O, corr.* ϛ   39 at *Barber*:
a *O*   a Rhodano *Postgate*: Eridano *Palmer*   40 cui *Guyet*   41 Virdomari *Itali*: Virtomanẹ *N*, *similia cett.*   42 Nobilis *P corr.*, ϛ euectis
Rothstein: e rectis *ed. Gryph.*: erecti *NF4*: effecti *F1LP1DV1Vo.* gesa *F4*:
c(a)esa *O*

illi ut uirgatis iaculans it ab agmine bracis
　　torquis ab incisa decidit unca gula.
nunc spolia in templo tria condita: causa Feretri,　　45
　　omine quod certo dux ferit ense ducem;
seu quia uicta suis umeris haec arma ferebant,
　　hinc Feretri dicta est ara superba Iouis.

XI

DESINE, Paulle, meum lacrimis urgere sepulcrum:
　　panditur ad nullas ianua nigra preces;
cum semel infernas intrarunt funera leges,
　　non exorato stant adamante uiae.
te licet orantem fuscae deus audiat aulae:　　5
　　nempe tuas lacrimas litora surda bibent.
uota mouent superos: ubi portitor aera recepit,
　　obserat euersos lurida porta rogos.
sic maestae cecinere tubae, cum subdita nostrum
　　detraheret lecto fax inimica caput.　　10
quid mihi coniugium Paulli, quid currus auorum
　　profuit aut famae pignora tanta meae?
non minus immitis habuit Cornelia Parcas:
　　et sum, quod digitis quinque legatur, onus.
damnatae noctes et uos, uada lenta, paludes,　　15
　　et quaecumque meos implicat unda pedes,
immatura licet, tamen huc non noxia ueni:
　　det Pater hic umbrae mollia iura meae.
aut si quis posita uindex sedet Aeacus urna,
　　in mea sortita iudicet ossa pila:　　20

---

43 illi . . . bracis *ita Postgate*: Illi uirgatis (nigratis *F1*, Iurgatis *in mg. F2*,
uirgatis *F4*) iaculantis ab agmine (agmina *N*: inguine *P corr.*) brac(h)is (pracis
F: brutis *L*) *O, quo seruato* illi *ad Claudium referunt nonnulli.*
XI *priori continuat N*　　8 euersos (-uorsos) *Richmond*: herbosos *NF3LP*:
erbosos *F1*: umbrosos Δ　　13 Non *NDVo.*: Num *FLP*:　　habui *ς*　　14
En *ς*　　17–76 om. *N uno folio interciso*　　19 uindex *scripsi*: iudex *codd.*
20 iudicet *LP*Δμν: uindicet *F*

assideant fratres, iuxta Minoia sella, et
   Eumenidum intento turba seuera foro.
Sisyphe, mole uaces; taceant Ixionis orbes;
   fallax Tantaleus corripiare liquor;
Cerberus et nullas hodie petat improbus umbras;   25
   et iaceat tacita laxa catena sera.
ipsa loquor pro me: si fallo, poena sororum
   infelix umeros urgeat urna meos.
si cui fama fuit per auita tropaea decori,
   Afra Numantinos regna loquuntur auos: 30
altera maternos exaequat turba Libones,
   et domus est titulis utraque fulta suis.
mox, ubi iam facibus cessit praetexta maritis,
   uinxit et acceptas altera uitta comas,
iungor, Paulle, tuo sic discessura cubili: 35
   in lapide hoc uni nupta fuisse legar.
testor maiorum cineres tibi, Roma, colendos,
   sub quorum titulis, Africa, tunsa iaces,
†et Persen proaui stimulantem pectus Achilli,
   quique tuas proauo fregit Achille domos,†   40
me neque censurae legem mollisse neque ulla
   labe mea uestros erubuisse focos.
non fuit exuuiis tantis Cornelia damnum:
   quin et erat magnae pars imitanda domus.
nec mea mutata est aetas, sine crimine tota est: 45

---

21 minoia *FLPΔμv*: Minoida *ʒ*   sella et *P2VVo.μv*: sella *FLP1D* iuxta
et Minoida sellam *ʒ*   24 tantaleo *FLPΔμv, corr. ʒ*: Tantaleo corripere
ore *Auratus*   26 lapsa *Fv*   27 fallor *FLPΔμv, corr. ʒ*   29 troph(a)ea
decori *μv1*: decora troph(a)ei *FLPDV1Vo.*: fama decori *V2*   30 Afra
Scaliger: (A)Era *F4V2μv*: Et *LPDV1Vo.*   31 ligones *FLPΔμv, corr. ʒ*
34 uitta Δ: uicta *FLPμv*   36 in] ut *Graevius*   38 tonsa *ʒ*   *post hunc u.*
duo uu. excidisse putat Munro   39 persen *F4Lμv*: persem Δ: proseu *F1*:
perseu *P*   te, Perseu, *Santen*   proaui *F corr., LP* Δ *μv*:proam *F primo*
(h)ac(h)illi *FLPDV1Vo. μv*: achillis *V2*   stimulantem *O*: simulantem *ʒ*
proauo stimulantem pectus Achille *Lipsius*   40 proauo *FLPDV1Vo.*:
proauus *V2v, Munro*: proauos *μ, quod probat Housman pro nominat. inter-*
pretatus   Auerne *Munro*: Achiue *Richmond*

uiximus insignes inter utramque facem.
mi natura dedit leges a sanguine ductas,
  ne possis melior iudicis esse metu.
quaelibet austeras de me ferat urna tabellas:
  turpior assessu non erit ulla meo,   50
uel tu, quae tardam mouisti fune Cybeben,
  Claudia, turritae rara ministra deae,
uel cui, iusta suos cum Vesta reposceret ignis,
  exhibuit uiuos carbasus alba focos.
nec te, dulce caput, mater Scribonia, laesi: 55
  in me mutatum quid nisi fata uelis?
maternis laudor lacrimis urbisque querelis,
  defensa et gemitu Caesaris ossa mea.
ille sua nata dignam uixisse sororem
  increpat, et lacrimas uidimus ire deo.   60
et tamen emerui generosos uestis honores,
  nec mea de sterili facta rapina domo.
tu, Lepide, et tu, Paulle, meum post fata leuamen,
  condita sunt uestro lumina nostra sinu.
uidimus et fratrem sellam geminasse curulem;   65
  consule quo, festo tempore, rapta soror.
filia, tu specimen censurae nata paternae,
  fac teneas unum nos imitata uirum.
et serie fulcite genus: mihi cumba uolenti
  soluitur aucturis tot mea fata meis.   70
haec est feminei merces extrema triumphi,
  laudat ubi emeritum libera fama rogum.

---

48 Ne possis *FL, P1* (Ne mel. possis), *DV1Vo.µv*: Nec possis *cod. Berolin.*
Diez B. 53   49 quamlibet *ς, Liuineius*   50 assessu *ς*: as(s)ensu
FLPDV1Vo.µv   51 cibelem *FL*   52 Claudia *L2PV2v*: Gaudia
F1L1DV1Vo.µ   53 cui, iusta suos *scripsi*: cuius iasos *µv*: cuius rasos
FLP Δ: cuius, sacros *Rossberg*   61 generosae *Turnebus*   63–4 *post* 74
Housman   63 ita *ς*: Te . . . te *FLPΔµv*   65–6 *post* 60 *Koppiers*   66
festo *Koppiers*: facto *FLPΔµv*   consul quo factus *Lachmann*   70 aucturis
ς: uncturis *LP Δ µv*: nupturis *F*   fata *FLPΔµv*: facta *ς*   malis *FLPΔµv*,
corr. ed. Brix.

nunc tibi commendo communia pignora natos:
  haec cura et cineri spirat inusta meo.
fungere maternis uicibus pater: illa meorum   75
  omnis erit collo turba ferenda tuo.
oscula cum dederis tua flentibus, adice matris:
  tota domus coepit nunc onus esse tuum.
et si quid doliturus eris, sine testibus illis!
  cum uenient, siccis oscula falle genis!   80
sat tibi sint noctes, quas de me, Paulle, fatiges,
  somniaque in faciem credita saepe meam:
atque ubi secreto nostra ad simulacra loqueris,
  ut responsurae singula uerba iace.
seu tamen aduersum mutarit ianua lectum,   85
  sederit et nostro cauta nouerca toro,
coniugium, pueri, laudate et ferte paternum:
  capta dabit uestris moribus illa manus;
nec matrem laudate nimis: collata priori
  uertet in offensas libera uerba suas.   90
seu memor ille mea contentus manserit umbra
  et tanti cineres duxerit esse meos,
discite uenturam iam nunc sentire senectam,
  caelibis ad curas nec uacet ulla uia.
quod mihi detractum est, uestros accedat ad annos: 95
  prole mea Paullum sic iuuet esse senem.
et bene habet: numquam mater lugubria sumpsi;
  uenit in exsequias tota caterua meas.
causa perorata est. flentes me surgite, testes,
  dum pretium uitae grata rependit humus.   100
moribus et caelum patuit: sim digna merendo,
  cuius honoratis ossa uehantur aquis.

77 mater *O, corr.* ϛ   79 quid *V2*: quis *O*   erit *O, corr.* ϛ   84 tace *O,*
corr. ϛ   94 ualet ulla uias *N*   97 lubrigia *NV2*: lubrica *FLP1DV1Vo.*:
corr. ϛ   sumptum *O, corr.* ϛ   102 aquis *NFL, P primo, V2*: auis *Heinsius*

NOTES

I

This long elegy falls into two halves.[1] Lines 1–70 (distinguished below as iA) are spoken by the poet; lines 71–150 (distinguished below as iB) are spoken by an evidently imaginary astrologer who in line 78 gives his name as Horos.

Formally, iB is a pendant to iA (as is viiiB to viiiA in Propertius' first book); and the link between the two is a warning given at the beginning of iB against an intention to write a certain kind of poetry that has been announced at the end of iA. This motive—the poetic intention that provokes a warning and is revised in consequence—is one that occurs elsewhere in Propertius, for instance in III, iii.

However, the two units iA and iB are widely diverse in their content and character. The greater part of iA consists in the development of an idea found in Tibullus II, v, 22–64: an imaginative picture of Rome's primitive past, against which is set the thought of the divine providence that brought the survivors of fallen Troy to Italy and caused Troy to rise again in the greatness of Rome. By contrast, iB is a genre piece, a speech in character depicting a type, the astrologer, just as

[1] Here and in what follows I assume that the reading *dicere fata* in line 71 is correct, and that lines 87–8 (which certainly do not belong where they stand in the MSS.) are rightly transposed to follow line 68 (or 70). Some may feel that *discere fata* is a more probable reading in line 71, and that no new position in the poem can be assigned with any confidence to the misplaced couplet. If that be so, there will be no direct link between iA and iB; they will be separate, though related, poems; and the astrologer in iB will be introduced replying to a supposed enquiry by Propertius, come to consult him, instead of intervening with unsolicited advice. The two poems will still be related, and their relationship will not in substance be different from that assumed above. Both contain statements personal to the poet. And both are concerned with his poetic programme. For, as indicated in the note on line 73, *auersus Apollo* in that line means that Apollo as god of poetry is unfavourable to some poetic project that Propertius has in mind.

IV, V, 21–60 below is a speech in character depicting another type, the *lena*.

Though so different from one another, the two units IA and IB have nevertheless this property in common, that each alike concludes with a statement personal to the poet. In IA this is the poet's announcement of a programme of patriotic poetry, partly prophetic (and presently abandoned) and partly aetio-logical (and fulfilled, up to a point, in the book which follows). In IB it is a summary account, in the mouth of the astrologer, of the poet's origins and personal history. This kind of material is evidently appropriate to an *introductory* elegy.

The relation between IA and IB is thus peculiar. They are neither (in the ordinary sense) a single elegy, nor two com-pletely separate elegies, but a pair, related by a certain com-mon function in their respective conclusions, and linked by a formal device at the point of transition. As mentioned above, Propertius I, viii is another example of an elegy that consists of a pair of distinct but related units.

IA

This first half of the elegy falls into three main sections. In lines 1–38 the poet reflects on the smallness and poverty of Rome's beginnings, as contrasted with her present grandeur. He imagines successively the rustic condition of the first settlement, the primitive forms of its worship, the crude methods and slight scale of its wars. Rome, he concludes, has risen from nothing. In lines 39–54 he proclaims his wonder at the providence which has brought this miracle about, a providence manifested in the safe coming to Italy of the survivors of fallen Troy (forerunners by ancestry or example of the great heroes of Roman history) and in prophecies delivered at that time. In lines 55–70 he promises to devote his poetic gift to the service of Rome, and to take for subject the prophecies[1] of Rome's rise and the origins of Roman customs and festivals and place-names.

The topics of the first two sections outlined above had been

[1] See footnote on p. 45.

treated already, in the same juxtaposition, by Tibullus (II, v, 22–64). This passage of Tibullus has obviously influenced both the form and the content of the present elegy and is worth reading in conjunction with it.

1-16. The poet stands with an anonymous visitor looking out over Rome. He invites him to imagine the scene as it was in a distant past, contrasting the pastoral landscape and primitive inhabitants of that time with the splendours of the scene contemporary. He thinks at first of a time before the coming of Aeneas (line 2) but moves on in imagination to the early days of the Roman community itself (see for instance lines 9 and 13).

Propertius had a lively visual imagination, and we can be sure that he has a real view over contemporary Rome in mind. Places identifiably mentioned are the temple of Palatine Apollo (3), the Capitoline hill (7), the Tiber (8), the Curia Julia (11), and (probably) the temple of Quirinus on the Quirinal (9). This suggests that the point of outlook is the north-west corner of the Palatine hill.

In some cases the language of the speaker may have been influenced by the names of things or places within his view, with or without a specific allusion being consciously intended. Thus *casa* (6) may be suggested by the *casa Romuli* on the Capitol (see note on line 6); *tonabat* (7) by the little temple of Jupiter *Tonans*, dedicated by Augustus in 22 B.C. in the vicinity of the above; *bubus* (8) by the *Forum Boarium*, lying between the Tiber and the viewpoint here assumed. The reference to the theatre (in line 15) may be suggested by the theatre of Marcellus, dedicated in 13 B.C. but under construction for long before that, and visible in the background from the same viewpoint, to the left of and behind the Capitoline hill. But this is of course conjectural.

1. hospes: for this motive whereby the poet addresses an imaginary visitor in the role (as it were) of a guide, cf. Cat. IV, 1 *phaselus ille, quem uidetis, hospites.* The imaginary situation which thus provides a context for the beginning of the poem is allowed to be forgotten later, when it has served its purpose; from line 39 on it is manifestly irrelevant. A similar shift of the initial conception will be found in Elegies vi and xi of the present book; in Elegy vi the poet begins as a priest announcing a ceremony and ends carousing in imagination with other poets to celebrate Augustus' victories. In xi the dead woman Cornelia begins by addressing her husband but presently embarks on an imagined speech in her own defence before the judges in the world below.

maxima Roma: 'mighty Rome'; cf. Mart. x, lviii, 6 *nunc nos maxima Roma terit* (of a man detained in town).

2. ante...Aenean collis et herba fuit: for this imagining of the rural scene that the site of Rome once presented cf. Tib. II, v, 25 ff. and Virg. *Aen.* VIII, 310 ff.

3. Nauali: this epithet is not elsewhere found applied to Apollo. It is applied to him here as author of the victory at Actium; cf. Elegy vi below, and also Virg. *Aen.* VIII, 704 ff., Ov. *A.A.* III, 389–90.

Palatia: this is poetic plural for *Palatium*, and means first the Palatine hill, then the buildings on it. These buildings included the house of the *princeps*, and the portico and temple of (Palatine) Apollo dedicated in 28 B.C.; hence *sacra...Phoebo*.

4. profugae: because their owner Evander was an exile from his original home in Arcadia.

concubuere: where this verb is found in other authors it is used specifically of sexual intercourse, and so in Propertius too at II, xv, 16. But Propertius is independent in his use of compounds; and at IV, viii, 36 he uses *concubitus* of the arrangement of guests at table. Here he perhaps intends to suggest a picture of the cattle lying in groups in the pasture, as cattle do.

5-6. fictilibus...casa: 'the gods of the temples which have risen to this gilded splendour which you see were humble figures of clay in those days; and a simple cottage was not disdained.' The second sentence may refer either to the gods or to the humans of those days.

5. fictilibus: Pliny *N.H.* XXXIV, 34 says that until Rome's conquest of Asia (189 B.C.) the images dedicated in Roman temples were commonly of wood or terracotta.

aurea templa: cf. II, xxxi, 1–2 *aurea Phoebi porticus*; Virg. *Aen.* VIII, 347–8 *Capitolia...aurea nunc*; Sen. *Contr.* I, vi, 4 *auro puro fulgens praelucet Capitolium.* The roof of the Capitoline temple of Jupiter was in the poet's day entirely gilded.

6. nec fuit opprobrio...casa: cf. Tib. II, v, 26 *et stabant humiles in Iouis arce casae.* According to Vitruv. II, 1 there was on the Capitol (at about the date of this poem) a *Romuli casa stramentis tecta*; and this is mentioned specifically by Sen. *Contr.* II, i, 4 and implied by Virg. *Aen.* VIII, 654 and Ov. *Fast,* I,

199 and Mart. VIII, lxxx, 6. Dionysius of Halicarnassus (I, lxxix) also refers to such an edifice, but places it on the Palatine, on the side looking towards the Circus. Perhaps there was a duplicate. In any case, this primitive *casa* was carefully preserved by the Roman state as a historic monument.

7. Tarpeiusque...tonabat: i.e. there was no temple of Jupiter on the Capitoline hill. The wording may have been suggested by the little temple of Jupiter Tonans (on the Capitol) which was still a novelty at the date of this poem; but of course the dominant reference is to the great temple of Jupiter Capitolinus, and to thunder as a regular attribute of Jupiter.

8. et Tiberis...aduena bubus erat: the Tiber, to the poet's contemporaries Rome's own river, flowing through the centre of the metropolis, was then an alien stream, emerging from unknown territory and flowing through the pastures on the outskirts of the tiny settlement. For the cattle suggesting a pastoral landscape cf. line 4 above and Tib. II, v, 25 and 55.

9. quot gradibus...se sustulit: 'see on how many steps the house of Remus (= temple of Quirinus) yonder has reared itself'. (*quot* is a conjecture. N here reads *quod*; as also at IV, iii, 36, where *quot* is needed. The other branch of the tradition here gives *quo*: which could be translated 'see how high. . .'.) For *Remus = Romulus* cf. II, i, 23 *regna . . . prima Remi* and IV, vi, 80 *reddat signa Remi*; also Cat. LVIII, 5 *Remi nepotes*. For *Quirinus = Romulus* cf. IV, x, 11 (of Romulus' opponent Acron) *hic spolia ex umeris ausus sperare Quirini* and Juv. XI, 105 (of the twins Romulus and Remus) *geminos . . . Quirinos*. For *domus* of a temple cf. III, ii, 20 *Iouis Elei...domus*. The temple of Quirinus stood on the Quirinal hill, visible from the viewpoint apparently assumed in this elegy (see introductory note, p. 47) beyond and well above the Curia Julia (line 11). It was reconstructed by Augustus and the reconstruction dedicated in 16 B.C., so that it was a new feature at the time when this elegy was written. It had seventy-six columns (Dio C. LIV, 19) and so must have been of impressive size and magnificence. Like all Roman temples, it will have stood on a high stepped podium, and it also stood high on a hill.

[Many editors prefer to understand *domus Remi* here as meaning *casa Romuli* (for which see note on line 6 above), and read *quo* (or *qua*)...*se sustulit* as a relative clause. Then the sense will be: 'where now Romulus' house stands at the head of the

(?new) steps yonder, once upon a time…'. To find a point in *gradibus…se sustulit* we have to assume (what we do not know) that the *casa* stood at the head of a flight of steps that were new or newly embellished, conceivably the *scala Caci* on the south side of the Palatine or the *centum gradus* (Tac. *Hist.* III, 71) leading up to the *Tarpeia rupes* on the Capitoline hill. But, against this, *domus…se sustulit* surely suggests an imposing building; and the reference to the primitive *casa* as part of the modern scene does not fit well in a context in which throughout, the contrast is between present splendour beheld and past simplicity imagined. Moreover, the *casa* seems already to have been hinted at in line 6.]

10. fratrum maxima regna: 'the brothers' whole domain'; for a comparable use of *maximus* cf. II, xiii, 25–6 *tres…libelli, quos ego Persephonae maxima dona feram* (the best gift, *or* the only gift, that I can). The contrast is between the grand new temple of Romulus = Quirinus and the cottage he shared with his twin in the days when they lived as shepherds before their recognition (cf. e.g. Dion. Hal. I, lxxix, 11). *regna* is the more appropriate because they were in fact princes; but the rustic in Virg. *Ecl.* I, 69 also says *mea regna* of his little property.

11–12. Curia…Patres: 'the Curia is now a lordly sight to see, with its senators resplendent in purple-bordered robes: the fathers that filled the Curia in those days were rustic souls, clothed in the skins of beasts'.

11. Curia: the building that Propertius has in mind is the Curia Julia, built by the dictator Caesar and restored after a fire by Octavian and dedicated by him in 29 B.C. It is by a looseness of expression that he makes the same Curia apparently subject of line 12, which refers to primitive times. (The senate-house of the Republic was supposed to have been built by Tullus Hostilius, and so it too originated at a date later than that which Propertius is contemplating in his picture of olden days.)

praetexto: for *praetextato*, i.e. wearing the *toga praetexta*, a *toga* with a purple border worn by those who had held curule magistracies. For the abridged form of the adjective cf. II, xxxi, 4 *femina turba*; IV, iii, 64 *carbasa lina*, etc.

alta: the Curia Julia was in fact a lofty building, and *alta* here partly refers to this, but it also carries the secondary meaning 'grand', 'exalted' as in Hor. *Od.* III, iv, 37 *Caesarem altum.*

12. rustica corda: for this use of *corda* cf. Virg. *Aen.* x, 87 *cur grauidam bellis urbem et corda aspera temptas?*

13. bucina: the herdsman's horn, a rustic instrument; cf. IV, x, 29. A sophisticated version of it was used for certain purposes in the Roman army in historical times; with this cf. IV, iv, 63.

14. centum illi...senatus erat: probably 'sometimes the Hundred of those days would meet as senate in an open field'. By *centum illi* seems to be meant the hundred senators originally supposed to have been created (as was well known) by Romulus; cf. Liv. I, viii, 7 *centum creat senatores*. And *senatus* can mean 'a meeting of the senate', as in Cic. *Fam.* XII, xxv, 1 *eo die non fuit senatus*, etc. The verb *erat* takes its number from the adjoining predicate.

15. sinuosa: 'billowing' or 'rippling' in any breeze; cf. III, xviii, 13 *pleno fluitantia uela theatro* of awnings in a theatre.

16. sollemnis: 'at the annual festivals'.

crocos: saffron perfume, which in the sophisticated days of Rome used to be sprayed about the theatre to abate the other smells.

17–26. The buildings mentioned or suggested in lines 3–16 above, Palatium, Capitoline temple, Curia, temple of Quirinus, (?)theatre of Marcellus, were all built or restored or improved by Augustus. The religious institutions now to be mentioned were no doubt all involved in his plans, whether in prospect or already fulfilled, for the revival of religious traditions.

17. nulli...diuos: i.e. in contrast with Propertius' own day, when many were attracted by foreign cults, though these were disapproved by the authorities; cf. the advice attributed to Maecenas by Dio C. LII, 36 τὸ μὲν θεῖον...σέβου κατὰ τὰ πάτρια ...τοὺς δὲ δὴ ξενίζοντάς τι περὶ αὐτὸ καὶ μίσει καὶ κόλαζε.

fuit: for this scansion cf. *petiit* in I, x, 23, also immediately before a strong caesura in the third foot. The *i* in these perfects had originally been long, though in Propertius' day it was normally short.

18. cum...sacro: 'in those days when the people, in rapt attention, thrilled (with awe) at the rites they had received from their fathers'. For the required meaning of *pendula* cf. Pliny *Ep.* I, x, 7 *sequaris monentem attentus et pendens*; Lucr. VI, 51–2 *(mortales) pauidis cum pendent mentibu' saepe.* [But some take *pendula turba* quite otherwise, as suspended masks or puppets in some old rite; cf. Virg. *Georg.* II, 389.]

19. annuaque...faeno: 'and the Parilia was kept each year with bonfires of straw'. The Parilia, which fell on 21 April (incidentally the foundation date of Rome), was a shepherds' festival. One feature of it was the leaping of merrymakers over fires of straw; this is mentioned again at IV, iv, 77; cf. Tib. II, v, 89 and Ov. *Fast.* IV, 781. The point seems to be that this typically primitive and rustic procedure was then regularly followed in what was later to be the heart of the metropolis.

celebrata: *sc. sunt:* the preterite is easily appropriate here to recurrent action in the past because *annua = quotannis*; cf. IV, iv, 25 *saepe tulit*, etc. (But Propertius is apt to use the simple preterite, without such assistance, in a general statement about the past, even when the action he refers to is evidently one that was continuous or recurrent; cf. III, xiii, 34 *dedere* and 40 *reduxit*; IV, v, 64 and 70; IV, vi, 28 and note.)

20. qualia...equo: 'just as still today they sever the horse's tail to renew the cleansing magic (year by year)'. The horse is the so-called October Horse, and the reference is to an archaic rite described by Festus, p. 190 L.: a chariot race took place in the Campus Martius each year on 15 October and a horse of the winning pair was sacrificed and the blood from its tail allowed to drip on the hearth of the Regia; this blood later (see Ov. *Fast.* IV, 733) formed one ingredient of a magic compound used for religious purification (*lustra*). As *nunc* shows, the rite was still kept up in Propertius' day; so that the reference would be intelligible. The point of *qualia* (which, though grammatically constructed with *lustra*, goes really with the sentence as a whole and stands for *sicut*; cf. III, xvii, 40) seems to be that this quaint survival, within the reader's experience, is offered as an illustration of the general character of religion in the primitive settlement.

curto: the adjective means 'having lost a piece of itself'—in this case the tail.

21. Vesta...asellis: 'Vesta was poor, and proud of her garlanded donkeys'. At the Vestalia on 9 June both cornmills and the donkeys that worked them were garlanded with flowers and the donkeys had loaves of bread hung around their necks; cf. Ov. *Fast.* VI, 311. The point here seems to be that in olden days this custom was not (as in the poet's time) merely a quaint survival, but an important part of the honours paid to Vesta. Though Vesta's cult was always relatively simple in character it must naturally have become more expensive as civilization advanced; thus Ov. *Fast.* VI, 261 observes that her temple used to have a roof of thatch but now has a roof of bronze.

22. ducebant...boues: this describes a religious procession. *ducebant* could mean either that the oxen drew carts containing sacred objects, or simply that they headed the procession as sacrificial victims: cf. Virg. *Georg.* III, 532–3 *quaesitas ad sacra boues Iunonis et uris imparibus ductos alta ad donaria currus*, and also *Aen.* VIII, 665; but on the other hand *Georg.* 11, 148 of the victims which *Romanos ad templa deum duxere triumphos*.

23. parua...porci: the reference here seems to be to a *lustratio* (*gregis*, or *agri*, or *pagi*, or *urbis*), in which sacrificial victims were led around an area to secure immunity or divine protection for its occupants; see for instance Virg. *Georg.* I, 338 ff., Cato *R.R.* 141. Typically the offering was of three victims (pig, sheep and ox, called collectively *suouetaurilia*), so that the mention of a pig only here corresponds to the smallness and poverty of the community (cf. *parua compita*).

compita: the junctions of paths (dividing fields) in the country or streets in the town; then, secondarily, a sort of shrines erected at these points and sacred to the *Lares*. Augustus specially revived and encouraged the cult of the *Lares Compitales* by the inhabitants of the various *vici* of the city of Rome.

24. pastor...ouis: the sheep here may be alternative to the pig in a rite of lustration such as that just mentioned; it is in any case a relatively humble victim; cf. Tib. I, i, 21 *tunc uitula innumeros lustrabat caesa iuuencos: nunc agna exigui est hostia parua soli.* So also the shepherd's own pipe contrasts with the music of the professional flute-player which accompanied formal sacrifices in later times.

litabat: i.e. his sacrifice was acceptable to the gods.

25–6. uerbera...habet: 'and skin-clad ploughmen plied their hairy thongs, forerunners of the wanton rite of the Fabian Luperci (of today)'. As in line 20 the poet illustrates his account of the old religion by reference to a primitive rite still practised as a survival in his own times. However, the Luperci of his time were not rustics but persons of some rank. At the Lupercalia on 15 February the Luperci (drawn from two *collegia*, the Fabii and the Quintilii) ran around the boundary of the old Palatine settlement, striking with their goat-skin thongs any woman who came in their way; this was a charm to promote

fertility. For an account see Plutarch, *Romulus* 21 and Ov. *Fast.*
II, 267 ff.

27. nec rudis...armis: 'no gleaming weapons armed the
rude warriors of those days'. *rudis* is not negatived; it carries the
connotation that the warriors of those days were unskilled
amateurs beside the expert soldiers of later Rome. *infestis* shows
that by *armis* offensive arms primarily are meant; for the use of
in cf. Virg. *Aen.* v, 37 *horridus in iaculis et pelle Libystidis ursae.*

28. nuda presumably = *inermia*, which may be used to
indicate absence either of offensive or of defensive arms, so that
probably both ideas are present here.

29. prima galeritus posuit praetoria Lycmon: Lycmon is
the Etruscan captain who came to Romulus' aid against Tatius
and the Sabines; cf. Dion. Hal. II, xxxvii, ἧκε δὲ αὐτῷ Τυρρηνῶν
ἐπικουρίαν ἱκανὴν ἄγων ἐκ Σολωνίου πόλεως ἀνὴρ δραστήριος καὶ
τὰ πολέμια διαφανής, Λοκόμων ὄνομα. The name is formed from
lucumo, the Etruscan word for a chieftain.

The point here is in line with the thought of the preceding
couplet. The word *galeritus* carries a heavy emphasis in the sentence. Even Lycmon, general though he was, made do with a
cap of skin instead of the helmet (sometimes very magnificent by
Propertius' time) of later days. The *galerus* is worn by a rustic
warrior in Virg. *Aen.* VII, 668; in historical Rome a version of it
was worn by the holders of the most ancient priesthoods.

prima ... posuit praetoria is simply an indirect way of saying
that Lycmon was a general; it defines his status in terms of a
function characteristic of a general; namely (as stated by
Polybius VI, 27 and illustrated by Liv. IX, ii, 12) to mark the
place and give the signal for an army to encamp by setting up his
own tent (called the *praetorium*) first. This may explain the point
of *prima* here. Or perhaps we can take *prima...praetoria* as
= *primi ducis praetorium*; for *primus dux* cf. Virg. *Aen.* VII, 107;
Lucan VII, 223. Or perhaps *prima* here may = 'primitive'; cf.
Quint. *Inst. Or.* VIII, iii, 36 *illi rudes homines primique.*

[Some prefer to understand that Lycmon was the first to
make an advance on the primitive conditions of the preceding
couplet by introducing organized methods of warfare, typified by
the characteristic Roman system of encampment. This gives an
easy construction, but extends rather drastically the natural
meaning of *praetoria*. It also introduces a new idea, which is not
carried on in the following pentameter.]

30. magnaque pars Tatio rerum erat inter ouis: Tatius is the Sabine king who first made war on Romulus and then became his colleague in the kingship of Rome. He too is represented as a primitive and pastoral figure. The sentence means either (*a*) 'and most of Tatius' feats were in the pastures (i.e. in pastoral affrays)'; or (*b*) 'and most of Tatius' business was in the pastures'. The former of these better fits the military context of lines 27–9; and for *res* = 'feats' cf. II, i, 25 *bellaque resque tui memorarem Caesaris*: Hor. *Sat.* II, i, 10 *Caesaris inuicti res dicere*; Hor. *Ep.* I, xvii, 33 *res gerere et captos ostendere ciuibus hostes attingit solium Iouis*; Ov. *Met.* IV, 639 *seu gloria tangit te generis magni, generis mihi Iuppiter auctor; siue es mirator rerum, mirabere nostras*; Val. Flacc. I, 98 (the word is spread) *iam stare ratem remisque superbam poscere quos reuehat rebusque ad sidera tollat*.

31. hinc: 'from such conditions...'; or 'from such a kind of men...'.

Tities Ramnesque uiri Luceresque Soloni: 'the Tities and brave Ramnes and the Solonian Luceres'. The names of the three original Roman tribes supposed to have been constituted by Romulus here stand for the warriors (cf. *uiri*) of early Rome. The Luceres are called Solonian as coming from Solonium (or *ager Solonius*, as the name elsewhere appears); see the passage from Dion. Hal. quoted on line 29 above.

32. quattuor hinc...equos: i.e. with such men (or, with such resources) Romulus won his triumphs.

33. quippe: the immediate connexion of thought seems to be 'for there were wars to be fought, since...'. But the point illustrated by what follows is that Rome was a tiny place and her wars still miniature affairs. In line 34 *maxima turba* is half-ironical.

suburbanae paruae minus urbe Bouillae: i.e. Rome's little suburb (as it now is) Bovillae was in those days not as little as (and so more than a match for) Rome itself. [The text is uncertain here.]

33–6. Bouillae...Gabi (contracted for *Gabii*)...**Alba... Fidenas:** these were all Latin towns near Rome, later extinct or reduced to mere hamlets; cf. Liv. I, xxix, Cic. *Planc.* IX, 23, Hor. *Epist.* I, xi, 7. The furthest was Alba, rather more than twelve miles from Rome, the nearest Fidenae, about five miles.

34. nulli = (here) 'reduced almost to nothing'; cf. I, v, 22 *cur sim toto corpore nullus ego*.

35. albae suis omine: the reference is to the sign of the white sow with thirty young, seen by Aeneas after his landing in Latium and interpreted to him as promising the foundation of Alba after thirty years; cf. Virg. *Aen*. VIII, 41 ff.

37–8. nil patrium...lupam: in its context this must refer, figuratively, to the Roman people, and summarize the thought of all that has been said: that Rome has risen 'from nothing' to her present greatness. In this sense it can be translated: 'the breed that Rome has nurtured owes nothing to inheritance, except its name; no shame to own a she-wolf foster-mother of the race'. But in their literal sense the words apply unmistakably to Romulus, first suckled by the she-wolf and then brought up as the supposed child of a landless shepherd; and in this sense, which must also be present, the same words can be translated: 'the Roman nursling has no inheritance except his name; no shame to own the she-wolf for foster-mother'. The phrase *nil patrium nisi nomen habet* looks like a proverbial tag for a poor man's son who starts in life with nothing. The point of *non pudet* seems to be that the thought of the she-wolf might seem to a superficial observer out of place in the context of Rome's present grandeur, but is not so in the context of Rome's or Romulus' humble beginnings; moreover, the Romans, secure in their present grandeur and power, look back with pride to their humble beginnings and with pride and gratitude to their humble benefactress in that distant past: cf. Sen. *Contr*. I, vi, 4 (the Romans) *humilitatem suam, cum obscurare possint, ostendunt; et haec non putant magna, nisi apparuerit ex paruis surrexisse*. This thought will be pursued in lines 55–6 below; the connexion is obscured by the long parenthesis 39–54 which now intervenes.

39–54. On the content of this section and its relation to what precedes and follows it, see the general introduction to this elegy above. For the subject cf. Virgil's *Aeneid* and Tib. II, v, 19 ff. and 39 ff. It will be noticed that 39–54 forms a parenthesis, and that line 55 follows naturally on line 38.

39. melius: 'well was it that...'. *melius*, adverb (as here) or adjective, is sometimes used in this sense, without any real comparative value: cf. Juv. II, 139 *sed melius* (well it is) *quod nil animis in corpore iuris natura indulget*. (The English 'you'd better...' is not equivalent in meaning, but is another instance of the loss of comparative force.)

40. heu: 'ah'. *heu* conveys emotion, but not necessarily (though commonly) grief: cf. Housman on Lucan v, 354.

quali...aue: 'with what good augury'.

41ff. iam bene..., etc.: the favour of destiny was made plain from the beginning. Lines 41-4 amplify the idea propounded in line 40: similarly lines 49-54 below will amplify the idea contained in the word *felix* ('of happy destiny') in line 48.

iam bene spondebant: for the final vowel left short before initial *sp-*, etc. cf. IV, iv, 48 *tu cape spinosi* and IV, v, 17 *consuluitque striges*; also III, xi, 53 and 67, III, xix, 21. Tibullus and Ovid allow themselves this only before intractable foreign words (*smaragdus, Zacynthus*).

illam: the *Dardana puppis*, i.e. the Trojan ship or fleet (singular for plural) which was to bring Aeneas and his companions to Italy; here representing or at least including those who were to travel in it.

uenter apertus...equi: the opening of the belly (womb) of the Wooden Horse to let out the Greek warriors who captured Troy.

pater: Anchises.

45. hinc...secures: 'hence came the heroism of Decius and (stern) Brutus' axe(s)'. The virtues of the heroes who made Rome great were derived, by descent or example, from the Trojan immigration. Decius and Brutus are cited as typical Roman heroes, notable for their *uirtus* but above all for their *pietas*, devotion to their country. Decius sacrificed himself to the gods of the underworld to ensure his soldiers' victory in battle; Brutus, liberator of Rome from Tarquin and one of the republic's first pair of consuls, put his own sons to death for conspiring against the state. The *secures* are the axes in the lictors' *fasces*, symbol of consular office, and used to execute offenders; here the mention of them denotes the execution by the consul of his own sons. Brutus and Decius occur in proximity also as typical heroes in Virg. *Aen.* VI, 819-24 and in Juv. VIII, 254-68.

[*hinc* here is an emendation for *tunc* of the MSS. It is possible that *tunc* should be retained, for *uenere* is then in accord with *uexit* in line 46; on the other hand, *uenere* in the sense 'came to

Italy' with *secures* for subject makes a rather harsh figure of speech. If kept, *tunc* = 'then was it that . . .'.]

46–8: uexit et . . . deos: 'yes, and Venus brought us Caesar, her warrior son (*Caesaris arma*), when she bore hither the conquering arms of Troy resurgent; blessed by fate was this land that received Iulus' gods'. Venus is said to have borne or conveyed the arms of Troy (i.e. the armed warriors led by Aeneas) to Italy because she protected them on their voyage; this she is represented as doing in the Aeneid, and Servius on *Aen.* 1, 382 quotes Varro for a legend that her star actually guided them all the way from Troy to their destination. She is said in so doing to have brought the arms of Caesar (i.e. the great warrior Caesar, much as *Bruti . . . secures* in line 45 stands in effect for the stern executioner Brutus) because Aeneas' son Iulus (line 48) = Ascanius was supposed ancestor of the Julian family and so of Julius Caesar and (by common convention) of his adopted son Caesar Augustus. The reference here is to Augustus; Propertius elsewhere (e.g. II, i, 25, II, vii, 5, II, x, 4, III, iv, 1) dwells more on his military than on his other achievements, and at IV, vi, 37 calls him *mundi seruator* for his victory at Actium.

48. felix: 'blessed by destiny', as the outcome has shown.

deos: the household gods of the *Iulii*, symbolizing the family. Inevitably in the background is the thought of the Penates of the Roman state, supposed also to have been brought by Aeneas from Troy.

49. si modo: this construction is most easily understood as dependent on the idea of *felix*, echoed from the preceding line; Italy must have been favoured by destiny from the beginning, if the rise of Rome was being prophesied long beforehand. In a conditional sentence of this kind, the speaker sometimes assumes that his audience know that the condition is fulfilled. The prophecies here alluded to appear to be that of the Sibyl delivered to Aeneas in Tib. II, v, 39 ff. and that of Cassandra reported to Priam in Lycophron, *Alexandra* 1225 ff.

Auernalis tremulae cortina Sibyllae: 'the shuddering Sibyl's tripod by Avernus' shore' or 'the inspired prophetess of Avernus, the shuddering Sibyl'. The Sibyl's *cortina* is the tripod on which she is conceived as sitting, like the prophetess at Delphi, to receive inspiration. It is called *Auernalis* because the Sibyl of Cumae, also associated with lake Avernus, is here in mind. For *cortina Sibyllae* as subject of *dixit* cf. on *Bruti . . .*

secures (45) and *Caesaris arma* (46) above. The Sibyl is said to be 'shuddering' because she is thus affected when possessed by the god.

50. dixit...Remo: i.e. (?) spoke (in prophecy) of the site, still rural then, for which (one day) Remus, (unlucky patron) of the Aventine, was to make atonement (with his death). A dark saying in which much is left to be supplied. The context (cf. lines 48 and 54) requires a prophecy of the rise of Rome, de-livered about the time of the fall of Troy and coming of the Trojan remnant to Italy. Such a prophecy is delivered by the Sibyl to Aeneas in Tib. II, v, 19 ff.: the place of it is not clear in Tibullus, but Cumae would inevitably come to mind because of *Aen.* VI. The word *rura* here refers to the site of Rome and is explained by Tib. II, v, 55–6 *carpite nunc, tauri, de septem montibus herbas dum licet; hic magnae iam locus urbis erit*; cf. also Car-mentis' prophecy in Ov. *Fast.* v, 96 *nam locus imperii rus erit istud, ait.* That *Remus* here is Romulus' twin and not (as in line 9 above) another name for Romulus himself is shown by Tib. II, v, 24 *moenia consorti non habitanda Remo* (a reference to the quarrel of the two brothers and Remus' death in consequence) and by the epithet here *Auentino* (which contrasts Remus with Romulus, who—see IV, vi, 44 below—*ire Palatinas...uidit aues*). But the *rura pianda Remo* cannot in this context be the site un-successfully preferred by Remus for his augural observations or for the proposed new city; the *rura*, subject of the Sibyl's pro-phecy, must be the site on which the city of destiny was actually founded. The only way in which Remus could be said to *piare* this site would be by his death, conceived as a sacrifice (*pia-culum*), and so as (*a*) making amends for his impious leap over the wall, or (*b*) rendering the wall inviolable for the future (cf. III, ix, 50 *caeso moenia firma Remo*); or (*c*) more generally, hallowing and so protecting from harm the site and city as a whole. Of these, (*a*) or (*b*) is recommended by the known re-ligious status of the walls of Rome; cf. Cic. *N.D.* III, 94 *urbis muros, quos uos pontifices sanctos esse dicitis.* On the other hand (*c*) is recommended by *rura*, which seems too wide a term to refer to the walls specifically. For the sense of *piare* required by (*b*) or (*c*) cf. Ov. *Fast.* II, 29 *quodcumque est quo corpora nostra piantur* (of religious purification).

51. Pergameae...uatis: Cassandra, who is represented in Lycophron's *Alexandra* as prophesying the fall of Troy and the rise of Rome; not indeed in Priam's presence, but in the presence of a servant who reports her words to Priam.

sero rata: = ὀψιτέλεστα = 'fulfilled long after'.

51–2. si...uera fuere: the context suggests that this is parallel to *si modo* in line 49, and that the meaning is not 'if Cassandra's prophecy, fulfilled long after, was true', *uera* duplicating *sero rata*, but rather 'if the story is true of that prophecy of Cassandra delivered to old Priam, long after to be fulfilled:...'.

53–4. uertite equum...arma dabit: an imaginary specimen of Cassandra's prophecy, which in Lycophron's *Alexandra* is partly concerned with the future woes of the Greek victors (see e.g. lines 1281–2) as well as promising the rise of Rome from the Trojan survivors. She is not of course really addressing the Greeks or trying to warn them; the apostrophe is part of the prophetic style: cf. 117 below. The *equus* is the Wooden Horse. *male* ('to no avail' or 'to your hurt') is said from the Greeks' point of view.

huic cineri...arma dabit: 'will arm these ashes'; i.e. will make a race of warriors arise from the survivors of the burning of Troy.

55–70. optima...oportet equus: for the general content of this section and its relation to what precedes see introductory note above.

55–6. optima...tuo: after the parenthesis which has occupied lines 39–54 the poet now reverts to the she-wolf (cf. line 38).

56. moenia: 'city', as often, e.g. Virg. *Aen.* IV, 74 *media Aenean secum per moenia ducit*.

57–8. moenia namque...sonus: i.e. for I am preparing to discourse of our city in my poems, and honour her as in duty bound; alas that mine is not a lofty style.

disponere: this seems here to mean 'expound' or 'set out the story of'.

paruus in ore sonus: cf. Virg. *Georg.* III, 294 *magno nunc ore sonandum*; Hor. *Sat.* I, iv, 43–4 *os magna sonaturum*. Different degrees of grandeur and elevation are appropriate to different types of poetry and to different subjects; and some poets who command a style adequate for success at a modest level could not do justice to a 'high' theme. Both Propertius and Horace are always professing to know their limitation in this respect.

[*conor* in line 57 is an emendation for *coner* of the old MSS., which may be due to *-oner-* in the word next following.]

59–60. sed tamen...meae: for this conception of literature as a service to the state cf. Livy, *Praef. iuuabit tamen rerum gestarum memoriae principis terrarum populi pro uirili parte et ipsum consuluisse*; Cic. *Leg.* I, 5 *uideris...patriae debere hoc munus* (viz. writing history), and *Brutus* 253–4, and *Tusc. Disp.* II, 5; also Sall. *Jug.* 4, etc. Sometimes the service consists in praise, sometimes in the addition of a new (literary) achievement to the existing achievements of Rome.

59. exiguo...riui: he has in mind the ὀλίγη λιβάς, ἄκρον ἄωτον of Callimachus, *H. Apollo*, 112.

61. Ennius...corona: an Ennius may be content to crown his poetry with 'a ragged wreath'. The quality of the wreath symbolizes the quality of the poetry: Ennius was considered by the Augustans to be powerful but rough and unfinished; cf. Ov. *Trist.* II, 424 *Ennius ingenio maximus, arte rudis*.

62. hedera: sacred to Bacchus, and often treated by Propertius as a symbol of poetic inspiration; he associated it apparently with his own kind of poetry, the kind that is delicate and sophisticated. For his ideas on poetry and view of his own capacities see especially II, i, II, x, III, i, III, iii, III, ix; also II, 34 and III, 2.

64. Romani...Callimachi: the reference is to Callimachus of Cyrene, third century B.C., the most important poet of his time, and the professor of literary principles which are often reflected in the elegies of Propertius listed in the note on line 62 above. In calling himself here the Roman Callimachus Propertius has in mind (*a*) in general Callimachus' eminence as a writer of elegiac verse, and (*b*) in particular his celebrated poem called the *Aitia* (= Origins), on subjects similar to those which Propertius in lines 69–70 below announces that he is intending to treat himself.

For the claim to have matched in Latin literature one of the great masters of Greek literature or the achievement of the Greeks in some given department cf. the similar claim of Cicero in respect of philosophical exposition, of Virgil in respect of Theocritean pastoral and Hesiodic didaxis, of Horace in respect of Archilochus and Lesbian lyric, etc.

65. scandentis...arces: this describes the steep hills crowned by small towns or fortresses (*arx* can mean either a height or a fortress) that are characteristic of the Umbrian landscape; it is to Umbria as a whole that Propertius here is hoping to bring honour, not specifically to his own town; cf. line 64.

66. ingenio muros aestimet ille meo: the ablative is not of price, but of the source of value; cf. Mart. I, lxi, 3 *censetur Aponi Liuio suo tellus*; similar though not identical is the use in Hor. *Epist.* II, i, 48 *uirtutem aestimat annis*. The verb *aestimo* seems to be used here much as we sometimes use 'value' in English to denote positive approbation. The *muros* are the *arces* of the landscape in 65.

67–8. candida...omina: words of fair omen, in the form of good wishes or prayers for his success.

87–8. dicam 'Troia, cades...sepulcra canam': this couplet is obviously misplaced in the MSS. Placed here it fits the style and the sense; and the echo *canam...canam* resembles that of *boues...boues* in IV, ix, 16–17. Propertius announces (*a*), in this couplet, that he will write poetic prophecies of the fall of Troy and rise of Rome, such as we find in Tib. II, v, 39–64 and Hor. *Od.* I, xv and III, iii; and (*b*), in lines 69–70, that he will write aetiological poems on the origins of old rites (*sacra*) and festivals (*dies*) and place-names, etc., as Ovid was later to do in the *Fasti* and as Callimachus had done before in the *Aitia*. Both types of writing have been foreshadowed in the present poem already; and prophecy, like aetiology, had been cultivated as matter for poetry by the Alexandrians. In the event, we find in the remainder of the present book a number of aetiological poems but no prophetic ones; and this fits with the fact that in lines 71–2 of IB below the poet is warned against proceeding with the first part of his design.[1]

(A similar misplacement appears to have occurred in elegy VIII below, where the couplet that stands after line 18 in the MSS. should, to all appearance, stand after line 2.)

88. et maris...sepulcra canam: the meaning of this is uncertain, and the text may be corrupt. It may be that the poet intends to tell stories purporting to derive place-names (cf. *cognomina prisca locorum* in line 69) from the death or burial of legendary persons, such as Misenus, Palinurus, Caieta, etc. For the then required value of *longa* cf. II, xiii, 19 *longa...imagine* = 'a long line of busts'. [But perhaps the old emendation *pericla*

[1] See however footnote on p. 45.

should be accepted, and the adventures of Aeneas and his companions, or of later Roman heroes, are the subject proposed.]

69. sacra diesque...et cognomina prisca locorum: for the meaning of these terms see the note on 87–8 above.

I B

This second half of the elegy falls like the first into three sections, though the first of them is extremely brief. In lines 71–4 the astrologer takes his cue[1] from the programme announced by the poet at the end of iA and warns him that the fates are unfavourable to the execution of the part of it to which lines 87–8 (above) refer. In lines 75–118 he expatiates, first on his own qualifications and professional successes, and then on the superiority of astrology as such over other techniques of divination. In lines 119–50 he gives a summary of the content of Propertius' horoscope (*astra*); his birthplace, early personal history, present servitude to a tyrant mistress, and future prospect of remaining in that condition. In conclusion he warns him to beware of the influence of the sign of the zodiac called the Crab.

What we have here is a genre study in the form of a monologue, such as we find in many contexts of ancient literature (good examples are some of the mimes of Herodas) and again in the speech of the *lena* in iv, v below. It stands as such in its own right.

But Propertius has had the idea of using this established form —by the convenient choice of an astrologer as the character type to be depicted—as a means of conveying some brief personal particulars about himself to posterity, and in particular identifying his birthplace. Information of this kind is conveyed by Virgil at the beginning of *Georgic* iii and the end of *Georgic* iv, by Horace at the end of the first collection of his *Odes* (iii, xxx), by Ovid at the end of his *Amores* (iii, xv); later Ovid furnished a full autobiography at the end of Book iv of the *Tristia*. This kind of personal material obviously asks for a significant position in any collection, either the last poem or the first.

On the connexion, such as it is, between this second half of the elegy and the first half, see the introductory note to the whole elegy above (including the footnote on p. 45) and the notes on lines 87–8 (above) and 71 (below).

[1] See however footnote on p. 45.

71. quo ruis...dicere fata, Properti?: 'what folly is this that you are rushing into, Propertius, wayward man, proposing (as you say) to prophesy?'. There seems to be in the Latin a not unnatural conflation of two different constructions: 'whither are you hurrying...' and 'why are you in a hurry to...'. The astrologer is a newcomer on the scene, not the *hospes* of line 1 above, concerning whom see note on that line.

fata: for the reference see note on 87–8 above. No more is said on this subject once it has served what is presumably its main purpose—to provide a 'cue' for IB and a formal link between it and IA; cf. on line 1 above.

[Concerning the possibility, and consequences, of reading *discere* in this line and understanding *fata* as Propertius' 'fortune' see footnote on p. 45.]

72. non sunt...colo: literally: 'it is from no propitious distaff that your thread is spun'; i.e. the fates that spin the thread of your destiny are not propitious to your present undertaking. For *condere* of the destiny spun by the *Parcae* cf. Stat. *Silu.* I, ii, 24 *iamque dies aderat Parcarum conditus albo uellere.* For *colus* masculine cf. IV, ix, 48.

73. accersis lacrimas: 'you are inviting grief'; so in Lucan IV, 484 a man courting death is said *accersere fata.*

auersus Apollo: for the opposite condition cf. III, ii, 9 *Apolline dextro*, Apollo being the god of poetry and giver of inspiration. For this role of Apollo in Propertius cf. I, ii, 17, I, viii, 41, II, i, 3, III, i, 7, III, iii, 13 ff., IV, i, 133, IV, vi, 69.

74. pigenda: either (*a*) 'that you will regret'; or (*b*) 'that it (the lyre) is loth to grant'.

lyra: for the lyre as symbol of poetic inspiration cf. II, x, 10 *nunc aliam citharam me mea musa docet.* It is Apollo's instrument; cf. IV, vi, 69.

76. aerata signa mouere pila: literally: 'to handle the signs (of the zodiac) on the bronze ball'. The object in question appears to be a globe of bronze, possibly adjustable in some way, with the signs of the zodiac and perhaps the other constellations on it; it is mentioned as the typifying equipment of an astrologer. *aerata* stands for *aerea. mouere* is a regular word for using an instrument; cf. Ov. *Am.* I, i, 12 *Aoniam Marte mouente lyram*; at Cic. *Rep.* I, 22 it is used specifically of someone turning, or 'working', a celestial globe (*hanc sphaeram cum Gallus moueret...*).

77. *Orops* and the speaker *Horos* are presumably fictitious characters. *Archytas* (fourth century B.C.) and *Conon* (third century B.C.) are the names of real people, celebrated figures in the history of Greek astronomy. Either (*a*) by *suboles* in line 77 and *domus* in line 78 something like 'disciple' and 'school' is meant; or (*b*) the speaker is depicted as a mountebank who claims these people as his ancestors for the sake of the impressive scientific associations of their names.

Astrology was a mixture of (*a*) false science, concerned with the supposed influence of the stars and planets on the character and destiny of individuals, and (*b*) perfectly genuine astronomical science, used to determine the positions of the various stars at given dates for the purposes of (*a*).

79. degenerasse has *me* (understood) for subject and *propinquos* for object.

81. fecere has for its subject an indefinite 'they'.

pretium facere here evidently means 'make into a source of profit'; cf. II, iv, 15 *cui non ego sum fallaci praemia uati?* (Elsewhere *pretium facere* is found with various other meanings: 'put up the price of...', 'offer a price for...', and 'get a return for' trouble taken, etc.)

81–2. fallitur auro Iuppiter: 'there are people who for gold pretend to reveal the will of Jupiter'; literally '(the will of) Jupiter is counterfeited for gold'. For an example of *fallere* in this sense cf. Virg. *Aen.* 1, 683 *tu faciem illius...falle dolo* (counterfeit his appearance), and the common use of the passive past participle *falsus* in the sense 'counterfeited', 'pretended', etc. [The text is uncertain here.]

82. obliquae signa iterata rotae: 'the signs of the slanting circle (i.e. the ecliptic) that the sun traverses in his (annually) repeated round'.

83–5. felices...rapaces...graue...animosa: qualities attaching in astrological lore to the planets and constellations mentioned.

84. in omne caput: 'to all alike'; for the use of *caput* cf. IV, xi, 10 and 55.

85. quid moueant: 'the purpose of...' or 'the influence of...'. The construction is loose but intelligible, the substantive clause in the form of an indirect question being parallel to the accusatives *deos* in line 81 and *stellas*, etc., in lines 83–4.

86. lotus et Hesperia...Capricornus aqua: a constellation disappearing beneath the western horizon can be said to be 'bathed in the western sea'. It is a question here whether simply the 'setting of Capricorn' is meant; or whether *lotus*, etc., is a general attribute of Capricorn, which is called in Hor. *Od.* II, xvii, 19–20 *tyrannus Hesperiae Capricornus undae*, and which never rises far above the horizon.

89–102. Arria...Lupercus...Gallus...Cinara: we cannot tell whether these are fictitious or real persons.

89–90. produceret...dabat arma: these expressions are used of a wife 'seeing off' her husband, and of a wife helping her husband to arm himself, in Ov. *Her.* XIII, 140–3 *ipsa suis manibus forti noua nupta marito imponet galeam Dardanaque arma dabit...producetque uirum.*

92. nempe: of an undisputed fact; here perhaps 'as you well know'.

93–4. quippe...eques...equo: the rider raises his hand (perhaps instinctively) to cover his wounded face, and through this error gets thrown (*sibi...non bene cauit*) when his horse stumbles (*prolapso equo*; the verb *prolabi* can be used either of horse or of rider; it is used of the horse e.g. at Liv. XXVII, xix, 10).

[The MSS. give *equi* in line 93; with which reading the horse has a head wound, and the rider is covering this when he falls. Persons with cavalry experience assure me that this is not an easily intelligible situation, so I have printed in the text and annotated above Heinsius' conjecture *eques*, which also removes the stylistic awkwardness of *equi...equo*.]

The reference in all this is very likely to the *clades Lolliana*, of 16 B.C., mentioned by Suet. *Aug.* 23 and Dio C. LIV, 20. The enemy were some German tribes who, according to Dio, τό τε ἱππικὸν τὸ τῶν Ῥωμαίων ἐπελθὸν σφισιν ἐνήδρευσαν, καὶ φεύγουσιν αὐτοῖς ἐπισπόμενοι τῷ τε Λολλίῳ...ἐνέτυχον ἀνέλπιστοι καὶ ἐνίκησαν κἀι ἐκεῖνον.

97. fatales...auarae: 'ill-fated lads, both victims of their mother's greed'. She had sent them to the wars in the hope that they would bring money home. *fatalis* can have a good, bad, or neutral sense according to its context.

98. fides: 'confirmation' or 'fulfilment' of his prediction; cf. Ov. *Met.* III, 527 *dicta fides sequitur*, VIII, 711 *uota fides sequitur*. By *ista* is meant 'afforded by you (i.e. by your fate)'.

inuito: sc. *mihi*.

101. Iunoni...uotum impetrabile: both text and punctuation are uncertain. The version printed means: 'make sacrifice to Juno (i.e. Juno Lucina, presiding over childbirth): your prayer is (*or* will be) granted'.

103 ff. Here the astrologer passes from advertisement of his own skill to a general eulogy of astrology as opposed to other kinds of divination.

103. hoc: i.e. this kind of problem.

harenosum Libyae Iouis...antrum: the oracle of Jupiter Ammon in Libya. The double genitive is softened by the fact that *Iouis* goes very closely with *antrum*, and *Libyae* with the whole phrase *Iouis antrum*.

104. fibra: i.e. (sing. for pl.) entrails, from inspection of which *haruspices* read the future.

sibi commissos...deos: i.e. the purposes of heaven, confided, as it were, to the entrails and there discerned by the *haruspex*.

105. si quis...senserit: i.e. an augur. *senserit* evidently here means 'discern the meaning of...'; cf. Virg. *Aen.* III, 360 *qui sidera sentis* (of the seer Helenus).

motas cornicis...alas: 'the flight of a raven'; an example of the material of augury.

106. umbraue...aquis: hydromancy, in which ghosts or other spirits (conjured up by the operator) appear in a bowl of water and declare the future.

107. uerus = (here) *uerax* = 'telling the truth'. The *trames per astra* is the zodiac.

108. zonis: the five zones (one hot, two temperate, and two cold) are not really relevant to astrology.

109 ff. The story which follows illustrates the danger of knowing something but not enough in these matters, and hence the danger of inferior methods of divination. Calchas knew how (at grievous cost) to enable the Greeks windbound at Aulis to proceed on their way to Troy; he did not know what evils awaited the Greeks, or how to bring them safely home again.

110. pia saxa: the rocky coast of Aulis is said to be either (*a*) 'righteous' or 'god-fearing', because it upholds the rights of Artemis, whose stag Agamemnon had killed, by detaining the Greek fleet; or (*b*) 'merciful' because by detaining the Greeks it tries to save them from the evils that lie ahead. These alternatives are not exclusive; both senses are present. The ships are called *bene haerentis* because it is really better for them not to proceed and for Iphigenia not to be sacrificed.

111. Agamemnoniae...puellae: Iphigenia.

113. nec rediere tamen: 'but (that was not the end of the story for) the Danaans did not...'.

114–18. Euboicos...sinus...Nauplius...Oiliade: at the taking of Troy, Ajax son of Oileus tore Cassandra away from the image of Athena to which she clung as a suppliant. Athena in her displeasure caused a storm to befall the Greeks on their home-ward voyage, as a result of which Ajax was shipwrecked and killed. Nauplius was father of Palamedes, whose death was un-justly compassed by Ulysses; in revenge he lit fires on the coast of Euboea to lure the returning Greeks to destruction by ship-wreck.

116. natat: the poet has floating wreckage and corpses in mind; cf. II, xxv, 24 *cum...fracta carina natet*; III, vii, 8 (a dead man) *piscibus esca natat*.

exuuiis...pressa suis: the wrecked ships are conceived as sinking more readily because heavily laden with the spoils of Troy.

117. nunc: this *nunc* with an ironical imperative (often in the form *i nunc et...*) may convey either (*a*) 'now you see how wrong it was of you to...'; or (*b*) 'now you see how little good it has done you that...'. Here both are appropriate.

rape nunc et dilige: 'drag from her sanctuary and ra-vish...'. For the reference, see general note on 114–18, above. The verb *diligo* is most commonly met meaning a virtuous affection, but that it can also be applied to gross desire is shown by a review of the adverbs and adverbial phrases found in association with it and listed in the *Th.L.L.* (e.g. *ardentissime, infamissime, turpi...amore, obscena...cupiditate*); cf. also Ov. *Met.* IX, 735 *ne non tamen omnia Crete monstra ferat, taurum dilexit filia solis.* Here the meaning seems to be extended from lust to an act of lust.

119–20. hactenus...nouis: the astrologer now turns to Propertius, having discoursed sufficiently about himself and his art. In 121 ff. he will recite some facts of the poet's past (for the benefit of the reader, but also in accordance with the practice of fortune-tellers), and in 139 ff. he will tell him that he is destined to remain the slave of a tyrant woman: this presumably is the 'bad news' (line 120) for which Propertius is now warned to prepare himself.

119. hactenus historiae: 'but enough of these tales'; cf. *haec hactenus*, and Plaut. *Bacch.* 158 *satis historiarum est*. He will now come down to business.

120. incipe tu lacrimis aequus adesse nouis: i.e. 'now prepare (*incipe*) to attend with composure (*aequus adesse*) to (?) more matter for tears (*lacrimis...nouis*). By *nouis* he might mean additional to the gloomy substance of the earlier part of his speech, or additional to the misfortunes which Propertius (as we are about to hear) has experienced already. But it is as likely that *lacrimis...nouis* is simply Propertian shorthand for 'bad news'.

121. Vmbria: Propertius has already told us in lines 63–4 that he was born in Umbria; the astrologer tells us whereabouts in Umbria.

123. Meuania: now Bevagna, in the plain below Assisi.

124. lacus Vmber: this also was in the plain below Assisi, but does not now exist, the ground having been drained long ago.

125. Asisi: the MSS. give *Asis*, but it seems reasonable to restore the appropriate case of the name *Asisium*. This name as it happens is nowhere extant in Latin literature, but Greek authors have Αἰσίσιον, and Ἀσισινοί as name of the inhabitants, whom Pliny calls *Asisinates*; see on the subject Butler and Barber, p. xviii.

uertice: this probably here means 'on its hilltop'; a conical eminence is suggested, crowned by an *arx*, and with buildings 'mounting' the hillside.

130. pertica: the surveyor's measure. Apparently Propertius lost his land, like Virgil, in the confiscations of 41 B.C.

131. bulla: the amulet worn on the neck by free-born children and abandoned when the *toga uirilis* was assumed; this would be at an age between 15 and 17. The ceremony took place in the presence of the household gods. These are said to be the mother's because, as we have been told, Propertius' father was by now dead.

rudi...collo: the epithet *rudis* implies both 'untried' and 'inexperienced'. In an English rendering we can transfer it from *collo* and say, e.g., 'when the amulet of boyhood was shed from my neck'.

133. de: not 'about' but 'from' (his store of poetic inspiration). Cf. on 73 above.

135–8. at tu...hostis eris: the promise of line 136, and the prophetic future tenses of 137–8 and the terms of the sentence in which they occur, are better suited to the beginning of Propertius' career than to a time when he had been writing for ten years about love and Cynthia and was already established in reputation (126) as a poet; so it seems best to take 135–8 as a quotation from the speech of Apollo implied by lines 133–4. [Some give 135–46 to Apollo; some give the whole speech to the astrologer himself.]

135. fallax opus: it is difficult to find an attested value for *fallax* that fits the context; perhaps it here approximates in meaning to *blandum*: cf. II, v, 5 *inueniam tamen e multis fallacibus unam quae fieri nostro carmine nota uelit*; Hor. *Od.* III, vii, 19–20 *peccare docentes fallax historias mouet.*

138. utilis hostis: 'a good antagonist'. Here *utilis* combines two senses: (a) 'doughty', as in Hor. *Odes* I, xii, 42 *utilem bello...Camillum*; and (b) 'useful' because providing good sport for a long time.

139. nam: '(and so it has proved) for...'.

140. eludit palmas: 'mocks your triumphs', or 'eludes your grasp'. The first meaning is required by the preceding line, the second is present as a pun, perhaps accidental.

una puella: this must be Cynthia, the subject of so many of Propertius' earlier elegies and of vii and viii below. It seems reasonable to infer from the terms here used (a) that the breach with Cynthia announced in III, xxiv and xxv was not effective; and (b) that elegy vii below, which refers to her death, is later in date than the present elegy—perhaps latest of all in the book.

141. discusseris: this verb usually means 'dash in pieces' or the like; but Propertius is independent in his use of compounds, and there seems no reason to doubt that he could use it to mean 'throw off by shaking your head this way and that'.

142. ansa: this word means elsewhere a big hook, a clamp, a shoehorn, a handle, etc. Just what it means here we do not know; perhaps the equivalent of a modern fisherman's gaff? If so the *rostrum* will be its big, sharp hook; the *uncus* of line 141 being the fish-hook. But text and sense are both uncertain.

[Many here read *rostro...tuo*, and understand it of the victim's 'snout'.]

143. illius arbitrio noctem lucemque uidebis: it is not clear whether this means (a) that he will always be at her orders, day and night, or (b) that he will believe her if she tells him it's day at midnight and vice versa.

145–6. nec mille...sat est: not only will she be tyrannical; she will also be unfaithful.

persuasae: 'resolved to...'.

147–50. nunc tua...time: in this passage *licet* does not mean 'although', but indicates things that Propertius is free to do, i.e. need not fear to do, as opposed to the peril presently stated in line 150 which he must fear. The speaker promises the poet, as victim of love, the traditional immunity of lovers from ordinary dangers: cf. III, xvi, 13 ff. *quisquis amator erit Scythicis licet ambulet oris; nemo adeo ut noceat barbarus esse uelit*; and II, xxvii, 11–12 *solus amans nouit quando periturus et a qua morte, neque hic Boreae flabra neque arma timet*. The sense of the present passage thus is: 'you can be storm-tossed; you can go unarmed to fight armed men; the earth can open under you; none of these things need make you afraid. But one thing you must fear—the sign of the Crab, fraught with ill omen for you.' The reason why he must fear the Crab is presumably astrological; one conjectures that when the sun or moon was in that sign of the zodiac, the time was supposed to be inimical to lovers generally, or to Propertius (because of his or Cynthia's horoscope) in particular. But it has been remarked that some gold and silver coins of 16 B.C. show a crab on the reverse; so that the warning here might be against money, e.g. a rich rival's.

149. cauo: ablative of *cauum* (substantive), here best taken as ablative of respect with *tremefacta*: 'earth, shaken in its hollow vault...'.

II

This is an aetiological poem, i.e. one which purports to explain the origin (or possible alternative origins, often fanciful) of some ancient name or thing or institution. The subject in this case is the god Vertumnus, and the speaker is an image of him which stood (see article *Vertumnus* in P.–W.) at the place where the *uicus Tuscus* ran into the *Forum*. The image is represented as addressing an imaginary passer-by. We are told where the god came from originally, what is the derivation of his name, and who made the image that is speaking; on the way we also learn about the god's principal characteristics.

We know hardly anything of Vertumnus beyond what we read in the present poem. Varro (*L.L.* v, 46) calls him *deus Etruriae princeps*. At Rome he had a temple on the Aventine, containing a picture of M. Fulvius Flaccus, who triumphed over Volsinii in 264 B.C.; cf. on line 4 below. Horace (*Sat.* II, vii, 14) says of an extravagantly mutable person that he is *Vertumnis quotquot sunt natus iniquis*. Ovid (*Met.* XIV, 623 ff.) tells a tale about the god courting Pomona in numerous disguises. Lastly, according to Porph. on Hor. *Epist.* I, xx, 1 he is *deus...praeses uertendarum rerum, hoc est emendarum ac uendendarum*.

2. signa paterna: 'the particulars of origin (ancestry)' of the god Vertumnus. *signa* is the word for distinguishing particulars of any kind; these for an individual, apart from his own name, are usually family and country. Vertumnus is supposed to be supplying the kind of information which Propertius himself says he has been asked for in I, xxii, 1–2 *qualis et unde genus, qui sint mihi, Tulle, penates quaeris*. Though Vertumnus is a god, he speaks like a human and though he names no father in what follows he says (line 3) not only that he is a Tuscan, but also that he is 'of Tuscans born'; this may explain the epithet *paterna* here.

This motive only serves to start the god on his discourse; he soon passes on to discuss the derivation of his name and to enumerate his attributes; these topics occupy lines 7–56. However, the idea of his 'origins' recurs in another sense at the end of the poem, when in lines 59–64 we are told who made the statue.

3. Tuscus ego: Tuscis orior: unless an *et* has fallen out— and the passage, which is brisk without it, becomes flat if it is inserted—this is the only place in poetry of the classical period where *ego* is to be scanned as an iambus, with a long *ō*. It is found frequently as an iambus in Plautus and Terence, and again, a century after Propertius, in Val. Flacc. VIII, 158 *nam quid egō quemquam* (where it gets no assistance from the punctuation).

nec here has the value of *nec tamen*, as not uncommonly; cf. IV, vi, 20, IV, ix, 13.

4. Volsinios deseruisse focos: the original *Volsinii* (on the site of the present Orvieto) was destroyed by the Romans in 264 B.C., and a new *Volsinii* (on the site of the present Bolsena) was founded. In the present passage the god may be saying either (*a*) that he bears no grudge against the Romans for removing him from his homeland on that occasion, or (b) that he does not regret having come to Rome (and so in a sense left home) on the much earlier occasion indicated in lines 53 and 60 below. Or he may be mixing the two.

5. nec templo laetor eburno: this might mean either (a) that he had no fondness for his temple on the Aventine (in which case we must suppose that that temple had some ivory ornamentation, e.g. of the doors), or (b) that he has no pleasure in a grand temple, i.e. does not want one. The latter seems more likely.

7. hac quondam: the region called *Velabrum*, through which the *uicus Tuscus* ran, lay between the *Forum* (*Romanum*) and the *Forum Boarium* and between the Palatine and the Capitol. It was liable to flooding and had in early days been permanently a marsh or stagnant elbow of the Tiber; cf. IV, ix, 5 and Tib. II, v, 33 ff.

9. tantum concessit: 'has granted this great favour', or 'has thus given much ground' to his foster-children.

10. dicor: this word must here do a double duty. It cannot mean that Vertumnus was so called, i.e. *did* get his name, from the retirement of the river, for this explanation will shortly be pronounced false in line 19. So the thought here, imperfectly expressed, must be *dicor dici*, 'I am said to get my name'.

11–12. seu, quia...credis id esse sacrum?: 'or is it rather because to me are offered first-fruits of the changing seasons that you suppose I am called Vertumnus, as the god to whom that offering is made?'. There is a heavy emphasis here on the name *Vertumnus*, and it is necessary to take account of this, and also to supply something from the context, in order to extract the meaning of the sentence. For *rursus* marking an alternative or contrast cf. I, iii, 41–2 *nam modo purpureo fallebam stamine somnum, rursus et Orpheae carmine fessa lyrae*; Lucan VI, 595 *mens dubiis perculsa pauet; rursusque parata est certos ferre metus.* For the construction cf. Liv. XLI, xii, 6 *arma lecta conici in aceruum iussit consul sacrumque id Vulcano cremari.*

[*credis id* is Postgate's emendation for *credidit* of the MSS.]

13. prima mihi: both words carry an important emphasis. The meaning is: 'to me are offered the first grapes that change colour as the clusters darken (on the vine); to me are offered the first of the bearded ears that swell with the milky juice (of the ripening corn)'. The verb *uariare* is naturally transitive but is used also intransitively with reflexive force; used reflexively it is a regular word for the change of colour of the ripening grape, indicating not so much a change from one colour to another as the occurrence of variations of colour (mottling) within the same object or mass.

18. inuito stipite: because there has been grafting the pear stock bears the alien fruit 'not of its own accord'.

19. mendax fama, noces: 'current report is a liar and misleads (*lit.* does harm)'. One need not preserve in English the vocative form of the Latin 'figure'.

alius mihi nominis index: either (*a*) 'I have another (viz. myself) to explain my name'; or (*b*) 'the significance of my name is other than what you say'; i.e. the phrase is a variant for *aliud est nominis mei indicium*, *index* standing for *indicium* by a process opposite to that whereby *hospitium* stands for *hospes* at I, xv, 20. Of the two alternatives the second is strange Latin, but the first is stranger sense.

21-40 (or 46). Here follows a list of the various guises that *Vertumnus* assumes, and the conclusion that it is from this versatility that he derives his name. Evidently the statue was dressed up in various ways (see, e.g. lines 23 and 24). Evidently also it was a jointed and adjustable figure (see, e.g. lines 39 and 63, perhaps also lines 35 and 36). Probably the position of the hands was varied according to the different articles carried, scythe, nets, fowler's pole, fishing-rod, flower-basket, fruit and vegetables. The occasion of these disguises is obscure.

23. non dura puella: in itself *non dura* could mean either 'not ungraceful' or 'not coy'; here the context makes the former more probable.

28. corbis in imposito pondere: for *in* thus used cf. on IV, i, 27; also (e.g.) Mart. IX, xvii, 7 *ne pulchrior ille in longa fuerit quam breuiore coma*.

29. ad lites: 'for (*or*, at) lawsuits'; presumably this means 'when I'm disguised as a pleader'.

31. mitra: a strip of material wound around the head (hence *cinge*), sometimes like a bandeau, sometimes like an incipient turban.

Iacchi: the name *Iacchus* is used by the Augustan poets as a synonym for Bacchus.

furabor: to us a rather strong metaphor; the point is that he will be infringing the proprietary rights of another god.

33. harundine: the fowler's pole, often jointed so as to be extensible (cf. II, xix, 24 *structo calamo*).

34. fautor...sum...aucupio: the substantive *fautor* is used sometimes with a genitive and sometimes (like the verb *faueo*) with a dative.

plumoso...aucupio: literally 'feathered fowling': we have to translate 'pursuit of feathered fowl'. For other striking examples of transferred epithet cf. line 63 below, iv, 60, vi, 32, etc.

35. est etiam aurigae specie Vertumnus: 'sometimes too Vertumnus has the appearance of...', or 'there is also a (version of) Vertumnus in the guise of...'; cf. Liv. XXI, lxii, 5 *multis locis hominum specie procul candida ueste uisos.* [*specie* is a conjecture; the MSS. have *species*.]

36. traicit...equo: a *desultor*, a trick rider who jumped from one to the other of a pair of running horses, to and fro. *alterno equo* = 'first to one, then to the other'. In *leue pondus* the adjective has evidently adverbial value; the point is that the man jumps lightly, not that he is light himself (though he may be).

37. sub petaso: the *petasus* was a round hat with a brim; for pictures of fishermen wearing it see Daremberg and Saglio, *s.v.* Piscator, figs. 5690 and 5691. [*sub petaso* is a conjecture, much recommended by the life and balance that it brings to the sentence and the couplet respectively. The MSS. have *suppat* (or *suppetat*) *hoc*: the latter phrase may be translatable as 'given the wherewithal'; for another loose (but not identical) use of *hoc* cf. IV, i, 103.]

40. medio puluere: we can only guess what picture the poet has in mind; perhaps a nurseryman bringing his flowers into town along a dusty highway; perhaps a flower-seller in a dusty piazza.

42. probata: 'choice' (an adjective); this participle, like *optatus* (see Virg. *Aen.* IV, 619) and *blanditus* (see IV, vi, 72) came to be used sometimes as an adjective, without any real trace of its participial force remaining.

in manibus...meis: we have to supply something to complete the sense, e.g. 'that are laid (*or* seen) in my hands'.

43. caeruleus: here evidently 'dark green', as also when used elsewhere of the foliage of the olive.

44. me notat: 'marks me', i.e. is a characteristic attribute.

46. ante: this is most easily understood if we suppose that specimens of any flower that begins to open are offered as first-fruits to the god, without waiting until it is fully open (*hiat*); just as in lines 13–14 specimens of the grapes and corn are offered before they are ripe.

47–9. at mihi, quod...haec tu, Roma, meis, etc.: 'now as for me, it was because of my changing shapes (21–40) that I got the name Vertumnus; as for these gifts of vegetables (41–6), they were (originally) brought by you Romans as reward to my Tuscans (from whom the Vicus Tuscus takes its name), on that famous occasion when...'. The gifts of vegetables do not help to explain the god's name, but themselves require explanation, and this is provided in lines 49–52.

[*haec* in line 49 is a conjecture, for *et* or *at* of the MSS. It creates a pattern of statement which makes intelligible the separation of the couplet 47–8 from the passage ending with line 40 to which it refers. But it is possible to keep *et* in line 49, and understand line 50 as description of the Tuscans' *praemia* instead of a parenthesis; though the couplet 47–8 then is left rather lonely, 41–6 are left unexplained, and there is some awkwardness in having to take *et* in line 49 with *meis...Tuscis* instead of with the *tu* which immediately adjoins it.]

48. patria lingua: he must mean Latin, not Etruscan, as he has derived his name from the Latin *uertere*; he speaks as a naturalized Roman.

50. Vicus...Tuscus: see introductory note.

51. Lycomedius: singular for plural, *Lycomedii* being a designation of the Etruscans who were led by *Lucumo* (the Lycmon cf. IV, i, 29) to help Romulus against the Sabine invaders under Titus Tatius.

53. tela caduca: weapons dropped by the defeated Sabines in their flight.

57. te, qui ad uadimonia curris: the imaginary passer-by is hurrying to the forum, where he is engaged to appear in some capacity at a trial or lawsuit. He has had to give security for his appearance, and this will be forfeit if he does not turn up. (It is always possible that an expression such as this may have lost its original force and come to mean by convention no more than 'appear in court'.)

58. haec spatiis ultima creta meis: i.e. 'I am coming to the end of my course'. *creta* is the finishing line.

60. grata: either 'in this city that I love' or 'in a grateful city'. [But it is not easy to see, either way, what *point* the epithet has in its context. Should perhaps *parca* be read? Or *parua*, or *ingrata*, the suggestions of friends?]

61. Mamurri: Mamurius Veturius was a legendary crafts-man, supposed also to have made for Numa the replicas of the *ancile* that fell from heaven.

caelator: an engraver or chaser of metal. In line 63 below *fundere* indicates that the figure was made, as one would expect, by casting; it would be finished by engraving, as in Quint. *Inst. Or.* x. iii. 8 *rectius erit...ab initio sic opus ducere ut caelandum non ex integro fabricandum sit.*

62. tellus...manus: the prayer is that the earth should lie lightly on the dead craftsman; and *terat* here must mean 'bruise' or 'crush', without any suggestion of its common meaning 'rub'. Apparently we are to understand that Mamurius was buried in Oscan territory; we know nothing of the circumstances.

63. tam docilis...in usus: the context shows that the meaning must be 'mould me so as to be thus adaptable in various ways'. The transfer of the epithet from *me* to *usus* is remark-able, and worth noting as a feature of Propertian style.

64. unum opus est...honos: 'my statue is one; the ways in which it is honoured are many'. Apparently the dressing-up, as well as the offerings of fruit, etc., is a form of worship.

III

This elegy purports to be a letter from a wife to a husband absent on a military campaign. She is named Arethusa and he Lycotas. We do not know whether these fictitious names conceal real persons or whether the whole situation is imaginary. Nor do we know whether the idea of imagining a letter in elegiac verse from a woman to her absent man came first to Propertius or to Ovid, who developed it in his *Heroides* with mythological characters for correspondents. Ovid was born in 43 B.C., and early made the acquaintance of Propertius, as he tells us himself in *Tristia* IV, x. This elegy of Propertius was probably written between 23 and 20 B.C.; for an elegy of the previous book (III, xviii) refers to the death of Marcellus in 23 or 22 B.C., while the references here to a campaign in Parthia would be unlikely after 20 B.C., when Augustus recovered the standards of Crassus from the Parthians by diplomatic means.

The content of the poem can be analysed as follows. In lines 1–18 the writer enumerates the absences of Lycotas, interspersing her account with references to her own distress and complaints at being thus denied the rights which marriage should have given her. In lines 19–28 she exclaims against the inventors of warfare, and expresses hopes of her husband's fidelity; a similar exclamatory passage of the same length follows later at 63–72 and concludes the poem; in between the two comes a long account of her own anxious and solitary life at home during his absence, punctuated almost centrally at 43–50 by a passage in which she wishes that she could be with him on his campaign. In the layout of 19–72 a certain symmetry will be observed.

5. tractu: the stroke of the pen that forms the letters.

6. morientis: 'fainting'.

erunt: the copula takes its number, as commonly, from the adjoining predicate.

7. iteratos...per ortus: 'on a second eastern campaign'. *per* is appropriate as the campaign ranges over a considerable area. For *ortus* = 'eastern lands' cf. Lucan II, 642–3 *totos mea, nate, per ortus bella feres*. For *iterare* = 'travel through repeatedly' cf. IV, i, 82 *obliquae signa iterata rotae*; here 'a second time' rather than 'repeatedly'.

8. Sericus hostis: though the Romans really had no contact with the Seres (Chinese) their name stands often in Augustan poets for a formidable eastern people beyond the frontiers of the empire, and so generally for an 'eastern foe'. Thus Hor. *Od.* IV, xv, 22 ff. *Getae...Seres...Persae*; *Od.* III, xxix, 26 ff. *Seres... Bactra...Tanais*; *Od.* I, xxix, 1 ff. *Arabum...Medo...(sagittas) Sericas*; *Od.* I, xii, 53 *Parthos...Seras...Indos.*

munito...equo: a reference to the cataphract, an armoured horseman on an armoured horse. This appurtenance of other eastern peoples is attached to the Seres here in the same way as the arrows usually characteristic of the Parthians are attached to them in Hor. *Od.* I, xxix (see above).

9. pictoque Britannia curru: both war chariots and paint were characteristic of the Britons, but usually we hear of the paint in connexion with the Britons themselves (as woad) rather than with their chariots. It may be that the two ideas are blurred in the poet's mind; cf. on iv, 71 (*Strymonis*).

10. tunsus et Eoa...aqua: for this use of *tundo* cf. Virg. *Georg.* III, 382 *gens effrena uirum Rhipaeo tunditur Euro*; and

Cat. XI, 2–3 *siue in extremos penetrabit Indos, litus ut longe resonante Eoa tunditur unda.* [*tunsus* or *tusus* is Housman's emendation for *ustus* of the MSS.]

discolor: because coloured differently from the normal. *discolor* is not found elsewhere applied to dark-skinned peoples, whereas *decolor* is; but Propertius is independent generally in his use of compounds.

7–10. Of the names mentioned in these lines *Bactra* and *Seres* (lines 7 and 8) indicate a campaign in central Asia, apparently to the north (47 below), and apparently prolonged for more than one season (7). *Getae* (9) indicate the Thracian frontier. *Britannia* (9) is another frontier. *Indus* (10) points to a tropical adventure; elsewhere Propertius mentions India in connexion with Arabia (II, x, 15 *India quin, Auguste, tuo dat colla triumpho, et domus intactae te tremit Arabiae*).

There was war with the Getae in 29 B.C. Augustus planned an invasion of Britain in 26–25 B.C. but did not in the end proceed farther than Gaul. Aelius Gallus made an expedition into Arabia in 24 B.C.; and this is the only campaign in the direction of Arabia or India of which we hear in this period. Operations against Parthia are often forecast or demanded by the Augustan poets, but talk of an actual or imminent expedition best fits the years immediately preceding the recovery of the standards in 20 B.C., though of course no campaign materialized.

The writer seems thus to refer, in loose and exaggerated terms, to a series of operations actually undertaken or contemplated between 29 and 20 B.C., and after mentioning the scene of the present operation first, to go through the rest in chronological order. It is perhaps a little suspicious that the activity attributed to Lycotas should be so systematically and so widely distributed. But we have no sufficient grounds for asserting either that Lycotas and Arethusa are fictitious persons, or that they are real ones.

11–12. et pactae tum mihi noctes, cum...: 'and (are these) the nights of love that were pledged to me on the day when...?'. [The text printed is conjectural.]

12. rudis: 'as an innocent girl'; cf. IV, i, 131 and note.

bracchia...dedi: 'I surrendered'; cf. the common expression *manus dare* (e.g. in IV, xi, 88).

13–16. fax...sum sparsa...uitta...deo: these are all features of the marriage ritual: the torch that lights the bride when she is brought home (*deducta*) to her husband's house; the lustral water with which she is sprinkled before she leaves her own; the headband which was part of her special coiffure; and the marriage-spirit Hymenaeus invoked in the marriage song.

14. traxit ab euerso lumina nigra rogo: i.e. it was a torch of mourning lit from the tumbled embers of a pyre. For *lumina nigra* cf. Hor. *Od.* IV, xii, 26 *nigrorumque memor, dum licet, ignium*; Virg. *Aen*, XI, 186 *subiectisque ignibus atris* (of lighting a pyre); in these expressions 'black' is said metaphorically, because of its funereal associations, but the thought of black smoke and sooty flame is present too. For *euerso...rogo* cf. Virg. *Aen*. VI, 226 *postquam conlapsi cineres et flamma quieuit*.

15. Stygio...lacu: i.e. with water from some pool or lake fed (as lake Avernus was supposed to be fed) by the infernal river Styx.

nec recta...uitta data est: the headband was put on awry (which would be a bad omen), in a technical sense 'not properly'; cf. the technical use of *recte* with reference to ritual in expressions such as *ludi recte facti, dona recte data*, etc.

16. deo: the marriage-spirit Hymenaeus.

17. omnibus heu portis pendent mea noxia uota: i.e. 'at all the gates hang votive offerings of mine, alas; and they have brought me only more unhappiness'. *omnibus...portis* shows that the *uota* meant are thank-offerings in payment of vows (cf. line 70 below), or less probably the vows themselves (cf. Juv. XII, 100ff.), for Lycotas' safe return from *previous* campaigns; for vows for his safe return on *this* occasion will not be hung at *all* gates but at the one through which he went and through which he is expected to return. Arethusa is complaining of his many previous absences (cf. line 1 above) in many diverse quarters (cf. lines 7-10 above). And though the prayers were granted for which she paid these vows, she calls them *noxia* because he returned safely only to go away and leave her again.

18. quarta lacerna: this carries on the idea of many absences on campaign conveyed by *omnibus portis* in the preceding line. If lines 7 and 8 above are regarded as alluding to one campaign prolonged for two years, the number of campaigns mentioned in lines 7-10 is in fact four.

19. occidat...qui...: 'perish the man who...'.

immerita: the tree has done nothing to deserve to be thus mutilated; also, it is innocent of the mischief which the use of its bough for warlike purposes will cause.

uallum: the *uallus* is a stake, used for making a palisade.

20. et struxit querulas rauca per ossa tubas: 'and contrived the trumpet, whose mournful note blares through the vibrant horn'. Here *rauca per ossa* is to be construed with *querulas*, which almost = *quae queruntur*. It may be that by *ossa* the poet really means bone, for it is used by primitive peoples to make musical instruments. But *ossa* might well stand by metonymy for the related substance horn, as *cornu* for instance is used of the tusk of an elephant, properly called *dens*. The *tuba* in historical times was made of metal.

19–20. It is worth noting that the important idea 'first' is left by Propertius to be understood in both these clauses.

21–2. dignior obliquo...famem: i.e. 'worthier than Ocnus to twist the rope for ever, as he sits athwart his task, for ever feeding the hungry donkey'. Ocnus was one of the figures in a celebrated picture of the underworld by Polygnotus, at Delphi (Pausanias x, 29); a proverbial character who let an extravagant wife waste the fruits of his industry, and was condemned to sit to eternity twisting (i.e. making) a rope, while a donkey standing by ate it up (it being no doubt of grass) as fast as he made it. The epithet *obliquo* is used because the ropemaker sits sideways on to his work and draws the strands across himself as he twists them into the finished article.

24–5. These questions illustrate the fact that *num* does not inevitably *expect* the answer 'no'. Here the speaker would *prefer* the answer to be 'no'; *num* gives a note of solicitude to the question.

24. imbellis: 'that were not made for war'; the epithet, like *teneros* in line 23, is chosen from *her* point of view; she thinks of him as her darling, not as a soldier.

26. det mihi plorandas per tua colla notas: here *mihi* must of course go with *plorandas*, not with *det*. (Or should it be taken with the whole sentence, as 'dative of the person affected'?)

32. lucis...auis: she is impatient to hear the singing of the birds (or crowing of the cocks) which promises the return of daylight.

33. castrensia pensa: *pensum* normally refers to the task of spinning—being in fact originally the amount of wool weighed out to a spinning-woman to be turned into yarn in a given time. There seems no reason not to take it here in this its usual sense. Arethusa is spinning yarn to be subsequently woven into articles of military attire for her husband.

34. et Tyria in chlamydas uellera lecta tuas: this is a possible though far from certain substitute for the corrupt MSS. text. The *chlamys* was a Greek military cloak, and there would be nothing odd in a poet using the word for the Latin *lacerna*; it is worn by warriors in Virgil, e.g. *Aen.* VIII, 588 (*Pallas*) and IX, 582 (*Arcentis filius*). [See here app. crit.]

35. qua parte: 'where'.

37. cogor: a favourite word of Propertius when speaking of the straits or expedients to which, e.g., a lover, is reduced; cf. I, i, 8, I, vii, 8, I, xii, 14, I, xvi, 13, I, xviii, 8, III, xxi, 1, etc. Sometimes it can hardly be translated; cf. I, i, 8 *aduersos cogor habere deos*; I, xviii, 8 *nunc in amore tuo cogor habere notam.* Perhaps here 'I find myself...' would be enough.

ediscere: she pores over the maps till she knows every detail by heart.

38. qualis et haec...dei: 'and to understand what is this order that the creator's cunning has devised'. *positura* is a regular word for the arrangement of parts within a whole. The creator is called *doctus* as a skilled artificer. For *deus* = 'the creator', cf. Sil. It. XVIII, 458. For the sentiment cf. III, v, 25-6 *tum mihi naturae libeat perdiscere mores, quis deus hanc mundi temperet arte domum.*

41. curis: some editors place the comma after this word instead of before, so that it goes as dative (= 'my cares' = 'me in my anxious state') after *assidet* instead of as causal ablative with *pallida*. But attached to *pallida* it adds point to that word.

42. peierat: she is said to 'swear falsely' because she does not really believe the reason she is giving for Lycotas' delayed return.

43. Hippolyte: the legendary Amazon queen.

47-8. cum Pater altas astricto in glaciem frigore nectit aquas: 'when the sky-god makes even deep waters icebound with frozen cold'. For *pater* = the sky-god, Jupiter, cf. Virg. *Georg.* I, 328-9 *ipse pater media nimborum in nocte corusca fulmina molitur dextra.* For the rest of the phrasing cf. Ov. *Trist.* II, 196 *astricto quae coit unda gelu*; *Pont.* III, iii, 26 *et coit astrictis barbarus Ister aquis*; Lucan I, 18 (*bruma*) *astringit Scythico glacialem frigore pontum.*

82

[*astricto* is Rothstein's conjecture, for *Affricus* of the MSS. There have been many others.]

49. omnis amor magnus, sed aperto in coniuge maior: 'the power of love is great always, but greater still (*or* especially) when man and wife are together'. The meaning here of *aperto in coniuge* (which is without parallel) has to be inferred from the context. Arethusa has been saying how much she wishes she could *be* with her husband, and how if she were with him no dangers or difficulties would prevent her from going wherever he went; so by *apertus* here Propertius must mean *praesens conspicuusque*, cf. the Greek ἐναργής; cf. Lucr. I. 915 *in rebus apertis*, of visible things as opposed to atoms. ('openly acknowledged' would lack point in this context.)

omnis here is used adverbially and has a value similar to that of *omnino*; cf. I, xi, 17–18 *non quia perspecta non es mihi cognita fama, sed quod in hac omnis parte timetur amor*; III, vi, 5–6 *omnis enim debet sine uano nuntius esse, maioremque timens seruus habere fidem*; and Kühner–Stegmann II (1), p. 236. *magnus* here = 'potent' or 'mighty'; cf. II, vii, 3–5 *diducere amantis non queat inuitos Iuppiter ipse duos. 'at magnus Caesar'. sed magnus Caesar in armis: deuictae gentes nil in amore ualent*; Cic. *Fam.* IV, iii, 2 *haec tibi ad leuandas molestias magna esse debent*; Ov. *Fast.* IV, 792 *haec duo* (fire and water) *magna putant* (as agents of purification).

50. hanc Venus...ipsa facem: 'for then Venus takes a hand (*ipsa*) and fans the flame to keep it burning'. Arethusa probably means that proximity encourages physical feeling and this reinforces conjugal affection in the wider sense.

51. quo: 'to what avail?'.

[*nunc* in this line is a conjecture for the impossible *te* of the MSS.]

52. crystallus...aquosa: evidently a translucent piece of crystal or crystal-like jewel, set in a ring.

53–4. rarisque assueta...Lares: there are two quite different ways of taking this:

(*a*) 'at most (*uix* and *raris*), one maidservant on the first of each month opens the closed shrine of the household Lares, as custom bids'. We are then to imagine a deserted house, the stillness of which is disturbed only when religious obligation absolutely requires. The household Lares were sometimes contained in a cupboard-like little shrine; in Propertius' day a monthly offering was regular, for cf. Tib. I, iii, 34 *reddereque antiquo menstrua tura*

Lari, and Horace's injunction to *rustica Phidyle* in *Od.* III, xxiii. It is to be noted that *puella* is only rarely found meaning a female servant.

(*b*) 'at most the door of the house is opened occasionally (*raris*) on the first of the month (*or* once a month) to admit the visit of a familiar woman friend'. Here *aperit* = 'causes to be opened' by an extension of meaning common with verbs in Propertius (e.g. IV, i, 46 *uexit*, I, xvii, 26 *soluite*, II, xxvi, 49 *persoluit*), and *Lares* = 'house' as at IV, viii, 50. From Mart. IV, lxvi, 3 *idibus et raris togula est excussa kalendis* it looks as though the kalends were a calling day.

My own preference is for the second of these interpretations. As a means of saying simply that there is only one maid in the house, this would be too roundabout. And if there is only one, what will have happened to the others? Moreover, the anxious piety of Arethusa (cf. 57–8 below) will ensure that the gods of the household get worship more than once a month.

55. Craugidos: the pet dog's name is Craugis, 'Yap', a Greek formation from the same root as κραυγή, κραυγάζω, etc.

[*Craugidos* is a happy conjecture for the MS. reading *Graucidos*.]

56. illa tui partem uindicat una toro: this cannot be translated 'she alone claims your place in our bed', for that would be in effect an affirmation of the speaker's chastity, out of place here and ludicrous in the form of its expression. We can, if we wish, assume a compression of two ideas: 'she is my sole companion, *and* claims your side of our couch for herself'. Or we can limit the value of *una*: 'she claims your side of our couch as her special (i.e. privileged) place'. *tui partem*: this use of the genitive of the personal pronoun instead of the possessive adjective is uncommon, except when the genitive is objective; cf., however, I, iv, 26–7 *amore...nostri* (my love); Tac. *Ann.* VI, 22 *initia nostri*; Sen. *Ep.* LXI, 3 *finem nostri*.

toro: i.e. on our couch.

57. uerbenis: certain kinds of herbs or foliage used for religious purposes are called *uerbena* in religious terminology.

compita: at the intersections of streets (*compita*) were shrines of the Lares Compitales. It may be these same shrines that are indicated by *sacella* earlier in the line.

58. herba Sabina: some kind of fragrant herb, burned like incense.

ueteres...focos: either (*a*) the reference is to the hearth of the speaker's house, where the household gods had their place; or (*b*) *foci* stands for altars and refers to altars of the gods at temples, etc.

59–60. We cannot be sure what is the significance of these omens. The cry of the *noctua* in Virg. *Georg.* I, 403 and νυκτερίη γλαὺξ ἥσυχον ἀείδουσα in Aratus, *Diosem.* 267 portends a return of fair weather. A lamp flickering and burning low in Aratus, *Diosem.* 302 portends storm; and an unsteady flame in IV, viii, 43 below is an unfavourable omen in its context though we cannot be sure how and why. On the other hand 'sneezing' of a lamp (? sudden flaring) is a favourable omen in Ov. *Her.* XIX, 151 and *Anth. Pal.* VI, 333 and portends the arrival of a loved one; moreover it is followed in the former passage by the application of wine to the lamp, as in line 60 here. This application of wine may however be a remedy that would be resorted to on any irregular burning of the wick, irrespective of its prognostic value; in which case the omen in line 60 will be indicated by the word *parca*.

60. parca: the lamp could fitly be called 'thrifty' or 'grudging' if it is burning low and so using less (too little) oil, because the wick is clogged.

61. Having received the omens, good or bad, she hastens to make sacrifice and prayers to the gods to fulfil their promise or avert their threat.

62. popae: these are temple attendants who help to kill the victims, and for this no doubt get perquisites or a tip or a fee.

63. ne...tanti sit, etc.: 'do not reckon the glory of storming Bactra to be worth so much as this', i.e. enough to compensate us for the pains of separation.

Bactra was the name of the Bactrian capital. *ascensis* refers to storming a citadel on a height, or scaling walls. Syntactically *ascensis...Bactris* is either ablative of origin, or an ablative absolute with an ellipsis of *quae tibi erit* or the like.

64. carbasa = *carbasea*: Propertius is fond of these short forms of adjectives; cf. IV, i, 11 *praetexto* (= *praetextato*) *senatu*; II, xxxi, 4 *femina turba*; IV, iv, 26 *Romula hasta*; IV, vi, 23 *Augusta ratis*, etc.

66. uersis...arcus equis: the Parthian horse-archers were adept at shooting backward while riding away from their enemy.

67. sic: the familiar formula, whereby a person asking some-one to do something prays for some good thing to befall the person addressed if he duly does what is asked.

68. pura...hasta: a spear shaft without a point, awarded as a prize of valour.

71. portae...Capenae: the gate of the *Via Appia* by which a man would leave Rome going to his port of embarkation for the East, or re-enter Rome coming back from the East.

72. subscribam SALVO...VIRO: in *saluo* is a double meaning: 'safely home' and 'still hers'. *subscribam* can be read as future or as subjunctive of wish.

IV

This elegy is formally an aetiological poem, like Elegy ii, pur-porting to explain the origin of the old name of the Capitoline hill, *mons Tarpeius*, or of the particular eminence of it that was still known as the *saxum Tarpeium* in historical times. But the real content of the poem, for which the aetiological motive serves as occasion, is an elaborately narrated tale of the guilty love of a Vestal virgin named Tarpeia. This narrative is related to the origin of the place-name by the concluding couplet of the elegy.

The story takes place in Romulus' day, when the Sabine king Titus Tatius makes war against him. There is a Roman garrison on the Capitoline hill. The invading Sabines are encamped below. The Vestal Tarpeia, while fetching water from a spring near their encampment, sees the Sabine king and falls in love with him at first sight. She betrays the fortress to him, having stipulated that in return for this service she is to become his wife. But when he has gained his object he tells his men to throw their shields on her and crush her to death.

From other accounts (Livy I, xi, Plutarch, *Rom.* xvii, Dion. Hal. II, xxxviii ff., Varro, *L.L.* v, 41) we gather that Tarpeia was the daughter of Spurius Tarpeius, captain of the garrison on the Capitoline; and that the garrison in question was an outpost, the rest of the Romans being on the Palatine and perhaps on other hills as well. It is not clear from Propertius' version whether he assumes the same background or not. He certainly differs from our other versions in making love the motive of Tarpeia's treachery[1]—and, this of course is the very essence of his story. In the standard version her motive is greed for gold.

Nearly half the elegy consists of a long soliloquy of the love-sick Vestal (lines 29–66). Immediately before and after this come two passages in which her state of mind and behaviour are described (23–8 and 67–72). Preceding and following the group thus formed come two narratives, the first of how she falls in love (3–22) and the second of how she betrays the citadel and is killed (73–92); each of these begins with a description preliminary to the narrative proper (see lines 3 ff. and 73 ff.). The first couplet announces the subject and the last couplet (93–4) relates the story to the place-name *mons Tarpeius*, etc. It will be noticed that there is a certain symmetry in the length and disposition of the members composing the piece.

1. Tarpeium...sepulcrum: 'Tarpeia's crime and Tarpeia's shameful end'.

scelus: this is a probable conjecture for *nemus* of the MSS. Propertius says nothing about a *nemus* in his conclusion in lines 93–4 below, nor has any reference to a *Tarpeium nemus* been found in any other author. Moreover, line 2 suggests strongly that what we are being promised in this opening couplet is not an explanation of anything but simply a story of past events; the aetiological significance of these will be noted later, at the end of the poem.

The introduction of *nemus* into the MS. tradition is probably due to the influence of *lucus* in the next sentence. But that *lucus* is described simply to provide a setting for the beginning of the story, and thereafter disappears from view.

sepulcrum: the choice of this word may have been influenced by the fact that, according to some accounts, Tarpeia was actually buried on the Capitoline hill. But her tomb was removed by Tarquin (Plutarch, *Rom.* 18) when he built the temple of Jupiter Capitolinus; so that it did not exist in Propertius' day to be made the subject of an aetiological study. Here *sepulcrum* probably stands for 'death', as *funus* often does.

3–6. lucus erat...ouis: this description sets the scene for the beginning of the story. We shall shortly learn (line 14) that it

---

[1] However, Plutarch, *Rom.* 17 mentions an exotic version by a Greek poet named Simylus, not otherwise known to us, in which Tarpeia betrays Rome to the *Gauls* (not the Sabines) for love of their king, Brennus.

was to the spring in the copse here described that Tarpeia went to draw water. (There is doubt what spring is meant. Some think of the spring that rises in the *Tullianum*, under the Capitoline hill; some of the *fons Iuturnae* under the Palatine.)

3. antro: (?)'nook'. *antrum*, properly the space sheltered by an overhanging rock, may in poetry mean anything from a cave to a ravine; cf. I, i, II and I, ii, II and Housman on Manil. v, 311.

6. fistula: the shepherd's pipe.

7–8. hunc Tatius contra...humo: 'over against this copse Tatius fenced his camp with a palisade of maple stakes, and piled a rampart of earth around it to make it safe'; here *castra* is to be construed with *praecingit* as well as with *coronat* by the construction called ἀπὸ κοινοῦ; for which cf. I, ix, 31 *illis et silices et possint cedere quercus*; II, xx, 19 *quod si nec nomen nec me tua forma teneret*; Tib. I. i. 11–12 *nam ueneror, seu stipes habet desertus in agris seu uetus in triuio florida serta lapis*.

[*contra* (an alternative would be *propter*) is a conjecture for *fontem* of the MSS., which must surely be corrupt: Tatius cannot have set a palisade either partly or wholly around the copse and spring, for that would be incompatible with Tarpeia going (as she will) to the spring to draw water; but cf. Liv. IX, ii, 14 *castra propter aquam uallo circumdant*.]

9–14. quid tum...equus: here another aspect of the scene is conveyed to us: the Sabine invaders in what was later to be the very heart of Rome but was then still village and farmland.

9. Curetis: an adjective (here agreeing with *tubicen*) formed from *Cures* (pl.; the Sabine capital) and meaning 'Sabine'.

12. Foro: i.e. 'where now the Roman forum is'.

13. murus erant montes: the point seems to be that the Romans depended for their defence on the hills, to which they had retired: there was no wall around the whole area which later constituted 'Rome', as indeed appears from the position of the Sabine encampment.

ubi nunc est Curia, saepta: *sc. erant*: 'there were sheepfolds'. The point is the primitive and pastoral condition of what was later the great metropolis. In all this line the poet is answering the question he asked in line 9 above: *quid tum Roma fuit?*

[Some punctuate otherwise and construe *saepta* with *Curia* as a participle; but the point of it is then obscure.]

14. ex illo fonte: i.e. the one described in lines 3–6 above. The narrator reverts to it now because it is the scene of what follows. *equus* may be the horse of Tatius or collectively the horses of the Sabines. (This detail has probably been suggested by reminiscence of another legendary tale—Castor and Pollux watering their chargers at the *fons Iuturnae* after the battle of Lake Regillus; cf. Dion. Hal. VI, xiii and Prop. III, xxii, 26.)

15. deae: i.e. for Vesta. Fetching water for the service of the goddess would be one of a Vestal's regular duties.

hinc: from the spring just recalled.

fontem: spring-water.

libauit: 'went to draw'. The perfect (preterite) tense here refers to a single past occasion, the one on which Tarpeia first saw Tatius.

at illi here and at IV, vii, 11 changes the grammatical subject but not the subject of thought, and adds a touch of description. More usually, *at ille* transfers attention to a different subject of thought.

16. medium...caput: i.e. the water-pot was balanced on her head.

17-18. et satis...Vesta, tuas?: this is an interjection by the poet as his story approaches its fatal moment, i.e. *uidit...Tatium* in the line next to come. Vesta is in mind from *deae* in line 15.

20. pictaque per flauas arma leuare iubas: the warrior is manœuvring his arms in the course of his practice; cf. Tib. III, vii (IV, i), 95 *quis parma, seu dextra uelit seu laeua tueri, (aptior)*. *picta arma* must indicate primarily a blazoned shield. The meaning of *per* is probably 'over' the mane, as the rider turns this way and that.

23-8. saepe illa...secta rubis: this passage describes the first phase of her passion; a further phase is described in the corresponding passage 67-72 below.

23. immeritae: the moon was really 'innocent' of having sent the omens which Tarpeia alleged as pretext for her excursions. We do not know what these omens were, or what the superstition was that necessitated hair-washing on account of them. Tarpeia wanted an excuse to go down the hill in the hope of catching a glimpse of Tatius.

25. blandis...Nymphis: perhaps here 'amorous' or 'indulgent'; cf. Sil. It. XVII, 81 *blando nimium facilique marito*. In its usual sense *blandus* is better suited to the person making the prayer than to the deities prayed to.

26. Romula...hasta: for the form of the adjective cf. on IV, iii, 64 above.

27. primo...fumo: 'as the smoke began to rise (from the evening fires)'; cf. Virg. *Ec.* I, 82 *et iam summa procul uillarum culmina fumant* (in an evening scene). The fires would be wanted in the evening for cooking and warmth at night. That evening is meant is clear from *ignes* in line 31, and from the context: Tarpeia's object in all this is to get a chance of *seeing* Tatius, so she goes down in the day and returns as darkness approaches.

28. hirsutis...rubis: perhaps because she used the path through the brambles to which reference is made in line 48 below; perhaps because she had been hiding in the undergrowth to watch Tatius.

29. Tarpeia...arce: 'the Tarpeian height', apparently anticipating the name which the hill was to receive; cf. 93 below.

34. conspicer: usually deponent, *conspicor* is here (and occasionally elsewhere) found as a passive. She fancies she would be looked at with admiration; cf. the value of *conspectus* in Virg. *Georg.* III, 17 *Tyrio conspectus in ostro*, etc.

36. probro Vesta pudenda meo: 'Vesta before whom my wickedness is ashamed'. (While *pudet scelerum* = 'I am ashamed *of* my sins', *pudet deorum* = 'I am ashamed *before* the gods'.)

37. meos...amores: 'my heart'; cf. Virg. *Aen.* IV, 28–9 *ille meos, primus qui me sibi iunxit, amores abstulit*. The horse that takes Tatius back to his camp will bear her heart with him, henceforth on the Sabine side.

38. dextras: cf. Virg. *Georg.* III, 86 *densa iuba, et dextro iactata recumbit in armo* (cited as an attribute of a potential war-horse).

39. Scyllam: Scylla, daughter of Nisus king of Megara, fell in love with Minos, who was at war with Nisus, and betrayed Nisus to him. She is sometimes (but not regularly) identified with Scylla the sea-monster, who is often represented with dogs growing out of the lower part of her person.

39–40. saeuisse...saeuos: such repetitions are not uncommon in Propertius, if the MSS. may be believed; cf. III, viii, 2 and 4, III, ix, 37 and 39, III, xi, 19 and 21 and other instances.

41. fraterni cornua monstri: the Minotaur. Pasiphae, mother of the Minotaur by the legendary bull, was also mother of Ariadne by Minos. Ariadne betrayed the Minotaur for love of Theseus.

42. lecto stamine: by following the clue of the thread.

torta uia: 'the winding way' (of the labyrinth).

45. Pallados...ignis: the fire of Vesta; here called 'of Pallas' because the Palladium, the image of Minerva (= Athena) supposed to have come from Troy, was kept in Vesta's temple.

47. potabitur: cf. line 78 below *ebria turba*. This is an emendation for *pugnabitur* of the MSS., which is incompatible with the rest of the story, if, as seems likely, we are to understand that the next day referred to by *cras* here is the day of the festival described in lines 73 ff., on which the betrayal takes place. [It is not certain however that we should so understand the chronology of the story. It may be, perhaps, that some time passes in lines 69–72 after Tarpeia has conceived the idea of treachery, before she gives effect to it; just as some time passed in lines 23–6 after Tarpeia fell in love with Tatius, before she conceived the idea of treachery. If this is so, the MSS. reading *pugnabitur* must be retained, and we must suppose that in Tarpeia's soliloquy (lines 30–66) we have a specimen or a summary of thoughts that went through her head on several occasions. On one of those, thinking of an expected general assault on the Roman positions, she wishes she could warn her hero of a safe and sure way that she knows to his objective. Regarding *tota...urbe* see the introductory note to this elegy; and cf. line 13 above.]

48. tu cape: soliloquizing, she addresses him in imagination.

cape spinosi: for the prosody cf. on IV, i, 41.

49–50. tacentis...aquas: i.e. a silent trickle. (Or perhaps simply 'hidden'; for cf. Val. Flacc. I, 463 where the abnormally penetrating vision of Lynceus is said to be able even to *rumpere terras et Styga transmisso tacitam deprendere uisu*.)

52. haec quoque...lingua: i.e. like Medea's in the famous story.

formoso: 'my fair one', the man she loves.

53. toga picta: the royal robe, of purple embroidered with gold; under the republic it was worn by a victorious general at his triumph. Tarpeia says that Tatius is worthy to be king of Rome, and in effect invites him to aspire to be.

55–6. sic hospes patria metuar regina sub aula, etc.: 'thus (i.e. by your becoming king of Rome) let me hold court (*metuar* = be revered) as a conqueror's (*hospes* = foreign) queen

in my native land (*literally* native court): I bring you no mean
dowry—Rome betrayed'. [Text and interpretation are uncertain here.]

57–8. si minus...repende uices: 'if not (i.e. if you will not
accept my offer to betray Rome, and so do not become its king),
at least avenge the rape of the Sabine women: bear me away, and
pay the Romans back for what they did, with a fair reprisal'.
According to the legend, Tatius' invasion of Rome was a consequence of the famous rape of the Sabine women by the
Romans.

59–60. [**commissas acies ego possum soluere nupta:
uos medium palla foedus inite mea:** the text thus amended
gives good sense. One might be tempted to retain the MS.
reading *nuptae*, punctuating before instead of after it and taking
it as a genitive in agreement with the idea 'of me' which is contained in the possessive *mea*. But it has been pointed out to me
that in this construction the genitive regularly *follows* the possessive adjective.]

60. uos medium palla foedus inite mea: 'do you (Sabines
and Romans) be reconciled through my marriage and make a
pact of peace'. The *palla*, an outer garment, was not peculiar to
brides; but in Ov. *Her.* XXI, 162 a *splendida palla* is attribute of
Hymenaeus, and here as there the word symbolizes marriage.
medius is applied to one who serves as a mediator, which is the
role in which Tarpeia sees herself here; cf. Lucan I, 118 *ut
generos soceris mediae iunxere Sabinae*; Sil. It. XVI, 220 *haud
deformis erit uobis ad foedera uersis pacator mediusque Syphax.*
Thus, though *medium* here is attached grammatically to *foedus*
(and is not altogether inapposite in sense, since *medium foedus*
might be a treaty of reconciliation), it really goes in thought with
palla mea. For other examples of transferred epithets cf. IV, ii,
34 and 63. (If we had here *media palla mea*, the construction
would be an ordinary ablative absolute. As it is, *palla mea* is an
unusual ablative of cause or attendant circumstances; cf. IV, xi,
96 *prole mea.*)

61. adde, Hymenaee, modos: 'on with (*or* raise loud) the
marriage song'; cf. *addere gradum* = 'hasten'.

62. credite, uestra...: she addresses the warring Sabines
and Romans, as in 60 above.

63. quarta...bucina: i.e. the horn which announced the
beginning (or end?) of the last of the four *uigiliae* into which the

night (sunset to sunrise) was divided. In summer the duration of a *uigilia* would not be long.

64. ipsaque...sidera...cadunt: here *ipsa* must emphasize the point of time and mean 'even now'.

67-72. dixit, et...aperta sinu: see on 23-8 above.

67. permisit bracchia: 'surrendered': cf. IV, iii, 12. (With *incerto* the phrase further suggests the restless arms of the troubled sleeper.)

68. nescia se furiis accubuisse nouis: 'not knowing that new madness was her bedfellow'; i.e. that worse passion was about to possess her as she lay. [The MSS. give *nefariis*; *se furiis* is a conjecture.]

69. Iliacae...fauillae: the embers of the perpetual fire of Vesta, which was supposed to have been brought by Aeneas from Troy.

felix tutela: 'saviour and guardian'. *felix* when applied to a deity means 'propitious' as promising success.

71. ruit: (?)'is swept away' (by her passion).

Thermodonta: the river Thermodon in Cappadocia would naturally be associated with Amazons, not with Bacchantes; see note on next line.

72. Strymonis: the river Strymon flowed between Thrace and Macedonia. *Strymonis* stands (poetically) for a woman of Thrace and (here, more specifically) for a Thracian Amazon, or Bacchante. *Thermodon* above points to an Amazon, as the Amazons were associated both with Cappadocia and with Thrace. But Tarpeia's behaviour as victim of an overpowering emotion is more plausibly illustrated by comparison with a Bacchante. The Amazons had no use for men; and when they are described by poets as in mad career, it is in the context of a military assault. The two figures, of Amazon and Bacchante, are evidently here confused to some extent (as is the geography) in the poet's mind; but we can have no doubt that the figure of the Bacchante is dominant.

[**abscisso pectus aperta sinu:** this is a commonly received emendation for the MS. reading *abscisso fertur aperta sinu*. For *pectus aperta* cf. Tib. I, vi, 18 *laxo pectus aperta sinu*.]

73. urbi festus erat: with this we supply *dies* from the following line.

Parilia: the festival of Pales, on 21 April. This was the supposed date of Rome's foundation. See note on IV, i, 19.

76. cum pagana madent fercula diuitiis: 'when the board at the village feast flows rich with plenty'. *madent* suggests both cookery and 'richness' of the food (with oil, etc.), also perhaps tipsiness; *diuitiis* suggests plenty and disregard of expense. *fercula* are dishes; then the 'courses' of a banquet.

77–8. cumque super...pedes: see note on IV, i, 19.

82. pactis ipsa futura comes: either (*a*) *pactis* is ablative, 'by the terms of the bargain', and we supply a dative (the Sabines or Tatius) after *comes*; or (*b*) *pactis* is dative after *comes* and means 'her betrothed and his men'; cf. Sil. It. XIII, 843 (Tarpeia) *pactis reserauit claustra Sabinis*. Either way, she is engaged to accompany the party who make the stealthy attack.

83. mons erat ascensu dubius: besides its primary meaning 'doubtful' *dubius* can bear the secondary meaning 'difficult'; and so *mons ascensu dubius* can be said in the same way as *res factu difficilis*. Here the context shows that this is said of this hill (strictly, of this way up the hill) to give one reason why it was not better guarded; so the viewpoint must be that of the defenders, and the meaning 'was known (or believed) hard to climb'. For this attachment of a subjective value to an objective statement cf. IV, xi, 101 *sim digna merendo* = 'may I be *judged* worthy...'.

festoque remissus: 'and the guard on it relaxed because of the holiday'. As in the preceding sentence we have had to understand *mons* as 'way up the hill', so here we have to understand it as 'guard on the hill'; this is made easy in the first case by the context, and in the second by the strong and definite meaning in *remissus* (cf. *custodia remissa*, etc.).

85. omnia praebebant somnos: 'all around was a scene of slumber'; cf. *corpora uicta sopore* in Ovid's description, *Met.* XIV, 779. For *praebebant* = 'displayed to view' cf. III, xiii, 42 *praebebant uestri uerba benigna foci* (of altars displaying inscriptions).

86. poenis inuigilare suis: 'to remain on watch and see the vengeance he was planning carried out'. [*suis* is an emendation of the MS. reading *tuis*.]

88. nubendique petit, quem uelit ipse, diem: 'and asks him to name what day he will for her to be his bride'. Here *petit* = *poscit ut dicat*: cf. Ov. *Fast.* III, 177 *disce...quod petis*. [*ipse* is a conjecture for *ipsa* of the MSS. Keeping *ipsa* one gets 'asks to be allowed to name the day'.]

93. a duce Tarpeium mons est cognomen adeptus: 'the

Roman (or Sabine) leader gave the hill the name "Tarpeian Hill"'. For this construction of *adipisci* with *a* of the person who bestows the thing received, cf. *adipisci a populo honores*; and for *adipisci* meaning 'get' without any implication that the thing got has been sought cf. expressions such as *adipisci dolores*.

[*Tarpeium*, printed in the text here, is a conjecture for *Tarpeio* of the MSS., as Tarpeius, Tarpeia's father in the legend, is nowhere mentioned in this elegy. An alternative conjecture is *Tarpeia* (ablative); we should then understand that the hill got its name from Tarpeia 'because she guided the enemy'; and the construction would be one familiar in Ovid: cf. Ov. *Fast.* IV, 420 *Trinacris, a positu nomen adepta loci*; *Met.* VIII, 151 *Ciris...a tonso...nomen adepta capillo*. But the fact that this construction is familiar to us from Ovid does not prove that it is compulsory in Propertius his predecessor. And though Tarpeia evidently had guided the Sabines (and cf. Ov. *Fast.* I, 262 *duxerit*), the word *duce* applied to her here would give no more point or clarity or colour than a simple mention of her name. Nor does it seem likely that she would be called *dux* in one line and *uigil* in the next.]

94. o uigil, iniustae praemia sortis habes: literally 'o you that kept watch, you have your reward for the treacherous watch you kept'; disregarding the apostrophe as foreign to English idiom we can translate 'such is her reward for the traitor's watch she kept'. Tarpeia is called *uigil* ironically, because she stayed awake while all the rest were asleep (line 85). Her *sors* here, carrying on the metaphor, must be the watchman's 'turn of duty'; for this sense of the word cf. Sil. It. IX, 91–3 *uestigia uallo...uigil extulerat, dum sorte uicissim alternat portae excubias*; Hor. *Od.* III, xxiv, 15–16 *defunctumque laboribus aequali recreat sorte uicarius*. Her *sors* in this sense is *iniusta* because it was a watch wrongfully kept, just as *iniusta regna* in Ov. *Met.* V, 277 means a kingdom wrongfully won, and *iniustus cruor* in Val. Max. III, viii ext. 3 blood wrongfully shed. It is not possible for *iniusta sors* here to mean (*primarily* at any rate) her 'cruel fate', for the concluding lines of the elegy must accord with its general sentiment; and there has been no suggestion anywhere that her fate was anything but fully merited by her treacherous conduct: cf. lines 1, 17–18, 69–70, 87, 89, 92. The point of *praemia* seems to be that all the reward she got for her treachery was to have the hill named after her, in memory of her shame; the reward she wanted she did not obtain.

[That Propertius should use *iniusta sors* in a sense, as determined by its context, so different from its common and obvious meaning is not incompatible with his practice elsewhere; cf. II, ix, 45 *ponet vestigia* = 'leave her marks' (instead of 'set foot' or 'tread'); III, iii, 24 *maxima turba* = 'most violent disturbance' (instead of 'largest number'). However, there is another possible way of printing and reading this passage that deserves consideration: *o uigil iniuste, praemia sortis habes* = 'o you that kept a traitor's watch, you have your reward for the watch you kept'.]

V

This elegy, like elegy iB, is a genre piece depicting a strongly characterized type, in this case the bawd or procuress. This particular type was already established in literature from of old—an early example is in the first mime of Herodas—and she appears more than once in the elegies of Tibullus: see Tib. I, v, 47ff. and II, vi, 44ff.

The elegy begins and ends with curses (1–4 and 75–8) called down by the poet on the bawd, now on her deathbed (or dead already if *fuerant* is read in line 72). Within this frame is an account of her evil powers (5–18) and of her miserable death and the wretched funeral in prospect for her (65–74). The central and longest part of the elegy (19–64) is a speech, a specimen of the old woman's advice to his mistress on how to exploit her lovers to best advantage to herself.

For the description of a witch's powers in lines 8–18 cf. Tib. I, ii, 43–54; and for the description of the bawd as a witch cf. Tib. I, v, 59. For the situation implied in lines 19ff. cf. Plaut. *Most.* I, iii, where the lover overhears another woman giving worldly advice to his beloved. For the idea of a lecture by a professional adviser in such matters cf. Tib. I, iv, 9–72 (where the adviser is the god Priapus and the advice is offered with a different object in view). It will also be found that many of the detailed motives in the bawd's speech resemble ones that are found, with different applications, in Tib. I, iv, 9–72 and II, iii, 51–8; in fact this is true of almost everything in the bawd's speech except the passage 29–44. Lastly, for the curses on the bawd cf. Tib. I, v, 49–66 (where the details are different).

The piece has all the appearance of an essay in imagination.

There is no ground for supposing that the *lena* is a real person; or that the *amica* of line 63 is Cynthia.

3. nec sedeant...Manes: 'may your spirit find no rest'.

cineri: i.e. *tuo cineri* = '(for) you, when you are dead and turned to ashes'.

4. ieiuno: hungry and therefore angry.

ossa: 'your ghost'. For *ossa* used of the spirit of the dead in the underworld cf. IV, xi, 20 and 102, where there can hardly be present any notion of a skeleton form. Here the thought of a skeleton-ghost would be appropriate enough, for this is a skinny old hag.

5–18. docta...equae: here the construction changes; after cursing the dead *lena* in lines 1–4 he now goes on to describe her powers and practices.

5. Hippolytus: son of Theseus and the Amazon Hippolyte; he is depicted in the play of Euripides which is named after him as abstinent on principle from sexual relations and for this punished by Aphrodite (= Venus).

6. auis: 'omen' (in this context).

7. rumore mariti: i.e. the reports reaching her that Odysseus was alive and on his way home.

8. cogeret: 'would have been able to get (her) to...' (*sc.* 'if she had been there').

Antinoo: Antinous is leader among Penelope's suitors in the *Odyssey*.

9–10. poterit: the tense is natural enough if the *lena*, though dying, is still alive; see note on line 71.

uelit: this subjunctive (and also *mouerit* in line 11 below) has the value of a conditional clause, just as in English we can say 'should she...' instead of 'if she should...'.

11–12. Collinas: this adjective is used with special reference to the Quirinal hill. On this hill was the *porta Collina*, and near it the *campus sceleratus*, where Vestal virgins convicted of unchastity were buried alive. Herbs growing in such a place would have evil associations and so be suitable for witches' spells, etc.

fossam: in Ov. *Met.* VII, 245 the witch Medea pours blood into two *fossae* as she invokes the help of the infernal powers for the rejuvenation of Aeson.

ad...mouerit herbas: perhaps 'bring to...'; perhaps 'ply at...', with *moueo* used as in IV, i, 76, etc.

mouerit...diluerentur: an uncommon mixture of tenses;

97

but cf. Liv. VI, xl, 17 *si hodie bella sint, quale Etruscum fuit...,*
possetisne ferre Sextium consulem esse...? The distinction between 'ideal' and 'unreal' is blurred. One might translate: 'let
her but..., and already the...would be...'.

stantia: these could be 'fixed objects' generically; but it is not
Propertius' way to use colourless terms. Possibly therefore the
reference is to 'standing crops': the witch has but to work her
spells, and lo! a standing crop is swept away by a rush of water.
With the meaning thus supposed for *stantia* cf. on the one hand
stantes segetes and on the other *arata, sata,* etc.: though such a
use of *stantia* is not met in the Latin literature that has come
down to us, it might nevertheless be common in ordinary speech.
The power to make water flow this way or that at will was one of
the recognized powers of witches (cf. Tib. I, ii, 44; Prop. I, i,
23–4), and so was interference with crops (cf. Virg. *Ecl.* VIII, 99
and Tib. I, viii, 19 where witchcraft moves a standing crop from
one farm to another).

13. cantatae: i.e. bewitched by incantation.

14. et sua nocturno fallere terga lupo: i.e. assume the
form of a wolf; cf. Virg. *Ecl.* VIII, 97. (The Latin can be construed in either of two ways: (*a*) 'disguise her skin (i.e. herself)
in (the appearance of, i.e. the fell of) a wolf that prowls by night';
for this use of *fallere* cf. Ov. *Fast.* III, 633 *falsumque Lauinia*
uulnus mente premit (she conceals or disguises her distress); Ov.
Met. VIII, 578 *spatium discrimina fallit* (distance conceals, or ob-
scures, the gaps between the islands of a group, so that they seem
one mass); (*b*) 'borrow (by counterfeiting) his fell from a wolf
that prowls by night'; for this use of *fallere* cf. Virg. *Aen.* I, 684
tu faciem illius...falle dolo (of Cupid assuming the appearance of
Ascanius); the strong possessive *sua* is explained by the fact that
the counterfeiting is conceived as a borrowing of the wolf's
property, much as *speciem furabor Iacchi,* etc. is said of Vertumnus in IV, ii, 31–2.)

15. posset ut...: final construction after *eruit* in next line,
where see note.

astu: 'by her arts'.

intentos: 'watchful' against the would-be seducer.

16. cornicum immeritas eruit ungue genas: 'she tore out
poor (*literally* undeserving) ravens' eyes with her nails'. The
procedure is one of 'sympathetic' magic; by blinding the *cornix*
(a proverbially keen-sighted bird) she expects to blind the man of

whom she thinks while performing the act. (This makes it plain that final *ut* is the right reading in line 15.) *genae* is used here by an extension of its normal meaning ('cheeks') for the sockets of the eyes and so for the eyes themselves; this extension occurs elsewhere in poetry.

17. striges: 'screech-owls'. These appear elsewhere as birds of ill omen, and (e.g. Ov. *Fast.* VI, 135 ff.) suckers of babies' blood.

nostro de sanguine: either (*a*) about killing him; or (*b*) about sucking his blood, since this activity of the *striges* may not have been confined to infants. If blood-sucking is meant, the object *may* have been to render him impotent: cf. Petronius *Sat.* 134.

18. hippomanes: this word is a neuter substantive of Greek formation. In Virg. *Georg.* III, 280 ff. it is the name of a discharge from pregnant mares, said to be gathered by *malae nouercae* and used for poison or in making bad magic. [In Plin. *N.H.* VIII, 165 the *hippomanes* is a growth on the forehead of a newborn foal, and is used in love magic; it is found so used at Virg. *Aen.* IV, 515.]

19–20. †exorabat…uiam†: the text of this heavily corrupt couplet is here printed as it is given in the MS. tradition; *perure* at the end of the hexameter is no word, but certainly more is amiss than that. Some conjectures (among which *exercebat* for *exorabat* seems fairly certain) are shown in the *apparatus criticus*: for others, and for discussion, reference must be made to larger editions. The way in which the old woman used to work on the young woman is illustrated by a comparison; but a comparison with what? [If by *saxosam…uiam* Propertius means (and such a use of the adjective in *-osus* would not be foreign to his manner) the same as the *strata…uiarum saxea* of Lucretius I, 315–16, there may be relevance in the phrase in the same Lucretian passage (313) *stillicidi lapsus lapidem cauat*, which presumably refers to water dripping from eaves on to a pavement; cf. then also Lucr. IV, 1284–7 *nam leuiter quamuis quod crebro tunditur ictu, uincitur in longo spatio tamen atque labascit. nonne uides etiam guttas in saxa cadentis umoris longo in spatio pertundere saxa?*]

21. si te Eoa Dorozantum iuuat aurea ripa: we do not know who (if they existed) were the Dorozantes nor what was the *aurea ripa* here referred to.

22. sub Tyria concha...aqua: the *murex*, the shell-fish from which the famous Tyrian purple dye was extracted.

23. Eurypylique: Eurypylus was a legendary king of Cos. For the double genitive cf. IV, i, 103 and note.

Coae...Mineruae: 'of Coan work', Minerva being the patron goddess of spinning and weaving, and her name standing for the work of which she is patron by a metonymy similar to that by which Mars may stand for 'war', Ceres for 'bread', etc. Coan stuff was very fine and translucent, made of a thread from the cocoon of a silkworm-like caterpillar (but not the true silk-worm).

24. sectaque ab Attalicis putria signa toris: Attalus, king of Pergamum, was celebrated as inventor of an art of weaving cloth of gold. Hence 'figures cut from Attalus' couches' means figured tapestry-work in cloth of gold, removed (presumably) from couches originally covered with it; called here *putria* be-cause fragile from age. For *signa* = 'figures' (in woven stuff), cf. Virg. *Aen.* I, 648 *pallam signis auroque rigentem.*

25. palmiferae...Thebae: i.e. Egyptian Thebes.

uenalia: 'goods for sale'. We do not know what these typical Theban exports were.

26. murrea: made of *murra*, a mineral substance of which cups, vessels, etc. were made. This is its first appearance in Latin literature; later references are fairly frequent, and agree with this one in indicating that *murra* was expensive. It is thought to have been a kind of fluorspar; which according to some techniques is heated in the process of working, so that *cocta* would apply. (See A. I. Loewental and D. B. Harden in *JRS* XXXIX (1949), pp. 31 ff.)

29. simulare uirum: i.e. 'to pretend that you are someone's mistress'; the phrase is a substantive and subject of *facit*. A *uir* in the elegists is usually not a real husband, but a man who has established a regular arrangement with a courtesan. Here the advice is that the woman should pretend to all her lovers that she has such a regular protector, as a pretext for being sparing with her favours and setting a high price on them.

pretium facit: 'puts up your price'; cf. on IV, i, 81.

causis: 'excuses', 'pretexts'.

30. dilata nocte: 'after an assignation has been postponed'.

32. mercata pace premendus erit: 'be sure to (*or* you will be able to) drive a hard bargain with him for terms of peace'.

34. puros Isidis...dies: the cult of Isis involved periods of abstinence from sexual intercourse. [*Isidis* is a correction: the old MSS. give *sideris*.]

35. ingerat...tundat...: 'keep talking of...harp on the fact that...'.

tibi: not dative of the person addressed, but of the person interested: 'see to it that...'.

Aprilis: for the plural used of a subject often talked of cf. Mart. IV, lxxvii, 8 *Sigerosque meros Partheniosque sonas* (Sigerus and Parthenius being important persons); v, xli, 4 ff. *theatra loqueris et gradus et edicta trabesque et idus fibulasque censusque.* April was Venus' month; and the woman's birthday was coming in May.

Iole and *Amycle* are maids.

39–40. morsus...litibus alternis quos putet esse datos: the force of *alternis* here is like that of *mutua* in Tib. I, vi, 13–14 *liuor quem facit impresso mutua dente uenus*; cf. also Juv. VI, 268 *alterna...iurgia. litibus* here must mean amorous tussles, but the word is not usually applied to physical conflicts.

41. probra: 'angry reproaches'.

sequacis: 'importunate', because in love herself.

42. nempe: 'of course', 'naturally', 'no wonder'.

43. mundi: 'urbane'.

Thais: i.e. her example.

pretiosa: i.e. charging a high price for her favours.

44. ferit: 'tricks'; cf. III, iii, 50 *austeros arte ferire uiros.*

45. si cantica iactat: 'if he strikes up a song', or 'if he's in a singing mood'. *cantica* are popular songs, from comedy, etc. *iactat* might in some contexts suggest that the man is vain of his singing or showing it off; but that is not likely here, because if it were so the woman would not please him (as is evidently intended) by joining in, *ebria.* The context here seems to be a jolly evening, and *cantica* fits well with this. *iacto* is used very widely of loud and usually intermittent utterance, taking a special colour from its context: entreaty (Virg. *Ecl.* II, 5), joy (*Ecl.* v, 62), complaint (*Aen.* I, 102), urgency (*Aen.* II, 768), indignation (*Aen.* x, 95); there seems no reason why tipsiness should not be added to this list.

47. si pulset inanis: 'if one with empty pockets should come knocking'.

48. in obductam somniet usque seram: 'let him doze on

(unheeding) by his still barred door (*literally* over the bar across his door)'.

50. nauta nec...si... = *nec nauta, si....*

51–2. aut quorum...foro: imported slaves had their feet chalked when offered for sale; cf. Tib. II, iii, 59 for a similar allusion. A slave for sale would have a notice hung on him specifying his qualities; and a buyer might have him made to jump, to test whether he was sound.

51. per must here mean 'around' their necks; cf. IV, vi, 72 *fluant per mea colla rosae.*

55–6. 'quid iuuat...sinus?': this couplet comes from Prop. I, ii, 1–2. It does not seem impossible that it should be quoted here by the speaker, with a sneer. (But many think it is here an interpolation, and they may be right.)

58. istius...sine aere lyra: 'his penniless lyre'.

tibi: dative of the person interested or making the judgement: 'as far as you are concerned', or 'to your ear'.

surda: this means here 'mute' or 'unheard', as often.

60. utere: *sc.* 'your youth' or 'your chance'. It is used in the latter sense, without a substantive expressed, at Tib. I, v, 75.

61. uictura: if (*a*) this is from *uinco*, we supply *rosaria* again (*rosaria uidi uictura rosaria Paesti*), and the meaning is 'roses (*literally* rose-gardens) that would have surpassed the (famous) roses of Paestum'. If (*b*) *uictura* here is from *uiuo*, the meaning must be 'roses of Paestum that ought still to have lived (*or* had long to live)'; cf. Lucan VI, 710 (a witch is addressed) *si quisquis uestris caput extaque lancibus infans imposuit uicturus erat.*

Paestum was famous for its rose-gardens (*rosaria*).

63. dum: i.e. in the days when his mistress was thus being worked on by the hag.

his: i.e. with advice of this kind.

nostrae...amicae: probably an imaginary character, like the *lena*; see introductory note to this elegy.

64. per tenuem ossa mihi sunt numerata cutem: 'the bones could be counted through this poor skin of mine'; i.e. he was reduced by anxiety and frustration to skin and bones; cf. Ov. *Trist.* IV, vi, 42 *uix habeo tenuem quae tegat ossa cutem* (where the poet's attenuation is due to illness and depression in exile). For the preterite *sunt numerata* cf. on IV, i, 19. For the phrase cf. Tac. *Dial,* 21 (*oratio*) *in qua non eminent uenae nec ossa numeran-*

tur. The epithet *tenuem* combines the ideas that the skin is transparent and that the poet is thin and worn.

[The text printed incorporates a commonly received conjecture. The MSS. give *per tenues ossa sunt numerata cutes.* This appears to be unmetrical (*ōssā sŭnt*). Furthermore, the plural *cutes* is strange. However, *cutes* may be a poetic plural like *sinus*, etc., and as such hardly more remarkable than *menta* = 'chin' in Virg. *Aen.* VI, 809; indeed, it might have a certain real value, as suggesting the various parts of the person where the bones were conspicuous through the skin; much as *carnes* carries a similar suggestion in Ov. *Met.* VII, 269 (*strigis*) *ipsis cum carnibus alas*, or Plin. *N.H.* XXVI, 7 *cute…ad ossa carnes adprimente.* Hence it seems possible that the MS. text should be retained, with the insertion of some suitable monosyllable after *ossa*, such as *haec* or *heu.* For the resulting rhythm cf. II, xi, 6 *nec dicet 'cinis hic docta puella fuit'*; II, xx, 16 *si fallo, cinis, heu, sit mihi uterque grauis.*]

65. torquatae…columbae: a ring-dove, Venus' own bird.

67. tussim: literally of course 'cough'; but here by an extension of meaning it must stand for the phlegm associated with a cough.

68. sputa…cruenta: symptom of a consumption.

dentis…cauos: not hollow teeth, but gaps in the row of teeth, as the context shows; similarly *caua rupe* in Liv. IX, ii means a gap in a rock face, and so a rocky gorge.

69. tegetes…paternas: the *teges* is a mat, made of rushes (Mart. XI, xxxii), and used as a blanket by the poor (Mart. XI, lvi). *paternas* is said with a certain irony: this is the old woman's patrimony; her father was a pauper too.

70. horruit: for the tense cf. 64 above and note on IV, i, 19.

pergula: a kind of lean-to shelter.

curua: sagging.

71. fuerint: this may be either future or subjunctive. I think the former is more effective, leaving the curse to begin at line 75.

[*fuerint* here is a conjecture, for *fuerant* of the MSS. If we retain *fuerant*, the old woman is already dead, and the future tenses of 9–10 seem strained.]

rari…capilli: genitive sing., used collectively.

furtiua: 'stolen'.

74. clatra: the grille or lattice of a window or door of open-work. (The word is neuter pl.; *clatri*, masc. pl., is the commoner form.)

76. caprifice: the wild fig was supposed to destroy monuments by the growth of its roots. Here there is no monument to destroy, and the tree is named simply for its bad associations.

VI

The central feature of this elegy is a narrative (lines 15–66) of the battle of Actium. This purports (11–12 and 67–8) to explain the origin of the temple of Palatine Apollo, so that the elegy in this respect has the character of an aetiological poem, like Elegies ii and iv. (The temple in question was in fact vowed to Apollo by Augustus during the war against Sextus Pompeius, though evidently thought of later as a thank-offering for Apollo's help at Actium.)

Faint echoes of Virgil's account of Actium (*Aen.* VIII, 675 ff.) appear to be audible here in line 23 *hinc Augusta...* (cf. *Aen.* VIII, 678 *hinc Augustus...*) and line 29 *puppim...flamma* (cf. *Aen.* VIII, 680 *puppi...flammas*).

The whole complex 11–68 is introduced, as is Horace *Od.* III, i, by a passage (1–10) in which the poet speaks as a priest preparing to initiate an act of worship; this appears to be a figurative application of an idea suggested by the arrangement of certain hymns of Callimachus (II and V) in which the praise of the god, the hymn proper, is similarly prepared. The conclusion of the elegy (lines 69–86) consists of a passage in which the poet prepares to feast in celebration of Augustus' more recent victories, and calls on his fellow-poets to join with him in this.

The reference to the conquest of the Sygambri in line 77 suggests a date after the *clades Lolliana*, suffered at the hands of the Sygambri and other German tribes in 16 B.C.; cf. note on IV, i, 93–4 above. The same year, 16 B.C., saw the celebration of a four-yearly festival in honour of Augustus' principate (Dio C. 54. 19), and this may have been the occasion of the present elegy.

1. sint ora fauentia sacris: i.e. *fauete linguis* = εὐφημεῖτε = 'keep silence'.

3. serta: feminine singular; cf. *demissae...sertae*, feminine plural, in II, xxxiii, 37, where the correctness of the gender is attested as an idiosyncrasy of Propertius by the grammarian Charisius. The normal form of the word is *sertum*, neuter, with plural *serta*. On the point of 'garland', see next note.

[The reading of the MSS. here is *cera*, but *serta* gives much better sense in the context and is a very likely conjecture.]

Philiteis...corymbis: the *corymbi* are ivy-clusters, and the ivy (*hedera*) makes the poet's crown and symbolizes his achievement: cf. IV, i, 62. Philitas (or Philetas) of Cos was a celebrated poet of the third century B.C. whom Propertius elsewhere also (e.g. II, xxxiv, 31, III, i, 1, III, iii, 52) claims to emulate; his works, all but a few fragments, are lost.

4. Cyrenaeas...aquas: the reference is to Callimachus of Cyrene: see IV, i, 64 and note. In a well-known passage of his *Hymn to Apollo* (105–12) water stands as a symbol of refined purity of style; hence no doubt the allusion to *aqua* in the present passage and in III, i, 6; cf. also III, iii, 52 *Philitea...aqua*, and the fact that Callimachus' followers were called *aquae potores* = ὑδροπόται. In the present passage the outward, as opposed to the symbolic, reference is to lustral water as used in religious ritual.

5. costum: spikenard.

blandi...turis: i.e. incense which accompanies prayers.

mihi: dative of the person interested: 'I bid you offer...'.

6. terque focum circa laneus orbis eat: cf. Virg. *Ecl.* VIII, 64 *molli cinge haec altaria uitta*.

8. (carmen) tibia Mygdoniis libet eburna cadis: 'let the ivory pipe pour libation of music from Phrygian jar'. A metaphor from libation describes the music of the pipe-player (accompanist of a religious rite), which is itself part of the elaborate metaphor sustained in all the poem so far.

'Mygdonian' is a poetic equivalent to 'Phrygian', and the epithet occurs here because the original pipe was supposed to have been inherited from Marsyas by the legendary Phrygian musician Olympus.

9. alio...aere: 'under another sky', and so 'far removed'.

10. pura: i.e. purifying.

laurea: the spray of foliage used for sprinkling the lustral water; cf. Ov. *Fast.* IV, 728 and V, 676 for this use of such a spray.

mollit iter: 'prepares (*literally* makes easy) his way'.

nouum: because what is to follow (a battle-piece) is a new and bold enterprise for an *elegiac* poet.

11. Palatini...Apollinis aedem: see introductory note to this elegy, and on IV, i, 3.

12. Calliope: later the Muse of Epic, but in Propertius' day the Muses had not yet come to be conceived as strictly specialized. Calliope is simply the Muse that Propertius chooses to invoke; he refers to her as source of his inspiration also at III, ii, 16 and III, iii, 38.

13. ducuntur: 'are being spun'.

14. uaces: 'pray attend'.

15. est...: a statement of the scene introduces the narrative; cf. IV, iv, 3 *lucus erat....*

fugiens: i.e. running far inland from the open sea. He refers both to the Ambracian Gulf and to the channels and the subsidiary bay between them that connect it with the Ionian Sea.

Athamana ad litora: either (*a*) with *est*, 'on the Epirot coast'; or (*b*) with *fugiens*, 'towards the shore of the Athamanes'. *Athamana* is a neuter plural adjective, from *Athamanes* a tribe in Epirus.

portus: 'haven'. The Ambracian Gulf is so called here because, though its area is very large, it is almost completely cut off from the open sea.

16. sinus: 'the (Ambracian) gulf'.

condit: 'stills'; cf. IV, iv, 61 above *tubicen, fera murmura conde.*

17. pelagus: 'an expanse of water'.

Actia Iuleae...monumenta carinae: literally 'Actian memorial of the Iulean ship (i.e. ships)'; in other words 'where the name of Actium keeps alive the memory of the (victorious) ships of (him who sprung from) Iulus'. *Iuleae* is a special adjective from Iulus, the son of Aeneas, from whom the *gens Iulia*, and Augustus as adopted son of the dictator Caesar, claimed descent.

18. non operosa: either (*a*) 'easy of access', or (*b*) 'not made by hands'—for at III, ii, 14 *operosa...antra* are artificially constructed grottoes.

uia: i.e. a way of refuge.

nautarum uotis: 'for sailors in need' (*literally* 'for sailors' prayers').

19–20. mundi coiere manus: 'the forces of the world met in conflict'.

stetit aequore moles pinea: 'their walls of (pine) timber rose towering on the sea'. The expression no doubt includes both fleets; but it suggests especially the vast size of the ships of Antonius, for which see Dio C. L, 23, and Plutarch, *Ant.* LXV and LXVI.

20. nec: 'but...not...' (here, as not infrequently; cf. IV, ii, 3, IV, ix, 13).

nec remis aequa fauebat auis: i.e. *sed non utrique classi par fuit ominum fauor*.

21. altera: i.e. on the other side; the antithesis comes with *hinc* in 23 below.

Teucro damnata Quirino: 'doomed by (*or* to be destroyed by) Trojan Quirinus'. For the construction cf. Hor. *Od.* III, iii, 22 *castaeque damnatum Mineruae*. Quirinus (originally a Sabine god) was identified with and gave his name to both Mars and Romulus; here (and cf. IV, x, 11) Romulus is meant; he is called 'Trojan' because as son of Ilia he was descendant (in some versions grandson) of Aeneas. For the deified Romulus as protector of the Roman state cf. Virg. *Georg.* I, 498.

22. pilaque...manu: i.e. (the *pilum* being the typical arm of the legionary) Roman soldiers fighting under a woman's (Cleopatra's) command.

23. hinc: i.e. *ex nostra parte*.

Augusta: *augustus* is of course an adjective to begin with, and becomes a substantive when used to make the title bestowed on Octavian ('august one'). Here it is an adjective (possessive) *from* that title, meaning 'of Augustus'; for the short form cf. IV, iv, 26 *Romula hasta*; IV, iii, 64 *carbasa lina*, etc.

plenis Iouis omine uelis: 'its sails, sign of Jupiter's favour, swelling (in the breeze)'; in fact the breeze *is* the sign.

24. iam...docta: 'by now accustomed to...'; the allusion is to earlier successes of Octavian against foreign foes; e.g. those against the piratical associates of Sextus Pompeius, or against the Illyrians; an allusion to earlier victories in the civil wars is not of course expressly excluded, but is not likely to be *intended*, as the stress here throughout is on the idea that the real enemy at Actium is a foreigner.

25. tandem aciem geminos Nereus lunarat in arcus: the sea-god is spoken of as agent of the action which is really the action of the fleets (on the sea). The description would fit either two concave arrangements opposed to one another, or a concave and a convex arrangement forming two parallel curves. That Octavian adopted a crescent-shaped formation with the horns advanced is stated by Dio C. L, 31.

27. stantem se uindice Delon: 'which stands fast fixed under his protection'. Delos was supposed to have been a floating island until it became the birthplace of Apollo, from which time it was anchored fast.

28. (non tulit iratos mobilis una Notos): '(at one time) it, alone among islands, was a moving island and was swept along before the raging of the winds'. For this sense of *non tulit*— 'give way before'—cf. IV, ix, 62 *nec tulit iratam ianua clausa sitim*. The parenthesis describes the island's original condition, for which cf. Callimachus *H. to Delos*, 193–4 ἀλλὰ παλιρροίη ἐπινήχεται ἀνθέρικος ὥς, ἔνθα νότος, ἔνθ' εὖρος, ὅπῃ φορέῃσι θάλασσα. This contrasts with the island's condition after Apollo's birth, for which cf. Virg. *Aen.* III, 77 (Apollo) *immotamque coli dedit et contemnere uentos*. The perfect *non tulit* is the 'historic' perfect which simply records that something occurred in the past without indicating anything about the frequency or duration of it; as in Cic. *Or.* 132 *dicebat melius quam scripsit Hortensius*; cf. in this book IV, v, 64 and 70, and note on IV, i, 19.

[The MS. tradition has *nam tulit...mobilis unda*. But *una* is required because the sentence plainly refers to Delos; and *non* is required because simply experiencing stormy winds belongs as much to any other island as to Delos, and as much to Delos' present as to its past; what distinguished it in the days of its bygone mobility was being swept along by such winds.]

29. noua: 'strange', almost 'miraculous'.

30. in obliquam ter sinuata facem: this seems to describe the conventional rendering of the lightning flash as a zigzag.

31. non ille attulerat...: 'he had not come with...'.

32. carmen inerme: 'the peaceful music'. But really the epithet 'peaceful' belongs to the god rather than the lyre, and the sense is: 'he had not come in peace, with flowing hair and lyre of tortoise-shell'.

33. sed quali: 'but with a countenance like that with which he looked on Agamemnon'. To complete the syntax one can supply (*attulerat*) *talem uultum*.

34. egessitque auidis Dorica castra rogis: 'and caused the Grecian camp to be emptied by (*or* on to) the greedy pyres'. For the action represented as directly an action of the god who caused it cf. the construction in line 25 above. The reference is to the plague sent by Apollo on the Greeks at the beginning of the *Iliad*. *Dorica* = 'Dorian' stands here simply as a poetic alternative for 'Greek'.

35–6. aut qualis…serpentem: 'or as he was when he made the snake Python relax his coils in death'.

36. imbelles quem timuere deae: '(the snake) of whom the gentle goddesses were afraid'. The *imbelles deae* are the Muses who lived on Helicon, conceived as terrorized by the great serpent Python which Apollo killed at his coming to Delphi.

[*deae* is a probable correction for *lyrae* of the MSS., which may well be an echo of *carmen inerme lyrae* in line 32 above, perhaps assisted by a recollection of Horace *Od.* I, vi, 10 *imbellisque lyrae musa potens*. Some, however, keep *lyrae* and suppose that it stands for 'Muses', citing Prop. II, xxvi, 18 *Arioniam…lyram* = 'the poet Arion'; but here the adjective *imbelles* does not contain a proper name as does *Arioniam*.]

37. Longa…ab Alba: because the Julians, and through them Augustus, derived themselves from Aeneas' son Iulus through the line of Alban kings which he began. Hence the many references to Alba in the Augustan poets: cf. III, iii, 3 and Virg. *Aen.* I, 7, XII, 826, etc.

38. Hectoreis: stands by an extension of meaning for 'Trojan'. It was Aeneas, not Hector, who was ancestor of the Julians. But the word suggests also Hector's prowess. So the total effect is 'yet mightier than your Trojan forebears and their champion Hector'.

39. uince mari: iam terra tua est: this echoes the phrase *terra marique* which appears in Hor. *Epod.* ix, 27 and on coins of the period; and cf. *Res Gestae* III, 1 *bella terra et mari ciuilia externaque toto in orbe terrarum saepe gessi*.

39–40. tibi militat arcus et fauet ex umeris hoc onus omne meis: 'my bow fights on your side, and this quiver on my back with all its load of arrows is ready to help you'. With *arcus* we have to supply in thought *hic* or *meus*; which is made easy by the possessive *meis* in the pentameter.

42. imposuit prorae publica uota tuae: turning it passively one could translate: 'your ship is laden with a nation's prayers'.

43–4. quam nisi…auis: the thought is that if Rome now is conquered by the foreign foe (Cleopatra) the promise of a glorious destiny given by the auspices before her founding will have been proved false. The reference of course is to the story of Romulus and Remus watching for auspices, on the Palatine and Aventine respectively, to decide which place and which founder had divine approval. *non bene* goes with the whole sentence and not specifically with *uidit* or *ire*: it seems to mean 'it was to no avail that...'; similarly in Martial IV, lxvii, 7 *male diues arca* is said of a money-chest that is well filled with money to no purpose, because the owner does not make good use of it.

45-6. Latinos...fluctus: 'Italian seas', i.e. it is a disgrace (to you) that the fleet of a (foreign) tyrant should venture so near to the shores of Italy, when you are our leader. *Latinos* stands here for 'Roman' or 'Italian'; cf. Hor. *Od.* II, i, 29 *quis non Latino sanguine pinguior campus*, etc.

[*Latinis* is the reading of the MSS., and would mean 'it is disgraceful for Italians (*or* Romans) that the sea should...'. But this weakens the point of *principe te*, and spoils the valuable contrast *Latinos...regia*. The change in transmission from *Latinos* to *Latinis* would occur easily.]

47. quod...remigat: 'the fact that...'. [The MSS. have *quod...remiget*, which may be right and mean 'the knowledge that...'.]

centenis...alis: i.e. the ships composing the *classis* have many oars apiece. *centum* may stand for 'a large number'. The oars are called *alae* here by a metaphor opposite to that which calls wings *remigium*.

49-50. quodque uehunt...experiere: either (*a*) 'and as for the fact that..., you'll find...'; or (*b*) the *quod* clause is parallel in construction to the *quod* clause in line 47 as subject of the verb *terreat*; the meaning of the whole being 'let not the fact that... alarm you, for...; and let not the fact that...alarm you, for...'. (The punctuation here printed assumes the first of the above alternatives.)

Centaurica saxa minantis: i.e. (*minantis* being accus. pl. = 'figures threatening...') figureheads in the form of Centaurs with rocks poised ready to be thrown; thus Virg. *Aen.* X, 195 says of such a Centaur-figurehead *ille instat aquae saxumque undis immane minatur*. For the transference of the epithet defining the figures from the figures to the rocks they hold cf. viii, 24 below *armillatos colla Molossa canis* (= 'Molossian dogs with...').

50. tigna caua et pictos experiere metus: 'you will find that they are (only) hollow (effigies of) wood and painted scares'.

53. ego temporis auctor: 'I, who tell you the time has come'; he has just said '*tempus adest*'.

54. ducam laurigera...manu: 'will lead with laurelled hand' = 'will lead to victory'.

57. fide Phoebi: 'by Phoebus' aid'; for this sense of *fides* cf. *implorare fidem*, etc. Better still, 'by Phoebus' *promised* aid', thus including another, and primary, sense of the word.

dat femina poenas: 'the woman is punished (for her presumption)'. (It is hardly possible to render the Latin sentence in English without making some of its implications explicit.)

58. sceptra...aquas: i.e. 'and her shattered power is borne away over the Ionian sea'.

59. at pater...astro: i.e. Julius Caesar, adoptive father of Octavian, deified (i.e. acknowledged officially to be divine and worthy of worship) since his death, looks down from his place in the sky and admires his adopted son's achievement. The epithet *Idalium* means 'belonging to Venus', because Venus had special associations with Mount Idalium in Cyprus. One might expect *Idalium astrum* to mean the planet Venus; but more probably it means the comet, called *Dionaei...Caesaris astrum* by Virg. *Ecl.* IX, 47, which appeared after Caesar's death and according to Suet. *Jul.* 88 was supposed by the populace to be his spirit, now divine.

60. est...ista fides: i.e. your achievement (*factum istud*) is proof (*fides*) of our inborn quality, i.e. (after *sum deus*) that we are divine. This, from the form of the statement (*sum...; est...*), must be the primary meaning; and there is an allusion to their descent from Venus as well as to their achievements. But no doubt there is also present the idea 'your achievement is worthy (fulfilment) of my fatherhood'. For the required sense, in either case, of *fides* cf. IV, i, 98 and note.

61. cantu: i.e. blowing his horn (or rather, an instrument made out of a big sea-shell, with the sound of which Triton was conceived as restoring calm after a storm).

63. cumba male nixa fugaci: *cumba* means strictly a small boat; this need not be stressed here, but it helps to suggest the abject condition of the fleeing queen. *nixa* = (*a*) 'relying on' as in *spe nixus*, etc.; (*b*) (?) 'reclining on' (cf. I, xvi, 33 *alterius felici nixa lacerto*); which suggests that Cleopatra is prostrate. *male* means 'to no avail' (as in Mart. IV, lxvii, 7 *male diuitis arcae*) and goes with *nixa* or *fugaci* or both.

64. hoc unum: this is in a kind of apposition to the rest of the line: all that she will achieve by flight is to be able to die at the time of her own choosing instead of being executed.

65. di melius!: this exclamation may mean either 'Heaven forbid!' or 'Heaven be thanked!' Here it means the latter, as in Ov. *Her.* XVII, 30 *di melius! similis non fuit ille tui.*

66. ductus...uias: understand *ducta per eas uias per quas Jugurtha ante ductus erat.*

67. hinc...monumenta: though the temple of Palatine Apollo was originally vowed by Octavian in 36 B.C. during his war against Sextus Pompeius, this line and line 11 above show that Propertius thinks of it as a thank-offering and memorial for Apollo's aid at Actium. As observed in the note at the beginning of the elegy, lines 11–68 are presented as an 'aetiological' poem.

traxit: (here) = 'got'.

68. una decem...ratis: we do not know anything from other sources about this event.

69. bella satis cecini: the phrase *bella satis cecini* calls attention to what Propertius must have considered a remarkable achievement: to have written in elegiacs a narrative of battle, usually supposed to demand the epic hexameter. There then begins the concluding section of the elegy, in which Propertius imagines himself as about to hold feast in honour of Augustus' achievements, in company with other poets.

71. candida...conuiuia: the *conuiuae* at the feast are dressed in white because it is a formal occasion. *conuiuia* stands here for *conuiuae* as does e.g. *hospitium* for *hospes* in I, xv, 20.

molli...luco: the feast is held out of doors, in a bower screened by trees or shrubs. *molli* (here) = 'pleasant' or 'luxurious'.

subeant: 'make their way to...', and so 'assemble in...'.

72. blanditaeque...rosae: 'sweet roses'; the past participle *blanditus* came to be used as an adjective, with the meaning 'pleasant', as can be seen from Pliny, *N.H.* IX, 35 *antemeridiano tempore blandito*, or X, 67 *blandita peregrinatione*. [The MS. reading here is *blanditiae*, and many editors prefer to retain this, taking *rosae* as genitive of a collective singular.]

per mea colla: 'around my neck'; cf. IV, v, 51.

74. perque lauet: 'drench'. [*perlavo* is not found elsewhere; in compounds *-luo* for *-lavo* is almost universal; no other example of *tmesis* is found in Propertius. For these reasons many editors here emend to *terque....* But *ter* with its implications of ritual will not do here. And there is nothing really unlikely about *per...lauat*, for Cicero has *per mihi mirum, perque iucunda* etc., and Virg. *Georg.* II, 366 *interque legendae.*]

spica Cilissa: this means saffron perfume, probably sprayed. *spica* is said with reference to the pistil of the flower, from which this saffron is extracted; *Cilissa*, because Cilician saffron was specially celebrated.

75. positis: 'as they recline at ease'; cf. II, xxxiv, 59 *me iuuet hesternis positum languere corollis*; Juv. IX, 52 *strata positus longaque cathedra*.

76. Bacche, soles...tuo: i.e. Bacchus (wine) is friend to (*tuo*) Phoebus (poetry), and quickens his creative powers; cf. Ov. *Met.* VII, 432 *carmina uino ingenium faciente canunt*.

77–8. ille...hic...: 'one...another...'.

77. Sycambros: the Sygambri (the name is variously spelt) were a German tribe, who took a part in defeating M. Lollius in 16 B.C., but retired and gave hostages soon afterwards; see Dio C. LIV, 20. *paludosos* alludes to the marshes of Germany.

78. Cepheam...Meroen: Meroe was a town in Ethiopia; of which country Cepheus (father of Andromeda) was a legendary king. An Ethiopian incursion into Egypt was repulsed by Petronius, prefect of the province, in 22 B.C.; see Dio C. LIV, 5.

79. confessum: the word here is used absolutely, or with something understood; the meaning must be 'owns himself defeated'.

80. reddat here begins a quotation; Propertius is imagining an effusion by one of the poets of the company (*hic* of line 79).

signa: the standards lost with Crassus in 54 B.C. were restored by the Parthians under diplomatic pressure from Augustus in 20 B.C., some years before the date of this elegy. The meaning here of *reddat* (*literally* 'let him give back' = 'never mind if he gives back') is fixed by its context: it must mean: 'never mind if he *has* given back our standards; that will not alter what is going to happen to him; soon...'.

Remi: with the same value as if it were *Romuli*; cf. II, i, 23 *regna...prima Remi*; Cat. LVIII, 5 *magnanimi Remi nepotes*.

81. pharetris...Eois: the 'quivers of the East' stand here for the Parthians, famous archers.

82. differat: 'defer those conquests only so that his sons can make them'. The *pueri* are Gaius and Lucius Caesar, born to her husband Agrippa by Augustus' daughter Julia, and adopted by Augustus in 17 B.C.

83. nigras...harenas: 'those sombre sands'. Crassus perished in the sandy plain around Carrhae. For the funereal associations of *nigra* cf. on IV, iii, 14 *lumina nigra*; here it may also suggest the darkness of the underworld which Crassus' ghost now inhabits. *niger* could be used literally of dark sand, but its value here is chiefly metaphorical.

85. patera: the flat, saucer-like vessel used typically for libations. In the course of their drinking they pour libations, and no doubt in this context libations in honour of Augustus especially are meant to be understood; for this was one of the honours decreed for him in 30 B.C. after his final victory over Antony and Cleopatra (cf. Dio C. LI, 19 καὶ ἐν τοῖς συσσιτίοις οὐχ ὅτι τοῖς κοινοῖς ἀλλὰ καὶ τοῖς ἰδίοις πάντας αὐτῷ σπένδειν ἐκέλευσαν).

85. ducam: here with *noctem* = 'pass'.

86. mea uina: the 'poetic' plural has here (cf. on IV, xi, 15 *noctes*) some real value, suggesting that the potations were repeated and lasted some time.

VII

In this elegy the ghost of the poet's mistress Cynthia appears to him, shortly after her funeral. The greater part of it, lines 13–94, consists of the ghost's speech to the poet. This falls into sections as follows: (13–22) she reproaches Propertius as forgetful of their love; (23–34) she complains of his perfunctory attention to her funeral; (35–48) she professes to believe that she has been poisoned, and that her place has been taken by a successor, who with Propertius' acquiescence is trying to obliterate her memory; (49–54) however, she will not reproach him further; for a long time they were happy together; she swears that for her part she has been faithful to him; (55–70) in the world below her place is with the heroines who have been true lovers in life, and who have suffered; (71–86) she gives directions to him to care for her favourite servants, and about the treatment of her grave; (87–94) she bids him heed her message, and declares that they will be reunited in time to come. Lines 1–12 and 95–6 provide the setting of the speech.

The dream motif was a favourite with the Hellenistic poets: witness for instance Theocritus XXI and the form of the *Aitia* of Callimachus (cf. Propertius, II, xxxiv, 32 *somnia Callimachi*); it occurs also in Tib. II, vi, 37–40 and repeatedly in the *Aeneid*. The lot of lovers in the underworld is described, and contrasted

with that of the wicked, in Tib. I, iii, 57–82. Further, in lines
1, 3, 8, 14 and 96 of the present elegy are apparent echoes of
Iliad XXIII, 103–4, 68, 66, 69 and 99–100, from the scene in
which the ghost of Patroclus appears to Achilles. However, there
is nothing in any of this to prevent us supposing that the poem
derives in some degree from a real experience.

It is not easy to reconstruct with confidence the background
assumed by the poem. The household referred to in lines 35–47
seems to belong to Propertius; the statements made about it are
not of course to be taken as all necessarily true; Cynthia's
imagination is fired by jealousy. The house from which Cynthia
used, in the early days of their intrigue, to slip away by stealth to
meet Propertius (lines 15–18) may be the house of a man who
kept her as mistress and from whom Propertius seduced her.
The terms of lines 5–6 might suggest that Propertius and Cynthia were still associated at the time of her death. But this interpretation of lines 5–6 is not inevitable; and the general effect of
the elegy may be felt to tend to an opposite conclusion. What is
clear is that the elegy as a whole presents a portrait of Cynthia,
and an unromanticized portrait at that. In this setting the impact
of the couplet 85–6, in the grand manner, is very powerful. It
will be observed that the tone of Cynthia's speech changes at
line 49.

1–2. sunt aliquid...rogos: 'the shades are no fable; death
is not the end of all; and somehow a wan ghost does survive the
pyre'. For the phrase *sunt aliquid...manes* ('there are such
things as...') cf. Juv. II, 149 *esse aliquos manes et subterranea
regna nec pueri credunt.* For *euincere* of getting past a hazard or
obstacle cf. Ov. *Met.* XIV, 75–6 *ubi...Charybdin euicere rates*;
Met. XV, 706 *euincit...Siculi...angusta Pelori.*

3. incumbere: she appears to bend over the bed; cf. Ov.
Met. XV, 21–2 *hunc super incumbens pressum grauitate soporis
clauiger* (Hercules, in a dream) *adloquitur.*

fulcro: the *fulcrum* is the raised head-end of a Roman bed, on
or against which the pillow is placed.

4. extremae...uiae: the edge of the road, i.e. the roadside.

5. penderet: 'hung back' or 'held off', i.e. 'would not come',
cf. Virg. *Georg.* I, 214 *dum nubila pendent* (before the rainy season). Either sleeplessness or fitful sleep may be meant. (The
ancients did not distinguish as clearly as we do between a dream-
apparition and a 'ghost'.)

ab: 'after'.

amoris: 'of her whom I had loved'.

6. et quererer lecti frigida regna mei: either (*a*) 'and I grieved that my bed was a cold and desolate domain'; or (*b*) 'and I grieved that she who once reigned in my bed was now a cold and lifeless corpse'; the abstract *regna* standing for the person, as do the abstracts in I, xv, 20 (*Hypsipyle*) *Haemonio tabuit hospitio* (= *Jason*), or IV, vi, 71 *subeant conuiuia* (= *conuiuae*) *luco*.

For *frigida* cf. on the one hand Ov. *Am.* III, v, 42 *frigidus in uiduo destituere toro*; and on the other Virg. *Georg.* IV, 506 *illa*... *Stygia nabat iam frigida cumba*. Both ideas are probably present; which we suppose to be dominant will depend on what we suppose to have been the relationship between Propertius and Cynthia at the time of her death.

7. eosdem: a similar synizesis occurs several times elsewhere in Propertius, but only here and in the next line (8) does it fall in the first syllable of the verse.

7–8. capillos...oculos: her hair arranged in the same way; the same (? fixed) look of the eyes. According to Pliny *N.H.* XI, 37, 155 the eyes were closed at death but opened again on the pyre—in this case apparently on the bier. (The word *oculos* is from ὄμματα in *Il.* XXIII, 66, where what is meant seems to be simply 'face' or 'expression'.)

10. summaque Lethaeus triuerat ora liquor: 'her lips were wet with the water of Lethe'; *literally* 'the water of Lethe had (?lightly) touched her lips'. For the pluperfect in descriptions of a state resulting from a past action, cf. (e.g.) IV, ix, 24 *fecerat*; Lucan X, 112–15 *laqueataque tecta ferebant diuitias crassumque trabes absconderat aurum* (describing a ceiling). There is no need to assign a strong value to *tero* in *triuerat*; cf. Virg. *Ecl.* II, 34 *nec te paeniteat calamo triuisse labellum*. *summa* need mean no more than 'the surface of', otiose in English here; but it may have an adverbial value, with the effect of 'lightly'. *Lethaeus liquor* may simply stand here, as at line 91 below and Tib. I, iii, 80, for water of the underworld; symbolizing the state of death because of the associations of the name, but without any specific reference to the power sometimes attributed to Lethe of making one forget one's past life—an idea prominent in our minds because of *Aeneid* VI and Plato, *Republic* X.

11. spirantisque: 'of the living (Cynthia)' (genitive).

animos et uocem misit: the verb *misit* is strictly appropriate to *uocem* and from it is supplied a sense appropriate to *animos* (= 'spirit', perhaps almost 'temper'); in fact, a zeugma.

at illi: adding a descriptive touch, with a change of grammatical subject but not (here) of the subject of thought; cf. IV, iv, 15 (and note), from which it appears that there need be no antithesis between what follows and what has been said already.

12. pollicibus fragiles increpuere manus: a regular meaning of *increpare* is 'reproach' or 'rebuke', and this may be assisted by an act or gesture: cf. Hor. *Od.* IV, xv, 1–2 *Phoebus uolentem proelia me loqui...increpuit lyra*. If we compare the phrase *crepare digitis* = 'snap the fingers', it seems clear that some form of gesticulation, reinforcing Cynthia's indignant speech, is being described. *fragiles* might suggest lean boniness as of a skeleton; but it *need* not refer to anything but the slenderness of Cynthia's hands (cf. II, ii, 5 *longae...manus*). *pollicibus* (literally 'thumbs') may stand simply for fingers, as at II, v, 24 *nec duris ausim* (? sc. *genas tuas*) *laedere pollicibus*; but possibly Cynthia's gesticulations included snapping the thumb and forefinger. Cynthia's manner, and style of speech and behaviour, are just as they were when she was alive.

13. perfide, nec...puellae: the sound is important in this line.

15. exciderant: 'had you forgotten...?', i.e. so that I found you asleep just now. Whether or not he was asleep, she professes to think that he was.

uigilacis: the termination *-ax* indicates a disposition, as in *minax, audax, loquax, mordax, sequax,* etc. Here the disposition is to stay awake all night, keep late hours, etc. The Subura was an area N.E. of the Forum, favoured by the demi-monde. So the sense is: 'had you forgotten the night-life of the Subura, and our adventures together there?'. She is recalling the early days of their affair.

16–18. et mea...manu: it is not clear what was the establishment from which Cynthia had to escape thus furtively in order to keep her assignation with Propertius. Perhaps that of some man whose mistress she was when she first became acquainted with the poet.

19. pectore mixto: the meaning is clear, but the expression is strange, perhaps deliberately so, to convey the closeness of the embrace.

21. foederis...taciti: presumably an understanding that

they would always remain lovers. *taciti* in view of what follows cannot mean 'unspoken', so must here mean 'secret (between them)'. The construction here used—the exclamatory genitive —is a very rare one in Latin.

23. at mihi non oculos quisquam inclamauit euntis: the verb *inclamare* is used ordinarily with an accusative of the person, and means 'call to' by way of summons or exhortation. Here the meaning appears to be 'call to me (to stay) as the light left my eyes'. With *oculos...euntis* (acc. pl.) cf. Ov. *Tr.* III, iii, 44 *labentes oculos* (of a dying person).

[It may be preferable here to read *eunti* (*sc. mihi*) = 'dying'; cf. Lucr. III, 526 *saepe hominem paulatim cernimus ire*, and Ov. *Am.* III, ix, 49 *fugientis* (genitive) *pressit ocellos*.]

24. unum...diem: this recalls the legend that Protesilaus was allowed to return for one day to Laodamia; cf. Stat. *Silu.* v, iii, 272.

25. nec crepuit fissa...custos: Propertius did not provide a watcher to stand guard by the corpse as it lay awaiting burial. The 'cloven cane' was probably a kind of rattle for scaring away bad spirits, or giving the alarm; a κρόταλον consisting of a split cane is referred to in a scholium on Aristophanes, *Clouds* 260 (quoted in Starkie's edn.).

26. laesit et...caput: (?)her head was propped on (and bruised or grazed by) a piece of terracotta instead of a pillow; evidence of cheap arrangements. (But uncertainty remains about the meaning of this line.)

27. curuum: 'bowed (from grief)'.

28. atram quis...incaluisse togam: this sentence in itself could mean either that he wore mourning but did not weep, or that he neither wore mourning nor wept. The second of these is the meaning required by the context here; Cynthia would not mention anything he had done right.

31. cur...non ipse...?: 'why were you not there to...?'.

33. graue: 'too much trouble (*or* expense)'.

nulla mercede...: 'that cost (little or) nothing'.

34. fracto busta piare cado: 'and break a wine-jar, as reverence requires, over the ashes of my pyre'. The wine was scattered over the bones after the burning, before they were put in the urn; cf. Virg. *Aen.* VI, 226–7 and [Tib.] III, ii, 17–19.

35. Lygdamus: a slave of Propertius; cf. IV, viii, 79–80.

uratur...candescat lamina: he is to be tortured with a

heated strip or plate of hot metal, to make him confess the plot on Cynthia's life. This plot is of course to be understood as part of the wild imagining of an angry and jealous woman; not as a real event, or even as one in which the speaker seriously believes. This is the way Cynthia used to carry on.

36. insidiis pallida: 'discoloured' by the poison. As will be seen from line 82 below, *pallida* means 'off-colour'; not necessarily (though frequently) what we should call 'pale' in colour.

insidiis must here either stand by metonymy for 'poison', as a furtive means of harm, or mean 'the assassin's arts'.

37. ut Nomas arcanas tollat uersuta saliuas: 'though artful Nomas hide away her secret liquors'. Nomas is a wise-woman who knows about charms and poisons and the like; as she too is to be tortured, she is probably a slave in the household, like Lygdamus. [*ut* is a conjecture, for *aut* of the MS. tradition.]

38. dicet...manus: 'will make her confess whose hands (*or* that her hands) are guilty'. Propertius has a way of taking for subject of a transitive verb someone or something other than the true agent; cf. I, xvii, 25 (the Nereids by bringing fair weather are said to unfurl the sails of the ship); II, xxvi, 49 (Amymone vows to accept Neptune's embrace on a certain condition, and he embracing her is said to be paying her vow); IV, vi, 25 (the sea-god is said to form into crescents the fleets which assume this formation on the sea). The *ignea testa* serves the same purpose as the *lamina* of line 35.

39. inspecta est: the historic perfect, saying simply that something happened in the past without specifying frequency (which here is indicated by *per...noctes*); cf. notes on IV, i, 19 and on *non tulit* in IV, vi, 28. The meaning is 'stood exposed to public view nightly, a common harlot and cheap at that'. The epithet *uiles* is the more easily attached to *noctes* because in the jargon of erotic poetry *nox* often has the special sense of a night or part of a night spent with a woman.

40. cyclade: a special kind of woman's dress, grand and long.

signat humum: her long dress sweeps the ground (*literally* 'marks' it).

41–2. at grauiora rependit...mea est: if any of the maids has forgotten to watch her tongue and has referred to Cynthia's beauty, she is punished by having extra big basketfuls of wool weighed out to her as her day's task, to be returned at the end of the day in the form of an equivalent weight of spun yarn.

43. Petale: another woman servant, now old.

44. codicis immundi: the *codex* was a block of wood, attached to the leg to prevent escape or by way of punishment.

immundus regularly means 'dirty', and in fact such a *codex* would collect dirt as it was dragged around. There is the further idea that this was an unbecoming and humiliating (*turpis*) form of punishment for an old woman such as Petale; *anus* standing in apposition at the end of the line and the sentence is evidently said with special point.

45. Lalage: another maid.

46. ausa rogare: a slave making a special request to master or mistress would do so 'by the name of...' someone dear to the person addressed.

47. conflauit: the subject is the new mistress.

48. dotem: either (*a*) this is meant literally, and the woman in question is accumulating a dowry in order to be able to enter into a regular partnership with some man of her own social order; or (*b*) the word is used in an extended sense to mean private capital, more generally.

rogo: in the context, this must be the fire on which the image (or a gold ring with a portrait on it) is melted. But the term suggests Cynthia's funeral pyre too.

49. non tamen: here Cynthia's tone changes (exactly in the middle of the elegy).

51. iuro...carmen: the accusative is of the thing sworn by. The idea in *nulli reuolubile* is taken from the thread which the Fates spin, and which can never be unspun; as they spin they sing a prophetic song (as in Cat. LXIV, 320ff.) and this is spoken of in terms more strictly appropriate to the thread.

52. sic...sonet: the familiar wish formula, used to reinforce a statement or a request; cf. iii, 67 above (a request).

55. sortita: 'separately assigned'. The participle is passive here, though the verb *sortior* is commonly deponent.

turpem: 'grim'.

per: the context shows that this must here mean 'beyond'.

56. turbaque...aqua: 'and the shades are ferried across the water two separate ways'. *omnis* need not be translated; it reinforces idiomatically the division indicated by *diuersa*, as in Caes. *B.G.* I, 1 *omnis Gallia diuisa est in partes tres*; Cic. *Cluent.* I *animaduerti, iudices, omnem accusatoris orationem in duas diuisam esse partes*.

remigat: here probably 'is rowed', i.e. travels in a rowed vessel. But at II, xxvii, 13 Propertius conceives the dead as rowing the ferry-boat themselves.

57. Clytaemestrae stuprum: i.e. *Clytaemestram adulteram.*

aut ea Cressae: if *aut ea* is right (it is a conjecture for *altera Cressae* of the MSS., which cannot stand with the preceding *una*, since Clytaemnestra and Pasiphae are grouped, not contrasted) the picking up of the subject by the demonstrative will resemble the kind illustrated by Kühner–Stegmann II (2), pp. 564–5 in respect of *et is, isque*, etc. [An alternative line of conjecture would keep *altera*, re-punctuate, and emend *una* at the beginning of the line to *unda*, thus: *unda Clytaemestrae stuprum uehit altera.* But it is then difficult to make the link with what follows.]

57–8. uehit...portat: for a similar combination of these two verbs cf. IV, i, 46–7.

Cressae...mentitae lignea monstra bouis: the reference is to Pasiphae, wife of Minos, king of Crete, who fell in love with the famous bull and had a wooden image of a cow made, under cover of which she let the bull serve her; in this way the Minotaur was conceived. The phrase could theoretically be construed in several ways, but as *Cressae* because of its position must surely be a substantive (= 'the Cretan woman' = Pasiphae) rather than an adjective agreeing with *bouis*, the effective possibilities are two, both requiring *stuprum* to be supplied with *Cressae* from what has gone before: (*a*) 'the incestuous crime of the Cretan queen, the wooden horror of the pretended (*mentitae* passive, like *sortita* in 55) cow'; or (*b*) 'the incestuous Cretan queen, whose fraud contrived (*mentitae* active, as usual) the wooden horror of the cow'. Probably most readers will judge (*a*) too strongly figurative, and so will prefer (*b*).

59. [*rapta* is an emendation. The MSS. give *parta*.]

60. ubi: we have to understand '*to the place* where'.

61–2. qua numerosa...choris: the tuneful lute, and the round bronze cymbals associated with the worship of Cybele, and the lyre accompanying turbaned dancers with music in the Lydian mode—none of these has any special association with the underworld, that we know of. They are here enumerated simply to suggest the musical delights that the blessed enjoy with their other blessings.

Cybēbes: genitive. This alternative form of Cybĕle's name has been favoured by many editors where a long penultimate is required. But the MSS. here have *Cybēles* or *Cybelles*, and neither of these is an impossible variant; cf. IV, xi, 51.

63. Andromedeque et Hypermestre: from what precedes it is clear that we are here thinking of virtuous heroines; from line 69 it is clear that they are also heroines who have suffered in this world. Hypermestra is an apt instance in both respects; she was the one of the fifty daughters of Danaus who refused to murder her husband at her father's command and was put in chains by her father (cf. Ov. *Her.* XIV) on this account. Andromeda, as we have her story, was exposed to the sea-monster because of her mother's vanity and not for any virtue or affection of her own; and while we hear that she married her rescuer Perseus, we hear nothing of her conduct as a wife. Hence Heinsius' proposal to emend *maritae* in line 63 to *marita*, restricting the term to Hypermestra. But the context makes it certain that Andromeda is cited here as a virtuous woman, whether as a famous example of such or not. Propertius and Cynthia may have known a version of the legend that we do not know. Or it may be that, finding in Andromeda a good example of a *suffering* heroine, he is ready to imagine her as notably virtuous too and cite her accordingly; much as in I, ii, 15ff. he cites various legendary beauties as dispensing with make-up, though this cannot really have been part of the legends about them.

64. narrant historiae tempora nota suae: literally 'relate the famous perils of their story', i.e. 'tell of the perils for which they are famed in legend'. For *tempora* in this sense cf. Hor. *Od.* II, vii, 1 *o saepe mecum tempus in ultimum deducte.* [Here *tempora* is an emendation for the MS. *pectora*. An alternative is to keep *pectora* and understand it as nominative in apposition to *Andromede* and *Hypermestre*, finding an object for *narrant* by reading *historias...suas.*]

65. maternis: a remarkable use of the adjective, for it must mean 'suffered on her mother's account'; cf. III, xxii, 29 *non hic Andromedae resonant pro matre catenae.*

67. magnum: 'a monstrous deed'; for *magnum* as a neuter substantive cf. Cic. *Verr.* IV, 2 *magnum videor dicere; attendite quomodo....*

69. sic mortis lacrimis uitae sanamus amores: 'thus with tears in death we console ourselves for (*literally* try to heal) the wounds love caused us while we lived'. Whatever may be the

case with Andromeda (see on line 63 above), this sentiment suits
the speaker and arises naturally from the reference to Hypermestra in the preceding line; and it is hard to think of any
alternative which would fulfil these conditions. We have to
suppose an extra sense ('wounds of') accruing to *amores* from
that of the verb *sanamus*, much as in IV, iv, 83 an extra sense
('guard on') appears to accrue to *mons* from that of the participle
remissus.

72. Chloridos herba: 'the magic herbs (i.e. drugs or spells)
of Chloris'. Chloris is either the successor complained of in lines
39–40 or a witch employed by her.

73. nutrix: Cynthia's, of course, and dependent on her.

74. potuit, nec tibi auara fuit: i.e. *potuit tibi auara esse, sed
non fuit*; she did not use her position, as she could have, to
extort bribes or hush-money from Propertius.

75. cui nomen ab usu est: because her name is Greek for
'maidservant', and Latris as the next line shows was personal
maid to Cynthia.

76. illa: either (*a*) resumptive, in the colloquial manner, without emphasis; or (*b*) emphatic: 'see that *she* doesn't...'.

78. ure mihi: either (*a*) 'burn as an offering to me'; or (*b*) 'I
bid you burn'.

laudes desine habere meas: either (*a*) 'keep no more the
poems that you wrote in my praise'; or (*b*) 'boast no more of
your possession of me'; for cf. II, xxi, 9–10 *dispeream si quicquam
aliud quam gloria de te quaeritur: has laudes ille maritus habet*.

79. pone hederam tumulo: 'plant ivy on my grave'.
[*pone* is Mr Sandbach's emendation for *pelle* of the MSS.;
required because Cynthia's tomb cannot yet be overgrown, and
still more because ivy for the ancients had good associations, not
bad ones; cf. the epigram quoted on line 80 below. Ivy is mentioned repeatedly in Propertius (e.g. IV, i, 62; IV, vi, 3) as a
symbol of poetic inspiration; and Cynthia wrote poetry too, as
appears from I, ii, 27 and II, iii, 21. *praegnante* also is an
emendation, for *pugnante* of the MSS.]

80. mollis: 'gently', with what follows; or perhaps 'gently
spreading', with *praegnante corymbo*. With this description cf.
Anth. Pal. VII, 22 (Simmias) ἠρέμ' ὑπὲρ τύμβοιο Σοφοκλέος,
ἠρέμα, κισσέ, ἑρπύζοις, χλοεροὺς ἐκπροχέων πλοκάμους . καὶ
πέταλον πάντη θάλλοι ῥόδου, ἥ τε φιλορρὼξ ἄμπελος ὑγρὰ πέριξ
κλήματα χευαμένη.

[In this line *alliget* is an emendation, for the MS. *alligat*, consequent on the adoption of *pone* in the previous line. *mollis* is an old emendation for the MS. *molli*; some prefer instead of it *mollia* = (presumably) 'crumbling', for which sense cf. perhaps Lucan IX, 627 where (*non*) *mollia sulco* is said of *arua*.]

81. incubat: as this word describes how the Anio fertilizes (cf. *pomifer*) the orchards (*ramosis...aruis*) of Tibur, it must here mean either 'spreads over (with its waters)' or 'descends on (to water)', by irrigation in either case. Regarding the waterfall and the irrigated orchards cf. III, xvi, 4 *cadit in patulos nympha Aniena lacus*; Ov. *Am.* III, vi, 45–6 *qui per caua saxa uolutans Tiburis Argei pomifer arua rigas*; Hor. *Od.* I, vii, 13–14 *uda mobilibus pomaria riuis*.

82. et numquam Herculeo numine pallet ebur: 'and ivory, by the grace of Hercules, never loses its brightness'. For some reason, ivory kept its colour better at Tibur than elsewhere; cf. Mart. IV, lxii and VIII, xxviii. Hercules was the patron god of Tibur. As ivory usually darkens with age, turning yellow, one can see from this line that the basic meaning of *palleo* is different from that of the English 'pale'; cf. on line 36 above.

83. media...columna: the reference is to a columnar grave-stone. The inscription might well be at half height, and would no doubt be centred from the point of view normally intended. But in such phrases *medius* often does duty for a simple preposition, with some extra value, slight or strong, arising from the context. Thus IV, iv, 16 *medium...caput* = '(balanced) *on* her head'; Ov. *Met.* V, 138 *media...nare* = '(right) *through* his nose'; Ov. *Met.* VII, 319 *auditur medio balatus aeno* = 'from (in) the pot', etc. Here, I think, the value of *media* is 'write on my tombstone (plain to see)'.

84. uector: 'traveller' (on horse or in vehicle).

86. Aniene: the spirit of the Anio would be called *Anienus*, as the spirit of the Tiber was called *Tiberinus*.

87. piis...portis: 'the gate of truth'. The conception of the two gates through which come respectively true and false dreams (cf. *Odyssey* XIX, 562 and Virg. *Aen.* VI, 894) is really distinct from that of the division of the inhabitants of the underworld into the good (*pii*) and bad which Propertius has alluded to in lines 55–70 above. Here he seems to be blending the two; but the word *pius* is not inappropriate to the authors of 'true' dreams, because 'true' in the sense of 'faithful' is one of its dominant meanings. (It is of course in any case not to be supposed that an agreed standard picture of the underworld existed. Rather, each poet gives his own picture, itself not necessarily or even probably a fixed one, based on literary recollections as modified by his own imagination at the time of writing.)

90. abiecta...sera: the *sera* is the bar that is fixed across a door to keep it closed. Here the bar is cast off, and the watchdog (who, it appears from IV, xi, 26, was sometimes chained to the bar) is free to wander.

91. Lethaea...stagna: as the next line shows, the idea here is not of the water of forgetfulness, but of a river such as Styx which marks the frontier of the underworld, and 'waters of Lethe' must stand for infernal waters generally.

92. nauta: Charon, ferryman of the Styx.

93. nunc te possideant aliae: the jussive–permissive subjunctive, meaning 'never mind if...' or 'let them, if they will,...'. The choice of *possidere* may be deliberate, to suggest temporary tenure as opposed to absolute ownership.

94. mixtis ossibus ossa teram: the word *ossa* at IV, xi, 20 and 102 below appears to mean simply the 'shade' of a dead person, without any insistence on the original meaning of *ossa* and the thought of a skeleton that it suggests. Likewise *pectore mixto* is used at line 19 above of two living human forms; and *tero* at IV, ii, 62 above must mean 'press hard' without any suggestion of friction. Thus the sentence as a whole perhaps is meant to say only that her shade will hold his in a tight embrace. But the primary meanings of the words composing it are hard to escape from.

95. querula...sub lite: 'to the accompaniment of bitter complaining'; for this use of *sub* cf. II, xxviii, 35 *magico torti sub carmine rhombi.*

VIII

This elegy recounts an anecdote (presumably real, but very likely embellished) of Propertius' association with Cynthia. She was on an excursion to Lanuvium with another admirer, and he decided to console himself with the company of two other women at table at his house. It proved a disappointment; and worse, for Cynthia returned unexpectedly and created a formidable scene.

But after the women had been driven out, and Propertius sufficiently humbled, peace was restored between the two.

The piece begins with four lines which state the subject. Next come twenty-two lines which elaborate the circumstances of Cynthia's absence; of these, twelve describe a rite at Lanuvium which was the object of her excursion, and ten describe the figure cut on the occasion by herself and her escort. A further twenty-two lines then describe Propertius' unsuccessful party, the guests, entertainment, and proceedings. The remainder of the elegy, forty lines, relates Cynthia's reappearance and the subsequent scene and reconciliation.

Though the piece purports (cf. *hac nocte* in the first line) to be written just after the event, there is no reason to take this as fact rather than literary artifice.

1. Esquilias...aquosas: we know from III, xxiii, 24 that Propertius lived on the Esquiline, and it will be seen presently that the episode about to be narrated in lines 27–88 takes place at his house. The adjective *aquosas* refers to the fact that on the Esquiline were many fountains.

hac nocte: 'last night'. But this may be a pretence, part of the 'manner' in which the anecdote is told.

fugarit: 'scared'.

2. cum uicina nouis...agris: 'when the people who live near the new gardens all came running' (to see what the commotion was about). The *noui agri* are presumably the *horti Maecenatis*—the gardens laid out by Maecenas on the Esquiline—called *noui horti* by Horace, *Sat.* I, viii, 7 and 14.

19–20. turpis...meae: these lines are obviously misplaced in the MS. tradition, and are welcome between lines 2 and 3 of the tradition, as the introductory couplet 1–2 is too light in content to stand unamplified so far ahead of the story it introduces. The *taberna* is evidently the *taberna* of line 62, into which Cynthia chases her evicted rivals; and though the poet does not say that she goes into the *taberna* after them, he likewise does not say that she does not: and in any case, the *taberna* will certainly have 'rung' with their account of the fight.

3. Lanuuium: here begins (and continues to line 14) an explanatory statement preliminary to the narrative; for the manner of this cf. line 29 below, also IV, iv, 3 and IV, vi, 15. Lanuvium, object of Cynthia's excursion (see line 15), was a

Latin town on the via Appia about fifteen miles south-east of Rome.

uetus est tutela draconis: this might mean either that the town is custodian of the snake (as Vesta is *Iliacae tutela fauillae* in IV, iv, 69 above), or that it is under the protection of the (sacred) snake (as, in a different sense, the garden of the Hesperides is *insopiti tutela draconis* in Lucan IX, 357). And in fact the relationship would be reciprocal.

4. sicubi, tam rarae non perit hora morae: i.e. 'here, if anywhere, the time spent on a visit is not wasted, so uncommonly curious a sight is there to see'. For the use of *sicubi* cf. Ov. *A.A.* II, 15 *nunc mihi, si quando, puer et Cytherea, fauete*; also in this book IV, xi, 29 *si cui fama fuit*. The construction seems to involve giving *morae* two of its recognized meanings at the same time: the time (*hora*) of a visit (*mora*) is not wasted, as the *mora* (object of the visit) is remarkable. [*sicubi* here is Mr Lee's conjecture for the MS. reading *hic ubi*.]

5. qua sacer...hiatu: i.e. where there is a steep descent into the sacred cavern with its dark and yawning mouth.

6. qua: 'by which way'; i.e. the cavern's mouth just described.

(uirgo, tale inter omne caue!): the point of this is mysterious. (?) the girl who carries the offering must tread carefully all the way. (?) young girls should never be taken to see this awful rite.

7. honos: the offering with which he is honoured.

8. ex ima...humo: 'from his lair deep underground'.

10. anguino creditur ore: we should expect the dative; the locative ablative is used instead with much the same effect as if in English one said 'hazarded in...'.

12. uirginis in palmis ipsa canistra tremunt: i.e. 'the basket quivers in the hand of the trembling girl'. The effect of *ipsa* (= even the...) can be rendered by repeating the idea of the verb.

15. detonsis...mannis: i.e. in a vehicle drawn by ponies with clipped manes. The clipped manes are an elegance; as we shall see presently, the vehicle belongs to a fashionable and extravagant young man.

16. causa fuit Iuno, sed mage causa Venus: the (professed) object of the excursion was to visit the temple of Juno Sospita (and perhaps also witness the rite just described) at Lanuvium; but the real object was love-making.

17. Appia: the via Appia, the great road running south from Rome, on which Lanuvium lay.

triumphum: 'triumphal progress'; the term is used ironic-ally, and *agere* is the technically proper verb with *triumphum*.

18. effusis...rotis: a variant on the common combination *effusae habenae*.

21. spectaclum ipsa sedens...: 'a fine sight to see she was, as...'.

primo temone pependit: 'she bent forward from (i.e. over) the front of the gig'. *primus* can indicate the edge of anything; and here the construction seems to be as in Lucan VIII, 590 *prima pendet...anxia puppe* (of a woman leaning forward over the side or end of a ship); *temone* must then be taken as standing by metonymy (part for whole) in the sense of 'vehicle', as it appears to do in Ov. *Met*. XI, 257–8 *Titan...inclinato...tenebat Hesperium temone fretum*, the metonymy being facilitated in both passages by the fact that the front of the vehicle is in question. (Some may prefer to take *temone* in its normal sense of 'yoke-pole', and construe it as a rather odd sort of local ablative, under-standing that Cynthia leans 'right forward over the pole'.)

22. per impuros...locos: i.e. amid the bumps and pot-holes; for the meaning of *impuros* required here cf. *purus* = 'free from obstacles' (e.g. Virg. *Aen*. XII, 771 where the Trojans have cut down a tree *puro ut possent concurrere campo*), and the ex-pression *purgare uiam* = 'level a road'.

frena mouere: i.e. steer her course, by manipulating the reins, etc.; for *mouere* of using an instrument cf. IV, i, 76.

23. serica: this here must indicate 'with silken upholstery (*or* hood)'.

carpenta: a *carpentum* was a kind of two-wheeled covered vehicle, used by women and luxurious persons. (The plural here is poetic.)

uulsi: 'smooth'. The smoothness (of any normally hairy exposed surface of the person) was achieved by plucking rather than shaving; it was a practice of the super-elegant, and was re-garded by ordinary people as degenerate.

24. armillatos colla Molossa canes: Molossian dogs, from Epirus, were a famous breed. The transference of the epithet is worth noting. *armillae* elsewhere are (*a*) armlets, or (*b*), by metaphor, metal rings used in construction, machinery, etc. The fact that they are here mentioned specially shows that what is meant is something less ordinary to a Roman than a dog's collar is to us.

25. qui dabit immundae uenalia fata saginae: i.e. who will sell himself to risk his life and eat the coarse mash of a gladiator. *fata* can mean both 'death' (as destined end of all) and 'life' (as our allotted span); the meaning here of the curious phrase *dabit uenalia fata* is fixed by the context. *sagina* is the diet of gladiators, a nutritious but unappetizing mash; here it connotes also the gladiators' 'school' to which the man sells himself, and in this connotation is construed as dative after *dabit*.

26. uincet ubi...genas: 'when to his shame the beard overruns (*literally* conquers) those carefully (*erasas*) shaven cheeks'. Presumably this means, when he has run through his money and can play the fop no more. (Or does *ubi* mean 'where', and the sentence refer to what will happen to him in the gladiators' school?)

28. castra mouere: the military term 'move camp' is here used of the man who transfers his attentions from one woman to another. Military metaphors abound in erotic elegy, a fact illustrated and exploited by Ov. *Am.* I, ix.

29. Auentinae...Dianae: i.e. the temple of Diana on the Aventine.

30. omne decet: 'everything (about her) is charming'.

31. Tarpeios...inter...lucos: i.e. living in the area called *inter duos lucos* in the depression between the Capitol and the Arx. The word order is remarkable, for *est altera, Teia, inter Tarpeios lucos.*

Teia: the adjective ('from Teos' in Asia Minor) is here used as a proper name, as its recurrence at line 58 below shows.

33. noctem lenire: i.e. to make the night more bearable for me.

34. et Venere ignota furta nouare mea: 'and vary my amours with a new adventure'.

35. herba: 'lawn', in a court of the house.

36. concubitus: this word usually means sexual intercourse; but here it means the order in which the members of the party recline at table; cf. on IV, i, 4.

37. Lygdamus: personal servant of Propertius: cf. also IV, vii, 35.

ad cyathos: regular, for the person in charge of serving the wine. The *cyathus* was the vessel used for drawing the wine from the mixing bowl; cf. Porph. on Hor. *Epod*. ix, 36 *cyatho hauriebatur ex cratere uinum*.

uitrique aestiua supellex: cf. *Copa* 29 *aestiuo te prolue uitro*; from this and the present passage it appears that cups, etc., of glass were used in summer. *supellex* here means table-ware.

38. Methymnaei Graeca saliua meri: Methymna was a town in Lesbos, and Lesbian wine was well known. *saliua* frequently means 'flavour'. So the whole phrase can be translated 'a fine-flavoured Greek wine of Methymna'.

39. Nile, tuus tibicen erat: i.e. 'there was a flute-player from the banks of the Nile'. (There is no need to reproduce the vocative form of the expression in English, which does not readily use this kind of 'figure'.)

crotalistria Phyllis: i.e. Phyllis had brought her castanets. (Phyllis may well be a performer as well as a guest at table on such an occasion; and a *crotalistria* may herself dance, or accompany another.)

40. et facilis spargi munda sine arte rosa: 'and there were roses, in their natural grace, (ready) for strewing'. Roses are part of the provision for a dinner-party; cf. Hor. *Od*. III, xxix, 2-3 *non ante uerso lene merum cado cum flore, Maecenas, rosarum...*, etc., and *passim*. These might be made up into wreaths and chaplets. But they might also be strewn or thrown around in sport, loose blooms in their natural state. This appears to be the point of *munda sine arte* in the present passage. For the practice of strewing roses, cf. Hor. *Od*. III, xix, 21-2 (where a festive party is being described) *parcentis ego dexteras odi: sparge rosas*: also Ov. *Fast*. v, 336 and 360. *facilis* with the infinitive can mean 'ready to', 'able to', etc.; for instance at Sil. It. VII, 199 *nec facilis laeto certasse sapori* is said of a man who cannot stand his wine. For the handy supply of roses thus put ready, cf. Ov. *Am*. I, ii, 40 *adpositas* (from a heap by her side) *sparget... rosas*.

41. Magnus et ipse suos breuiter concretus in artus...: 'and Magnus my mannikin' (*literally* 'shrunken in frame'). *ipse* need not be rendered in English: it coheres with and strengthens the following *suos*.

[*Magnus* might be a proper name given in irony to a dwarf. On the other hand *nanus* ('dwarf') might be corrupted into *magnus* in transmission; and many prefer to read *nanus* here.]

42. caua buxa: the castanets of line 39 could be boxwood;

but it is more likely that the *tibia* is meant here, for cf. Ov. *Fast.* VI, 667 *caua tibia* and 697 (of the same instrument) *terebrato buxo*. The plural *buxa* may be simply a poetic plural, but it could refer to a double pipe, or to pipe *and* castanets.

truncas...manus: 'his stumps of arms'.

43. sed neque suppletis constabat flamma lucernis: the unsteady burning of the lamp, though it has recently been filled up with oil, is an omen, evidently here unfavourable, as the context shows; see also note on IV, iii, 60.

44. reccidit inque suos mensa supina pedes: the collapse of the table is evidently another bad omen. As at line 51 below the verb *resupinat* is used of flinging back doors, it seems that *reccidit...supina* here describes a table with its top hinged on a central support, or with a hinged flap, which falls into a vertical position through a failure of a catch or supporting bracket. But we cannot be certain.

45. Venerem...secundam: this means both (*a*) that he was trying for a throw which would be an omen of Venus' favour for his love-making; and (*b*) that he was trying for the highest throw, called the 'Venus'. This occurred when all four *tali*—four-sided, unlike the six-sided *tesserae*—turned up showing different numbers. [*secundam* is an emendation for *secundo* of the MSS. It fits well with (*a*) above; but some may prefer to read *secundos*.]

46. canes: the worst throw, called *canis*; it occurred when all four *tali* turned up showing the figure 1. In gaming it would be a losing throw; in omen-taking it would be an unlucky one.

48. Lanuuii...solus eram: i.e. for all he knew, the women might not have been there; his mind was far away, at the gates of Lanuvium, looking for Cynthia.

49. rauci sonuerunt cardine postes: 'there was a grating noise, as the house door turned on its hinges'. These doors had projections at top and bottom which turned in sockets in the lintel and threshold; this arrangement served the same purpose as the hinging of our doors; *cardo* includes both peg and socket.

50. et leuia ad primos murmura facta Lares: 'and low voices were heard at the entrance of the house'.

murmura could refer to any muffled noises, but suits very well voices muffled by distance so as not to be intelligible; Cynthia speaking to the porter, saying goodbye to her escort, etc.

Ovid uses the word of the *inarticulate* animal sounds uttered by victims of metamorphosis. For *primos Lares* cf. Ov. *Met.* v, 284 *primas intrauimus aedes*. Here *Lares* (as often) = house.

51. totas resupinat Cynthia ualuas: she flings the double doors (leading into the court where Propertius is holding his party) wide (*totas*) open, so that they lie flat back against the wall, as it were with their backs to it.

52. non operosa comis: 'her hair still in disarray'; in III, ii, 14 *operosa antra* are artificial grottoes: Cynthia had had no chance to have her hair done after her journey.

sed furibunda decens: 'but lovely in her wrath'.

54. palluerant: the pluperfect may stand for a preterite, as in line 82 below (*riserat*) and sometimes elsewhere in Propertius; or it may describe a state ('had turned' = 'was' or 'were'). For the meaning of *palleo* cf. on IV, vii, 36 and 82.

palluerant ipso labra soluta mero: 'drunk as I was, my mouth hung open, and I went grey (*or* went white to the lips) with fright'. One cannot feel much confidence in one's ability to analyse this sentence.

ora soluere is quite common for opening the mouth, and an open mouth suits the context. *uino solutus* is common for a person who is drunk to the point of losing full control of his movements, etc. Combining these ideas we arrive at 'my mouth *hung* open'; and the sagging mouth of the fuddled man is well expressed by the word *labra*. In addition to having his mouth open, Propertius changed colour; and as the subject of *palluerant* is *labra* we must either understand that he went 'white to the lips' or we must extract from *labra* a meaning ('face') rather wider than its literal one. Such extension is not uncommon with related words like *os* and *genae*, and in Juv. III, 294 *ueruecis labra* stands for a sheep's chaps; moreover Propertius has a habit, after using a word in one sense in one part of a sentence, to extract a somewhat different sense from it in relation to another part (cf. notes on IV, iv, 83 and on line 25 of this elegy, above).

There seem to be two possible ways of taking *ipso*. Either (*a*) its attachment to *mero* is purely syntactical and its force really goes with *labra* ('even my lips'); for such treatment of *ipse* cf. Shackleton Bailey, *Propertiana*, p. 257 and for similar treatment of *primus* and *unus* cf. note on IV, ix, 30 below. Or (*b*) there is in this sentence a compression of two separate ideas, viz. (i) 'I turned pale, my mouth feebly agape *because of* the wine I'd drunk'; and (ii) 'I turned pale *despite* (i.e *flushed though I was with*) the wine I'd drunk'. On this supposition the idea 'flushed' (given the usual associations of wine) is provided by the contrast with *palluerant* which juxtaposed *ipso* notifies; and *mero* is ambiguous—as is the opening phrase 'drunk as I was', in the rendering suggested at the beginning of this note.

55. fulminat...quantum femina saeuit: 'her eyes shot looks that blasted like thunderbolts, and her fury was such as only a woman's can be'.

58. uicinas Teia clamat aquas: to shout 'triumph!' in Latin is *clamare triumphum*, and so to shout 'water!' is *clamare aquam*; the adjective *uicinas* is added because she is calling for water from the neighbours; the plural *aquas* suits the fact that it is 'the neighbours' (plural) to whom she is calling. She acts as if a fire had broken out, hoping thereby to bring others on the scene, or distract Cynthia from her onslaught; cf. Seneca, *Ir.* III, XLIII *saepe rixam conclamatum in uicinia incendium soluit*.

59. lumina sopitos turbant elata Quiritis: i.e. carrying torches, they, or some neighbours, rush out (into the street) and the glare wakes and alarms other citizens of the neighbourhood.

60. semita: 'alley'.

insana...nocte: 'with the fury of the nocturnal brawl'. One of the common secondary meanings of *nox* is a night with a woman: here is another, for which cf. Mart. x, lxxxvii, 11 *pugnorum reus ebriaeque noctis*.

64. peruersa: as the first meaning of *peruersus* is 'back-to-front', it seems that Cynthia turns her hand and gives him a backhanded slash with her nails.

67. nostris...plagis: 'with striking me'.

68. ad plutei fulcra sinistra: the *fulcrum* is the raised end of the couch or bed; cf. IV, vii, 3 and note; there might be a *fulcrum* at one end or at both. *pluteus* strictly means the 'back' of the couch; here as sometimes elsewhere it may stand for the couch itself. Lygdamus is crouching under the raised *fulcrum* at one end.

69. geniumque meum...adorat: a servant would swear by or appeal to the *genius* of his master; the *genius*, being the divine spirit supposed to attend each individual, could be an object of worship in a way that the mortal man himself could not be.

71. tum demum: i.e. then I gave in and....

ad foedera ueni: 'I made submission, suing for peace' cf. I, ix, 3 *supplexque uenis ad iura puellae*.

72. cum: this is (I think) an example of the 'inverted' construction of *cum*, which accordingly here means 'whereupon'. For this variety of the inverted *cum* cf. Kühner–Stegmann II (2), pp. 340–1 (section 204, 2).

uix: i.e. but only after much entreaty.

75. Pompeia...in umbra: the portico of Pompey, in the Campus Martius. Such places of public resort, as also places of public entertainment (see lines 76–7), are later specified by Ovid (*A.A.* I, 67 ff. and 89 ff. and 163 ff.) as ones where prowling flirts of either sex might strike up an acquaintance. Hence Cynthia's veto.

76. lasciuum...Forum: gladiatorial shows were given in the Forum on occasion; when it would need to be sanded. The epithet *lasciuum* refers proleptically to the nature of these occasions: 'when the Forum is sanded for holiday-time'.

77. summum...theatrum: where the women sat; cf. Suet. *Aug.* 44, and Ov. *Am.* II, vii, 3 *siue...respexi summa theatri*.

78. aut lectica tuae sudet aperta morae: this means in effect *sit tibi morae* = 'engage your attention', or, giving more value to *morae*, 'keep you dallying in conversation'. The verb *sudet* serves as a verb of motion, appropriate to a litter because the men carrying it were normally sweating, in the hot Italian sun: cf. Mart. IX, xxii, 9 *ut canusinatus nostro Syrus assere sudet*. The use of a word of such apparently strong colour in a context where English would use a verb of neutral colour (for these litter-bearers are not hurrying, rather the reverse) surprises at first, but it is in fact in the Latin manner; thus in Juv. VIII, 103–4 *cum Parrhasii tabulis signisque Myronis Phidiacum uiuebat ebur* means essentially that (in the provinces in days gone by) there used still to *be* works of Parrhasius and Myron and Phidias, and the verb *uiuebat* only notes parenthetically the familiar fact that the works of Phidias are lifelike; *sudet* here is used in just the same way. For the situation cf. Mart. V, lxi, 3–4 *nescioquid dominae teneram qui garrit in aurem, et sellam cubito dexteriore premit*.

80. ueneat: 'must be put on sale', and chained until the sale actually takes place; for the meaning of *ueneat* here cf. Fronto, *ad Am.* I, xvi *numquam uenierit, ueneat semper*.

82. riserat: pluperfect for preterite, as, e.g. at I, xix, 10 *uenerat*, II, ii, 13 *uiderat*.

imperio…dato: '(exulting) in the power I had given her over me'.

85. totas iterum mutare lucernas: 'to change the oil in the lamps completely'. For *mutare lucernas* = 'change the oil in the lamps' cf. 87 below where *mutare lectum* = 'change the covers on the bed'. *totas* has here adverbial force and means 'completely'. *iterum* is probably pleonastic, as in II, xviii, 12 *iterum…redire* and many examples with *rursus* quoted by Kühner-Stegmann II (2), p. 575; for *suppletis* in line 43 does not in itself indicate that there had been a previous change, and Cynthia's proceedings are evidently exceptional. The lamps have been contaminated by the presence of the other women.

87. mutato per singula pallia lecto: i.e. when every single cover on the bed had been changed.

88. respondi: i.e. he functioned normally again, in regard to sex, after the phase of frigidity implied in line 47; *respondere* is used thus of bodily functions generally, for cf. Petron. *Sat.* 47 *multis iam diebus uenter mihi non respondet.*

et toto soluimus arma toro: the incongruity is deliberate. They make peace, and their peacemaking leads to (almost, consists in) affectionate exchanges which take place *toto toro*; for the metaphor here played on cf. III, xx, 19–20 *ante…dulcia quam nobis concitet arma Venus.*

IX

This elegy is a narrative, telling how Hercules after his fight with Cacus (for which see Virg. *Aen.* VIII, 185 ff., Liv. I, vii, 4–7, and later Ov. *Fast.* I, 534 ff.) on the Aventine was denied water to quench his thirst by the priestess of a women's goddess (apparently the Bona Dea; see lines 25–6 and note), and in anger on that account decreed that women should for ever be excluded from his worship at the Ara Maxima. It is thus an aetiological poem, purporting to explain the origin of this religious rule. But the narrative begins without preamble in line 1, and its aetiological significance is stated only in its concluding couplet, lines 69–70. The following last four lines of the elegy, 71–4, are distinct from the narrative, and contain a prayer for favour addressed by the poet to Hercules under the Sabine name Sancus. (Subsidiary bits of aetiology are brought in at ll. 5–6, 19–20 and 73–4.)

1. Amphitryoniades: Hercules was the son of Alcmene by Jupiter (= Zeus), who visited her in the shape of Amphitryon, her absent husband. The patronymic 'Amphitryon's son' is thus not strictly appropriate, though convenient, and common in poetry. The movement of this opening line is intentionally solemn.

iuuencos: the oxen of the triple-bodied giant Geryon which it was one of Hercules' labours to bring to Eurystheus.

2. stabulis: 'pastures' here, as in Virg. *Aen.* VIII, 207 and 213.

Erythea: the legendary island outside the straits of Gibraltar supposed to be inhabited by Geryon.

3. inuictos...montis: 'the invincible hills (of Rome)' in one sense; but strictly the apposition *Palatia...montes* limits the reference to one hill, the Palatine, *Palatia* being a common poetic plural and the grammatical number of *montes* influenced by it. The Palatine is 'the invincible hill' as site of Romulus' city and Augustus' residence. [*inuictos* here is an old emendation; the MS. tradition is corrupt; see *app. crit.*]

pecorosa Palatia: 'the Palatine (then) grazed by flocks of sheep'.

5. Velabra: another poetic plural. The Velabrum was an area between the Forum, Palatine, Tiber and Capitol. It was supposed, as is shown by this passage and by IV, ii, 7-8, to have been under water in early days; and evidently one etymology derived its name from the *uela* of boats.

suo...flumine: because it was then occupied permanently by a part of the river, instead of being (as later) a piece of ground occasionally flooded.

quoque: 'and where...' (i.e. to which point).

6. urbanas...aquas: 'water where now our city stands'.

7-8. sed non...Iouem: 'but Cacus, his treacherous host, did not leave the oxen unmolested; he violated the law of Jupiter by an act of robbery'. Jupiter is protector of strangers under the law of hospitality. The construction *infido...hospite Caco* is an ablative absolute, indicating the conditions under which something happens (i.e. literally 'with treacherous Cacus for host...'). By calling Cacus *hospes* Propertius does not necessarily mean that he was in the formal sense Hercules' 'host', but perhaps only that as a local inhabitant he had an obligation under the law of hospitality to a traveller in passage such as Hercules was. Similarly, applied to the other party, *hospes* can mean either 'guest' specifically, or 'stranger from abroad' (as at line 53 below).

9. incola Cacus erat...: 'this Cacus was one who lived nearby...'. (*incola* is often used of one who is resident in a place without being originally a native of it.)

11. manifestae signa rapinae: the adjective has a predicative and proleptic value: 'evidence whereby the theft would have been revealed.'

12. auersos: two different meanings both fit here: (*a*) 'backwards', i.e. facing away from him; and (*b*) 'stolen', as in Virg. *Aen.* VIII, 207–8 *quattuor a stabulis...tauros auertit.*

13. nec = (here) *sed non*: cf. IV, ii, 3, IV, vi, 20.

deo: i.e. Jupiter, protector of strangers under the law of hospitality.

furem sonuere: 'by their lowing denounced the thief'. The construction is like that referred to in the note on IV, viii, 58; the oxen are said *sonare furem* in the same way as a person might be said *clamare furem* = 'cry "Thief!"'. (Note, however, that the *purpose* of the exclamation in the two contexts is different in kind: there to *ask for* water, here to *denounce* the thief.)

14. furis...implacidas...fores: 'the door of the savage robber's den', literally 'the robber's savage doors'. For the meaning of *implacidas* cf. Hor. *Od.* IV, xiv, 10 *Genaunos, implacidum genus:* these words of negative form in Latin often acquire (e.g. *implacidus, indomitus, inquietus*) a stronger positive force than English practice would lead one to expect.

ira: with this has to be supplied 'of Hercules', though Hercules has not been mentioned since line 4.

15. Maenalio...ramo: by *ramo* here is meant the famous club of Hercules, the *claua* of line 17 below. *Maenalius* means 'appertaining to Mount Maenalus' (in Arcadia), and so is often used in the extended sense 'Arcadian'; the reason for which it is here applied to Hercules' club is not (I think) known.

pulsus: the verb *pello* is not common elsewhere in the sense 'strike', except of striking the water with oars in rowing.

tria tempora: the anatomical kind of *tempora*, here put for Cacus' three heads.

16. Alcides: Hercules is often so called, as putative grandson of Alcaeus, the father of Amphitryon.

19. aruaque mugitu sancite Bouaria longo: the reference

is to the place known in Propertius' day as the Forum Boarium, between the Velabrum (see on line 5 above; the poet has perhaps forgotten about the Velabrum being then under water) and the Tiber; an open space or square in which stood a statue of an ox (cf. Ov. *Fast.* IV, 478). *arua* strictly means 'ploughland', but here as often stands more generally for 'fields'. *sancio* is used commonly of establishing or consecrating a law or institution; here it must somehow indicate the *naming* of the place, and so perhaps means 'to fix or confirm a title of honour or worship by addressing the recipient by it (or accordingly)'; so that we can (if the foregoing is correct) translate here: 'hail (*or* hallow) these fields as the Ox-fields henceforth'.

20. nobile erit Romae pascua uestra Forum: 'one day the place where you graze will be a famous market-square of the city of Rome'. For the syntax cf. on IV, iii, 6.

22. terraque non ullas feta ministrat aquas: 'and the earth, teeming with waters, proffered none to him'. *feta*, here metaphorical, is said elsewhere of female creatures in pregnancy or with young to suckle.

23. procul: 'some way off'.

24. lucus...nemus: a *lucus* is a group of *sacred* trees; a *nemus* is (here, and often elsewhere) a group of trees *enclosing a clear space*; for the form of the expression cf. Ov. *A.A.* III, 689 *silua nemus non alta facit*.

25. femineae...deae: evidently the Bona Dea. Her temple (called by Ov. *Fast.* V, 148 ff. *templa...oculos exosa uiriles*) was on the Aventine (cf. Ov. *loc. cit.*), and the Aventine was also the site of Cacus' cave (cf. Virg. *Aen.* VIII, 230–1 and Ov. *Fast.* I, 551 and VI, 82).

fontisque piandos: the verb *piare* means generally 'do what religion requires about...' in various contexts. A prominent special context is that of religious offences, respecting which *piare* = 'expiate'. So here *piandos* = 'which must be kept holy', with the connotation 'and violation of it expiated'.

26. impune et nullis...: i.e. *et nullis impune*...

27–30. deuia...auis: the following is a tentative rendering of these four lines: 'the door (of the shrine which stood) thus secluded had draped on it a garland of red (wool); inside the little age-worn building a fire fragrant of incense had been ablaze (*or* in front of the...blazed on the altar); the spreading foliage of a poplar (*or* poplars) made a brave canopy over the temple, and in its dense shade birds were singing'. Notes on individual points follow below.

27. limina: either the lintel specifically, or, by a common extension of meaning, the door itself.

28. putris: cf. Hor. *Epist.* I, X, 49 *fanum putre Vacunae*; Lucan VII, 403 *stat tectis putris auitis...domus*.

luxerat: this might be either (*a*) a pluperfect describing a resulting state, like *fecerat* in line 24 above or *triuerat* in IV, vii, 10 (and see note there); or (*b*) a pluperfect with the value of a preterite (as often in Propertius), and specifically of a preterite used as *horruit* is used in the description at IV, v, 70 (where see note); cf. also Prop. I, xv, 10 *fleuerat*. If we adopt (*a*) we have to give a very strong emphasis to *odorato*, for what is being described is then not the fire but the fragrance it has left. If we prefer (*b*) the fire is being described, and we have to suppose that the fire is burning on an altar in front of the temple, as the scene is described from the point of view of Hercules and the door is shut (cf. line 34). On the whole, the first alternative seems preferable; since it fits better with the subject *casa*, and *luceo* in similar contexts (cf. III, x, 19–20; Ov. *Fast.* I, 75–8) seems to refer to the flaring of the fire at the time when the incense is thrown on it; moreover the introduction of something invisible to the beholder affecting one of his other senses would correspond to the similar effect in the next pentameter.

29. populus is more naturally taken as a particular poplar tree overhanging the little temple than as collective for the trees of the grove, since we have not been told that it was a grove of poplars. The tree is likely to be outside the building, rather than growing in a central court (as we find in other contexts), since this building is such a small one.

longis...frondibus: this must refer to *leafy boughs*, or to *foliage* generally, reaching far out from the trunk of the tree; cf. II, xiii, 19 *longa...imagine* = 'a long *row* of busts'; Lucan X, 499 *longis...uaporibus* (of flames or heat spreading out from a fire).

[**ornabat:** this word in its literal sense is applied to accoutrements, furniture, decorations, etc., that are more intimately and subordinately attached to the thing or person they go with than is this tree here. Hence *longis ornabat frondibus* would more ordinarily describe garlands: cf. Ov. *Met.* VI, 163 *sua tempora frondibus ornant*; *Fast.* I, 203 *frondibus ornabant quae nunc Capitolia gemmis*; *Fast.* IV, 737–8 *frondibus et fixis decorentur* *ouilia ramis, et tegat ornatas longa corona fores.* Here garlands cannot be meant for we have had them already in line 27, and a tree is needed to prepare for line 30 with its birds singing in the shade. But the more ordinary meaning of the words is relevant to the value of the metaphor here.]

30. multaque...umbra tegebat auis: 'unseen in the shade of the poplar's abundant foliage birds were singing'.

[There is no need to disturb the meaning which normally familiar usage gives to this line. But the question may here be raised whether *multa*, despite its grammatical attachment as an adjective to *umbra*, may not have an adverbial value in relation to the rest of the sentence, giving (or adding) the sense 'concealed birds in plenty'. For *primus* in Virg. *Aen.* x, 427 (Lausus) *primus Abantem interimit* does not mean that he was first man to kill Abas but that he killed him as his first act; and in *Aen.* x, 241–2 *Aurora ueniente uocari primus in arma iube* it does not mean that he is to be the first man to do this when dawn comes but that he is to do it as his first act, as soon as dawn comes. Again, *una* in Prop. II, xx, 27 *cum te tam multi peterent tu me una petisti* must mean (because of the antithesis) that she 'wanted only him'; and in II, xvi, 11–12 *Cynthia non sequitur fasces nec curat honores, semper amatorum ponderat una sinus* it must mean (for the same reason) that she was not interested in men's rank or honours but 'only in the weight of their purses'.]

31. in siccam congesta puluere barbam: 'his parched beard thick with dust'. (The construction *in...barbam* and the usual meaning of *congero* invite one to suppose that he had clapped the dust in his beard himself. But this can hardly be meant. In Virg. *Georg.* IV, 243 the *congesta cubilia blattis* are 'filled thick' with beetles.)

puluis, feminine here and in I, xxii, 6 and II, xiii, 35, is masculine in IV, ii, 40 and elsewhere in Propertius and regularly in other authors.

32. iacit: for *iacio* = 'utter' cf. II, i, 77 and IV, xi, 84 below; also Ov. *Fast.* II, 590 *et iacit in medio talia uerba choro.*

uerba minora deo: 'words beneath a god', i.e. words that were humble for a god to speak.

33. uos...quae luditis: i.e. you whom I hear laughing together; cf. line 23.

luci sacro...antro: 'in the shady vault of this sacred grove'. *antrum* is used metaphorically by Juvenal of the interior of a covered litter; here it suggests the space under the overhanging boughs; cf. Sid. *Carm.* XXIV, 66 *qua nemus. . .non lucum arboribus facit sed antrum.* (In IV, iv, 3 a *lucus* is *in* an *antrum* in the sense of a rocky nook. But there has been nothing to suggest that this *lucus* is so situated.)

34. defessis. . .uiris: the plural seems to resemble that in Virg. *Ecl.* III, 7 *parcius ista uiris tamen obiicienda memento* = 'you'd better not be so ready to say that kind of thing about a man'; so here *uiris* = 'a (weary) man' as belonging to the class of (weary) men.

35. circaque sonantia lymphis: 'and all around (*or* nearby) is the noise of running waters' (*literally* 'and all around is a region noisy with. . .'). *circa* is adverb (not preposition), as (e.g.) in Liv. XXI, xxxvi, 4 *per inuia circa nec trita*; for the ellipse of the verb when such an adverb is predicate, as here, cf. (e.g.) Sil. It. IX, 254 *iuxta terribilis facies*; XV, 427 *antrum ingens iuxta,* etc. [If we were to take *circa* as preposition and construe *circaque sonantia lymphis* with *erro*, we should get a sentence whose force would be improved by omitting the *-que*; in a sentence such as Cic. *Am.* 13 *iisque. . .reditum in caelum patere optimoque et iustissimo cuique expeditissimum* the value of *-que* is 'and (more particularly)'; there is not an antithesis, as there is here.]

circa: this can mean 'near' alternatively to 'around', for cf. Ov. *Fast.* I, 708 where a temple is said to stand *circa Iuturnae lacus.*

36. et caua succepto flumine palma sat est: 'I ask no more than I can lift from the stream in my hollowed hand'. The ablative *succepto. . .flumine* is as in Virg. *Aen.* VI, 225 *fuso crateres oliuo*; it gets some further assistance from the fact that *caua. . .palma* suggests *palma plena.*

succepto: this form, given here by the most reliable of our MSS. instead of the more obvious *suscepto*, is said by some ancient grammarians to be proper in respect of the physical act of 'taking up', as opposed to 'undertaking' enterprises, etc.; Servius on *Aen.* VI, 249 says simply that it was the older of the two forms.

37. tergo qui sustulit orbem: a reference to the occasion when Hercules took the sky (or globe) on his back (i.e. bowed shoulders) from the giant Atlas who normally supported it.

38. terra recepta: either (*a*) 'the earth which he took upon his shoulders (from Atlas)'; for *recipio* is the proper word for accepting a commission from another, and is sometimes in this sense opposed to *suscipio* (undertaking something on one's own initiative); and while Atlas is commonly described as carrying the *sky*, he is *depicted* as carrying earth and sky together. Or (*b*) 'the earth which he reconquered', i.e. from the robbers, monsters, etc., who had been infesting it; for this sense of *recepta* cf. Manil. IV, 51 *post uictas Mithridatis opes pelagusque receptum.* From its position one might expect the sentence *Alciden...uocat* to relate to what has preceded, and so to bear meaning (*a*); but this is not inevitable, and indeed both ideas may be present.

40. uastas: 'monstrous'; *uastus* combines the ideas 'huge' and 'wild'.

ad...feras: for *ad* used thus like *adversus* cf. II, xxiv, 25 *Lernaeas pugnet ad hydras.*

41. atque uni Stygias homini luxisse tenebras: 'and that for one alone of human kind the darkness of Styx was (*or* was turned to) light'. Hercules was sent by Eurystheus to fetch Cerberus from Hades, and did. He saw his way through the darkness; and he returned from it into the light of day.

42. LACUNA: the reasons for marking a lacuna here, and for the transposition of lines 65-6 to stand after it, are discussed in the note next below (on the transposed lines 65-6). The missing line 42 will have concluded the recital of Hercules' previous feats.

65-6. angulus hic mundi...terra patet: either (*a*) 'and now (i.e. after the labours related) this corner of the world receives me, dragging the burden (cf. Sen. *Ep.* XLIV, 7 *sarcinas... trahunt*) of my destiny still: in this land my weariness has found a *brief* resting place' (cf. line 4 above); or (*b*) 'even now that I am come to this corner of the world the burden of my destiny is with me still; even this land *grudges* me a welcome'.

[In the MS. tradition these two lines stand later in the story, beginning the speech in which Hercules pronounces the 'stern decree' promised in line 64 below. The second of them, the pentameter, stands *also* after line 41, where the text here printed marks a lacuna instead. Some sense can be made of the pentameter in that position by emending it to read *accipite: haec fesso uix mihi terra patet.* But we are then faced not only with the repetition of the line, but with the following further improbabilities: (*a*) *accipite* in 42 and *accipit* in 66 would be almost identical in sound but quite different in construction and meaning; and (b) *haec fesso uix mihi terra patet* would have to be *pathetic* (brief rest at last) in 42 but *indignant* (grudging welcome) in 66. For these reasons it seems certain that the line cannot stand in both places; and if it is deleted it must be deleted after 41, which it follows with difficulty, and retained after 65, with which it is mutually complementary. But if we now look more closely at the couplet 65–6, we see that *nunc* in line 65 is much more appropriate after the recital of Hercules' past labours in 37 ff. than in the position in which it appears in the MSS. Likewise, the tone of pathos suggested by *angulus* in line 65 and *uix* in line 66 is more appropriate to the *uerba minora deo* (line 32) of the pleading Hercules than to the *tristia iura* (line 64) of the angry Hercules pronouncing sentence. In fact, the couplet is unhelpful at best after line 64, but helpful before line 43. The process of displacement supposed could arise through a copyist making a skip ahead to the wrong pentameter after line 41.]

43. quodsi...amarae: 'why, if the goddess you served were cruel Juno herself, even she, harsh stepmother though she is, would not have shut her door and refused me water'. Juno is called *amara* because of her animosity against Hercules; she is called *nouerca* (which she is not in the strict sense) because Hercules was her husband Jupiter's son by Alcmene and because the harshness of stepmothers was proverbial. The wording of the apodosis *non clausisset aquas...suas* shows that the protasis *si...sacrum faceretis* means in effect 'if you were priestesses of Juno (instead of whatever goddess it is) and this were Juno's temple', rather than simply 'if you were (now) engaged in sacrificing to Juno'.

45. saetaeque leonis: the rough mane of the Nemean lion, the skin of which Hercules wore after killing the animal.

46. Libyco sole perusta coma: Africa was the scene of several of Hercules' adventures, e.g. those concerned with Busiris, Antaeus, and the quest for the apples of the Hesperides. *perusta* ('scorched') presumably here means bleached by the burning sun.

47–8. idem ego...colo: at one time Hercules was temporarily enslaved to Omphale, queen of Lydia. According to some accounts she amused herself by setting him to women's work, while she admired herself in his lion-skin and club. A *palla* dyed with Tyrian purple is a grand robe; so presumably the clothes Hercules is wearing are those of Omphale, not of a slave.

48. colo: masculine here, as at IV, i, 72.

50. apta: 'deft'; cf. Ov. *Her.* III, 70 *est mihi quae lanas molliat apta manus*, where *apta...quae* = 'deft at' (not 'fit to').

52. puniceo...stamine: 'with scarlet threads', i.e. with a fillet or garland of red wool.

53. parce oculis: i.e. 'take care not to see what is not for your eyes'. The phrase combines the ideas 'abstain from using your eyes' and 'do not risk your eyes'; lines 55–8.

55. interdicta uiris metuenda lege piatur (ara): the sense is 'a fearsome law forbids men access to this holy altar (and ordains that any who violate it shall pay dear for their offence)'; cf. on line 25 above. Expiation of a religious offence is an idea prominently suggested by *piare*; but it comes to signify 'do what religious usage requires or recommends about...' in a wide range of contexts, so that often its value cannot be exactly fixed.

56. quae se...casa: 'the altar that hides itself from profanation in this little shrine, away from the world'. *uindico* has sometimes specifically the meaning 'preserve from corruption'.

57. magno: ablative of price. 'It cost Tiresias dear that...'. Tiresias (according to one version of the legend about him) accidentally saw Athena bathing, and was blinded in consequence but consoled with the gift of prophecy.

58. Gorgone: i.e. her aegis, in which was set the Gorgon's head.

60. unda: for the duplication with *lympha* cf. I, xi, 11–12 *aut teneat clausam tenui Teuthrantis in unda alternae facilis cedere lympha manu.* [*unda* is an emendation for *una* of the MSS.; cf. IV, vi, 28 above and III, xxii, 28. *una* would have to be taken in sense with *puellis* more closely than with *lympha*; and though it seems clearly to be treated thus elsewhere in Propertius (see note on line 30 above) the word order makes such a treatment here improbable.]

secreti limitis unda: 'water of a stream that is set apart'. *secretus* here is the opposite of 'profane'. For *limes* = 'channel' of a stream cf. Ovid *Met.* VIII, 558 *solito dum flumina currant limite.*

61. postis...opacos: as we should say 'the shady temple's door'; the epithet being as in Virg. *Aen.* VII, 36 *fluuio...opaco*.

postes for 'door' is a very common metonymy; but here 'door posts' would make equally good sense.

62. nec tulit iratam ianua clausa sitim: 'and the closed door gave way before the rage of the thirsty hero'.

64. uix siccis...labris: ablative absolute: 'almost before his lips were dry'.

ponit...tristia iura: 'pronounced this stern decree'. *ponit...iura* could mean either 'lay down a law' or 'pronounce a judgement'; for the latter of these cf. III, ix, 24, where *medio ponere iura foro* evidently means 'sit in judgement'; and cf. Sen. *Apocol.* 12 (*Minos*) *qui dat populo iura silenti*. Here the 'judgement' is also a 'law'.

67. Maxima...Ara: i.e. the Ara Maxima at Rome, in the Forum Boarium (cf. line 20 above), supposed by some to have been founded by Hercules (cf. Virg. *Aen.* VIII, 271).

deuota: for *deuoueo = uoueo* cf. *C.I.L.* VIII, 2620 *aram quam deuouit sua pecunia posuit*. (Commonly in literature the compound *deuoueo* is used of vowing a person or thing to destruction as an offering to the gods of the underworld.) Apparently at this point Hercules has vowed to build the altar but has not yet built it; and indeed there has been no mention of it in lines 15–22 above. If this is so (i.e. if Propertius has not extended the meaning of *deuota* to include 'dedicated'), *maxima*, etc. in line 68 is part of the terms of Hercules' vow: he has promised 'an altar, a mighty altar built by my own hands'.

69. nullis...pateat ueneranda puellis: 'is never to admit women to worship at it'.

70. Herculis aeternum ne sit inulta sitis: i.e. 'that Hercules' thirsting may *continue for ever to be* avenged'. [*aeternum* is an emendation for *exterminium* of the MSS.]

73ff. hunc, quoniam...inesse meo: his story ended, the poet concludes by invoking the favour of Hercules, who has been its subject. He invokes the god by his Sabine name Sancus, after first explaining that this is a name for Hercules, and why. For the identification of Hercules and Sancus cf. Varro, *L.L.* V, 66 (referring to Deus Fidius) *et putabat hunc...esse Sancum ab Sabina lingua et Herculem a Graeca*.

The following is a tentative translation of the passage as here printed: 'This hero, because by his labours he had purged *and cleansed* the world, the Sabines of Tatius' city *hailed as a god, and established in a temple, under a name that matches his deeds.* Hail holy sire, to whom cruel Juno now is kind; o Sancus, be pleased to accept with favour this place in my book.' There is no certainty about the italicised portions.

[In the text printed the couplet 73–4 which concludes the elegy in the MSS. is transposed to precede line 71. If the MS. order is preserved the poet is made (*a*) to turn jerkily from the reader to the god in line 71 and then back to the reader in line 73; and (*b*) after referring to Hercules by his usual name in line 70 to invoke him by an unusual one in line 71 without any previous explanation. The transposition removes both these difficulties, and makes the elegy end appropriately with the prayer to the god who has been its subject. But the text is subject to other uncertainties, as will appear from the *apparatus criticus* and the notes below.]

73. purgatum...orbem: the reference is to Hercules' services to mankind in cleansing the world of monsters, robbers, etc.

sanxerat: this seems here (I know no other instances of such a use of *sancio*) to stand for *sanctum fecerat* = 'had purified'. (*sanctus* means sometimes 'holy' or 'venerated', sometimes 'pure' or 'wholesome'.)

74. sic sanctum: here *sanctum* is (I think) best taken as past participle of *sancio* in the sense supposed for line 19 above (see note on that line); and *sic* with *sanctum* will then = *simili nomine* (cf. Cat. XXXIV, 21–2 *sis quocumque tibi placet sancta nomine*). The Sabines hailed Hercules as holy, or made him an object of their veneration, under a name corresponding to his deeds, a connexion being assumed between the name *Sancus* and the sense of *sancio* supposed for line 73 above.

composuere: with the god for object the thought must be of establishing him in a temple. But *composuere* is really appropriate only to the construction of the temple itself; and indeed is found with *templa* for object at Ov. *Fast.* I, 708. In effect therefore Propertius has here succeeded in saying in one sentence what Ovid says in two (of this same god) at *Fast.* VI, 217–18 *hunc igitur ueteres donarunt aede Sabini inque Quirinali constituere iugo.* The irregularity of Propertius' compressed expression is perhaps softened by the fact that to use a god's name when his temple is really meant is a common metonymy; e.g. at Liv. V, lii, 10 *Iuno...dedicata* refers to the dedication of a new temple (cf. Liv. V, xxxi, 3), not a new image.

[Many prefer in this line to read *sic Sancum...composuere*, translating 'have established him as they have (*or* accordingly) as (i.e. under the name of) Sancus'.]

Cures: the name (plural) of the chief town of the Sabines here stands for the people. The epithet *Tatiae* is formed from Tatius, the Sabine king, concerning whom see on IV, i, 30 above. [*Cures*, feminine here in our MSS., is masculine at Ov. *Fast.* II, 135.]

71. Sancte pater salue: this title of honour, *sancte pater*, may be applied to any god; e.g. at Mart. X, xxviii, 7 Janus is so addressed. A special use of *salue*, as here, is in saluting a person or god by a title of honour, sometimes also thereby conferring it on him as a permanent attribute: cf. Virg. *Aen.* VIII, 301 *salue, uera Iouis proles...* (Hercules is addressed); Liv. I, xvi, 3 *deum deo natum, regem parentemque urbis Romanae saluere uniuersi Romulum iubent* (the people salute Romulus with these titles after his translation).

[Some would read *Sance* here, as well as in the next line.]

cui iam fauet aspera Iuno: Juno persecuted Hercules in his life on earth; now she is reconciled.

72. Sance: here the proper name is certainly required. (The MSS. have *Sancte*.)

X

This is another narrative and aetiological elegy, describing the three combats in which a Roman general had killed with his own hand the enemy's commander, and purporting to explain the name of the temple (the temple of Jupiter *Feretrius*) in which the arms of the victim were dedicated by the victor on these occasions under the name of *spolia opima*. For an account of this temple, or rather shrine, and of its legendary foundation by Romulus see Dionysius of Halicarnassus II, xxxiv and Livy I, x. In 29 B.C., a decade or so before this elegy was written, Marcus Licinius Crassus as proconsul killed Deldo, king of the Bastarnae, in single combat, and there was a question whether he could dedicate *spolia opima* on this account and so add a fourth to the series; but it was ruled apparently (see Dio C. LI, 24) that he was ineligible, as not being supreme commander in his own right but deriving his command from Octavian.

The elegy begins with four lines of introduction, and ends with four lines of etymology. In between, the feats of Romulus,

Cossus and Marcellus are narrated in eighteen, sixteen and six lines respectively.

1. Iouis...causas...Feretri: i.e. the origin of the *temple* of Jupiter Feretrius and of the *name* Jupiter Feretrius. The temple was supposed to have been founded (though Propertius does not specifically tell us so) after the feat described here in lines 5–22; the derivation of the name is discussed in lines 45–8.

causa is here the Latin equivalent of the Greek αἴτιον and means, in such a context, much the same as 'story behind...'; cf. Ov. *Fast.* 1, 1 and for the construction Sil. It. XII, 568 where Hannibal surveying Rome *discit...locos causasque locorum.*

2. trina: three sets (of arms).

recepta: this verb (*recipio*) is found elsewhere of taking towns, conquering territory, etc. It is chosen here probably because its form suggests both 'capturing' and 'bringing back'.

3. gloria: here, as often, 'the hope of fame', i.e. 'ambition'.

4. non iuuat...iugo: i.e. my pride is in a garland gathered on heights that few can scale; the image of the mountain is suggested by Parnassus, where the Muses lived.

5. imbuis exemplum primae...palmae (huius): 'you, Romulus, were first to set the example of such a prize'. *palma* means the palm that is token of victory (and then, often, the victory that earns it). *imbuo* is often said of doing something *to* or *with* a thing for the first time; here, unusually, it is said of doing *something* for the first time. *primae* has here an adverbial value and goes with the whole sentence rather than specifically with *palmae*; or one can regard it as 'transferred' from *tu* (*primus*) or *exemplum* (*primum*).

6. exuuio: as from *exuuium*. This form of the word is not found elsewhere; the usual form is *exuuiae*. Cf. *delicium* = *deliciae* in Mart. 1, vii, 1, etc.

plenus: 'laden with'.

7. Caeninum Acrona: *Caeninum* is an adjective; the town's name was *Caenina*. It was a Sabine town.

[The accusative of the king's name is here printed in the form it has elsewhere; our MSS. give *Acronta* in this passage; it is not really possible to decide which Propertius wrote.]

9. Herculeus: 'sprung of Hercules'; this particular comes to us only in Propertius' version of the story.

11. Quirini: i.e. of Romulus; cf. on IV, i, 9 and IV, vi, 21.

12. sed non sanguine sicca suo: 'and those drenched in his own blood'. *sed* is used here as in Mart. I, cxvii, 7 *scalis habito tribus sed altis*. The ablative after *sicca* is of the same kind as is regular after *uacuus*. The negative form of *non...sicca* is a litotes, i.e. expresses a positive idea with an extra (here sinister) emphasis; cf. Virg. *Georg.* IV, 453 *non te nullius exercent numinis irae*.

13. ante...turris: Propertius does not say what is the city outside which the encounter takes place. In Livy it is (apparently) outside Caenina; in Dionysius outside or possibly inside Caenina. The people of Caenina had invaded Roman territory and were driven back into their own.

cauas...turris: for the point of the epithet cf. Virg. *Aen.* IX, 46 *armatique cauis exspectant turribus hostem*.

14. et uotis occupat ante ratis: here *occupat* can mean either 'forestalls', i.e. gets in his blow or his vow ahead of his enemy, or 'attacks'; in either case *ante* (= 'beforehand') can be taken with *occupat*, for the pleonasm that results then if *occupat* = 'forestalls' is comparable with *praesensit prius, prius praemittere, ante praedicere*, etc. (cf. Kühner–Stegmann II (2), p. 575). By *uotis* is meant a vow accompanied by or implying a prayer; the ablative, if not of means, is of manner or attendant circumstances; *ratis* then = 'that was fulfilled'.

15. haec: one can construe either (*a*) 'here is a victim, Acron, that shall...'; or (*b*) 'this Acron here shall fall a victim in your honour...', *haec* going in sense with Acron but by grammatical attraction (cf. IV, vi, 60 *ista fides*) with *uictima*. But nothing is gained by analysis in such a case.

17. urbis uirtutisque parens: cf. Liv. I, xvi, 3 *parentem... urbis Romae saluere...Romulum iubent*; Cic. *Fin.* II, I *Socrates parens philosophiae*, etc. By *parens urbis* is meant sometimes the same as *pater patriae* (cf. Cic. *Att.* IX, x, 3 *me quem...istius urbis...parentem esse dixerunt*); but in the case of Romulus also 'founder'. By *uirtus* here must be meant the military *uirtus* characteristic of the Roman race, and so one can translate 'father of Rome and Roman valour'.

18. qui tulit a parco frigida castra lare: 'who could stand cold campaigns (*or* quarters), coming from a frugal home'.

19. idem eques et frenis, idem fuit aptus aratris: if we understand this as *idem eques fuit et aptus frenis, idem fuit...*, we find that *eques* put thus by itself as predicate lacks value; if we understand *idem aptus eques* (cf. IV, ix, 50) *et aptus frenis, idem fuit*... we still have a tautology. It is better to take *eques* as subject of the whole in agreement with *idem*: 'that same (bold) horseman who knew how to manage bit and bridle knew also how to guide the plough'; for *et* in the first of a pair of phrases linked in asyndeton by repetition of a word; cf. Ov. *Fast.* VI, 224 *monstratur Iunius...utilis et nuptis, utilis esse uiris.*

20. et galea hirsuta compta lupina iuba: 'and his helmet was of wolf-skin, decked with a bristly crest' (? of horsehair).

21. picta neque inducto fulgebat parma pyropo: 'and his shield was not bright with glittering overlay of bronze and gold'. *pyropus* was a mixture of gold and bronze. [The words could mean that his shield was not overlaid with *pyropus* but *was* painted instead, like that of Tatius at IV, iv, 20. But as *picta* thus emphasized would imply a certain degree of ostentation, it is better not so taken in a passage which stresses throughout the simplicity of the equipment.]

22. praebebant caesi baltea lenta boues: the plain leather is contrasted with the sumptuously decorated sword-belts of later times, such as have influenced the description of the *balteus* of Pallas in Virg. *Aen.* X, 496 ff. The same contrast has run through all of lines 20–2.

23. Cossus: Aulus Cornelius Cossus, of whose exploit (in the late fifth century B.C.) an account differing in some respects from this one is given in Liv. IV, xviii–xx.

insequitur: just as we say 'next came...with..'.

24. laboris erat: i.e. it was a matter of difficulty, for the Rome of those days, to succeed in conquering Veii.

25–6. necdum ultra Tiberim...Corae: Rome's wars had not hitherto extended to the Etruscan side of the Tiber and on the near side they had been confined to places not far removed from Rome—Nomentum lay about 15 miles off to the north-east, Cora a little further to the south-east. This statement is not really true of the time at which Cossus performed his feat. But Propertius was not necessarily as attentive to the details of early Roman history as we are taught to be. He is speaking in poetical terms of a very distant and largely legendary stage of Rome's development. [Some move 25–6 to precede 23.]

26. iugera terna: 'three acres apiece'; this small amount was the share of each of the victors.

28. aurea sella: the royal chair of an Etruscan king, actually of gold and ivory, taken over by the Romans as their 'curule chair'.

29. lenti: as applied to the herdsman this must mean 'slow-moving', perhaps 'slow-witted'; but it suggests also by association the long-drawn winding of the horn (the *lentum murmur* of IV, iv, 10).

30. in uestris ossibus: i.e. 'on your grave'.

31. portae...arcem: the fortification over the gate; perhaps a gallery linking two towers.

[*Veiens* is an emendation for *Veius* (or *Veiius*) of the MSS., which should perhaps, however, be retained and scanned *Vēius* or *Vēiius*.]

32. fretus: 'confident'; *fretus* usually has an ablative of the grounds of confidence, but cf. Liv. x, v, 5 *fretus esse iam...* (confident that...) and Stat. *Theb.* IV, 182–3 *fretus doctas anteire canendo Aonidas* (confident that he could...).

33–5. dumque aries...pulsabat...Cossus ait...: the normal construction with *dum*, when as here time-within-which rather than coextensive time is in question, would be the *present* indicative; but there are occasional exceptions, e.g. Livy V, xlvii, 1 *dum haec Veiis agebantur, interim arx Romae...in ingenti periculo fuit* and other examples in Kühner–Stegmann II (2), pp. 375–6.

34. ductum...opus: (?)'its long-drawn work'; cf. Hor. *Od.* III, iii, 29–30 *nostris...ductum seditionibus bellum.* By contrast, Cossus now brought about a quick decision.

35. forti melius: 'it better befits a brave man to...'.

37–8. desecta...ceruix: the word *deseco* is a proper one for cutting something *off.* We think of the head as what is cut off in such a context; but the Latin poets include part of the neck with the head; cf. Plaut. *Merc.* 308 *decide collum stanti...*; Virg. *Aen.* VIII, 438 *Gorgona...desecto...collo*; Lucan VIII, 674 *trunco ceruix abscisa recessit*; Sil. It. v, 418 *auulsa est...ore simul ceruix.*

38. Romanos sanguine lauit equos: apparently Cossus carries away the severed head; in Livy IV, xix, 5 he sets it on his spear-point. The *equos* must be the horse of Cossus and those of Roman cavalry-men riding next him; unless Propertius is bringing (not quite appropriately) a triumphal chariot into the picture.

39. Claudius: Marcus Claudius Marcellus, who defeated a Gallic horde at Clastidium in 222 B.C. and killed Virdomarus, a chieftain, with his own hand; see *inter alia* Plutarch, *Marcellus* 8. The main enemy on this occasion were the Insubres, from

Cisalpine Gaul, but they had allies from further afield. Propertius here speaks of the enemy as coming from beyond or near the Rhine and of Virdomarus as a *Belga*; in so doing he may be simply indulging his poetic imagination.

Rheno traiectos: 'who had crossed the Rhine', i.e. coming from beyond the Rhine: the ablative of the river crossed, with *traicio*, is a regular construction in Livy. [The MSS. have *Claudius a Rheno*. But the conjecture *at* gives a good transition from what has gone before (cf. line 23), and a relation between *Rheno* and *traiectos* which lends more point to both.]

40. cum: a not very common variety of the 'inverted' construction of *cum*. One can translate: 'and on that occasion it was that...'. [*cui* = 'by whom' has been conjectured.]

42. mobilis euectis fundere gaesa rotis: 'quick to ride forward in his chariot and throw his spears'. *euehi* is used regularly of a warrior who rides out ahead of the rest; cf. (e.g.) Liv. v, xxxvi, 7 *euectus ante aciem equo*. Though strictly *euehi* should apply to the rider or passenger, we have *euecta classis* in Liv. xxxvii, xxix, 8 and *euectae...habenae* (= *currus*) in Val. Flacc. II, 35. Thus *euectis* is a good conjecture; cf. app. crit.

[*mobilis* here is the reading of all our old MSS. Later MSS. read *nobilis*, no doubt the product of conjecture. In the context *nobilis* has rather more force than *mobilis*, and should perhaps be adopted. For this is a notable enemy (cf. *uasti...ducis, genus... Rheno...ab ipso*) and *nobilis* could be construed before *fundere* in the same way as in Hor. *Od.* I, xii, 25–7 *puerosque Ledae, hunc equis, illum superare pugnis nobilem.*]

43. illi ut uirgatis iaculans it ab agmine bracis torquis ab incisa decidit unca gula: 'as the Gaul in his striped trousers charged forward from the enemy line to throw his javelin, his throat was severed (by Claudius' stroke) and the bent torque fell from it to the ground'. Here *illi* is dative of the person affected and refers to Virdomarus. *agmine* stands where *acie* would be strictly proper, by an extension of meaning common in poetry. The Gaul wears striped garments like the Gauls depicted on Aeneas' shield at Virg. *Aen.* VIII, 660, and a torque like the Gaul killed by Manlius in Liv. VII, x. *incisa* means 'severed' as in Virg. *Aen.* III, 667, where it is used of cutting away mooring-ropes. The torque is called *unca* because it is shaped like a horse-shoe with the extremities brought close together.

[The text printed is an emended version; the MSS. give *illi uirgatis iaculantis*. This can be translated, by referring *illi* to Claudius and taking it as dative of the agent as in Sil. It. X, 28 *cadit ingens...uni turba uiro*; *ab* in *iaculantis ab agmine* has then to be given the value 'as he advanced from...', as in line 18 above it has the value 'coming from...'.]

45. condita: 'are preserved'.

causa Feretri: 'the explanation of (the name) Feretrius'.

46. omine...certo: ablative of attendant circumstance like Cic. *Phil.* I, 9 *Brutum uidi, quanto meo dolore non dico*; it is most easily rendered here in English by an apposition to the sentence, e.g. '—a sign not to be mistaken of heaven's (*or* the god's) favour'.

47. seu: 'or perhaps'.

XI

This is a funeral elegy for Cornelia, daughter of an unidentified Cornelius Scipio and Scribonia (who subsequently was married for a short time to Octavian and bore him his daughter Julia). Cornelia was wife of L. Aemilius Paullus Lepidus (consul suffectus in 34 B.C. and Censor in 22 B.C.) and mother by him of the three children mentioned here in lines 63 and 68. Her brother, who bore the same name as his father, was consul in 16 B.C.; and as it appears from lines 65–6 that Cornelia died in the same year we are able thus to infer the approximate date of the elegy's composition.

The piece is in the form of a monologue spoken by the dead woman. Its opening lines recall a familiar type of monumental epigram in which the dead person is represented as speaking from the tomb; but this conception is not long maintained. Cornelia begins by addressing her husband (1–14); then she appeals to the powers of the underworld for merciful treatment (15–28), and by way of this passes to an apologia which she imagines herself as delivering on her own behalf before the judges of the dead; this apologia formally occupies the whole of the rest of the poem (29–102), but it includes a long passage (73–98) in which she turns to exhort her husband and children to comfort one another now that she is gone. This address to her husband and children occupies the place occupied in a normal speech by the peroration, in which it was a regular practice (see Quintilian, *Inst. Or.* VI, i, 23–4) for a defendant to invoke the thought of his or her dear ones (perhaps apostrophizing them or producing them in court) in order to excite the sympathy of the judges.

For a considerable part of the elegy (lines 17–76) the evidence of *N*, normally the most reliable of our MSS., is not available, a page being lost from it at this point. It is represented by two descendants, designated μ and υ.

1. desine...urgere: he is imagined as importuning her tomb with tearful entreaties, as though these could bring her back.

3. funera: here 'the dead'; but with the verb *intrarunt* the idea of a *funeral procession* also comes to mind.

intrarunt...leges: i.e. have passed the boundary beyond which runs the writ of the infernal powers.

4. non exorato: 'the way is barred with adamant that no prayers can move'. For *non exorato* = 'inexorable' cf. *inuictus* = 'invincible'.

The construction of *stant* with the ablative is the same as in Virg. *Aen.* VI, 300 *stant lumina flamma*; *Aen.* XII, 407–8 *puluere caelum stare uident*: the translation appropriate to *stant* in each case depends on the associated words.

5–6. te licet...bibent: i.e. though the god may hear you and be inclined to mercy, the river (Styx) will remain an impassable barrier between us; and your tears will fall unheeded on its shore and disappear as quickly and ineffectually as does water dropped on sand.

6. nempe: of an undisputed fact: 'you know that...', 'be sure that...'.

7. portitor: sometimes 'toll-collector', sometimes 'ferry-man'; here the reference is to Charon, who admits the dead to Hades by ferrying them over the Styx, and the *aera* (neuter plural) is his fee.

8. obserat euersos lurida porta rogos: (?)'the wan door (of death) shuts fast on the burned-out pyre'. The text is uncertain and obscure; but the underlying conception seems to be that the pyre is a passage from this world to the underworld, in which, at a certain point, a door closes irrevocably on the departing spirit of the dead. If *euersos* (an emendation for *herbosos* or *erbosos* of the MSS.)...*rogos* is right, its meaning will be illustrated by Virg. *Aen.* VI, 226 *postquam conlapsi cineres*, or *Aen.* XI, 210–11 *maerentes altum cinerem et confusa ruebant ossa*. For the word itself cf. IV, iii, 14 *euerso...rogo*.

luridus denotes a ghastly pallor, as of a corpse, and is applied here to the door by a metaphor.

9. sic maestae cecinere tubae...: 'this the trumpet's mournful sound proclaimed'. The sounding of the trumpet was a characteristic (though not universal) feature of funeral procedure.

9–10. cum subdita nostrum detraheret lecto fax inimica caput: 'when the cruel torch lit the pyre under my bier and rent me away'. It seems easier to take *lecto* with *subdita* than with *detraheret*, and if we do this we have to supply *tibi* (or the like) with the latter. *nostrum caput = me*; cf. line 55 below, and IV, i, 84.

11. currus auorum: 'the triumphal chariot of my ancestors'. For *currus* without epithet standing for 'triumphal chariot' cf. Cic. *Fam.* XV, vi, 1 *quem currum aut quam lauream cum tua laudatione conferrem*; Lucan VIII, 810 *et currus quos egit eques*. The singular *currus* here may be a collective, or the Scipios may have used the same *currus*: a triumphal *currus* was preserved in the house of the *triumphator*. The sense in any case is 'triumphs'.

[Many here prefer to understand *currus* of the ἄρματα mentioned by Polybius VI, liii, 8 on which busts of ancestors were carried in the funeral processions of the nobility.]

12. aut famae pignora tanta meae: 'or all the certain pledges of my fame'. The words could apply to circumstances that assured her of high renown (cf. line 29 below), or that were proof of her virtue; for *fama* can mean virtue (as e.g. at I, xi, 17) as well as fame, and *pignus* can mean what proves a fact as well as what assures a promise. There is no need to fix on one meaning rather than the other here; but a reference to the virtues of the dead is usual at this point in a funeral elegy. The *pignora* could include any of the matters enumerated later, and especially will include her children, to whom the same word *pignora* (though in a somewhat different sense) is applied at line 73 below. *tanta* can (in poetry) include the sense of *tot* as well as emphasizing the value of the word to which it applies.

13. non minus immitis: 'no less stern for that...'.

15. damnatae: the word includes the ideas 'hateful', 'doomed' and 'full of anguish'.

noctes: the plural may be purely 'poetic' (perhaps influenced by *tenebrae*); but it may have a certain value, suggesting 'regions of the dark'.

16. implicat unda pedes: the phrase combines two ideas, illustrated by Virg. *Aen.* VI, 439 *Styx interfusa coercet* and Cat. LXV, 5–6 *Lethaeo gurgite manans...alluit unda pedem.*

17. immatura licet...tamen...: the point is that premature death may be brought upon one by one's own misdeeds.

18. det Pater hic umbrae mollia iura meae: i.e. 'may *Dis pater* deal gently with my shade'. *iura dare* is said sometimes of law-giving (cf. Virg. *Aen.* III, 137 *iura domosque dabam*), sometimes of dispensing justice (cf. the passages cited on ix, 64 above, and Ov. *Fast.* II, 492 *forte tuis illic, Romule, iura dabas*).

19. aut: or if, as we are sometimes told (as for instance in the myth at the end of Plato's *Gorgias*), there are stern judges in the underworld whose judgement all must undergo....

uindex sedet Aeacus: 'an avenging Aeacus sits in judgement', or, 'an Aeacus sits in judgement to punish sinners'. *sedeo* can be said absolutely of someone who 'sits' as judge, presiding magistrate, etc. in a law-court: cf. (e.g.) Cic. *Rosc. Am.* 153 *si idcirco sedetis ut....* For *uindex* cf. Hor. *Od.* IV, ix, 34–44 where the *animus* of a magistrate exercising judicial functions is said to be *uindex auarae fraudis.*

[*uindex* here is a conjecture for *iudex* of the MSS. *iudex* can hardly stand, with *iudicet* in the next line; and *iudicet* in the next line does not invite alteration, because it gives exactly the sense required by its context.]

posita urna: 'with urn at hand'. See next note for the point of this.

20. in mea...iudicet ossa: i.e. *sedeat iudex in...* ; for which expression cf. Cic. *Cluent.* 105 *sedissentne iudices in C. Fabricium.* Here *iudicare* is intransitive and means 'act as a *iudex*' just as *militare* means 'serve as a *miles*' and just as it is used in Hor. *Od.* II, xiii, 21–2 *quam paene...iudicantem uidimus Aeacum.* The subjunctive in *iudicet* expresses not so much wish as willingness, i.e. it is jussive–permissive; she means 'let him by all means...I am not afraid'. She is ready to face the judges because she is confident in her virtue. For *ossa* = 'shade' cf. 102 below.

sortita...pila: 'when my lot is drawn', i.e. 'when my case comes up'. Here *sortita* is passive, though *sortior* is deponent. *pilae* are balls used for drawing as lots after being shaken in an urn; here they serve to determine which case is to be taken next. For this practice cf. Servius on *Aen.* VI, 432 *non enim audiebantur causae nisi per sortem ordinatae*; and (in the light of this) Virg.

Aen. VI, 432 *quaesitor Minos urnam mouet*; Seneca, *Ag.* 24 *quaesitor urna Gnosius uersat reos*; Horace, *Od.* III, i, 14 *aequa lege Necessitas sortitur insignes et imos; omne capax mouet urna nomen*, where the meaning is 'all alike will come up for judgement in the end'. The *urna* of line 19 is for use in the process just described, not for collecting the votes of jurors; there is no jury in the picture here, only a judge, or judges.

[It would be possible to construe *in mea...ossa* with *sortita... pila* = 'when my ghost's turn for trial comes up'. So construing, F. H. Sandbach in *C.R.* (1962), pp. 274–5 reads *uindicet* in this line (supplying *mea ossa* or *me* as object), and retains *iudex* in line 19. For *uindico* = (?)'discharge with honour' he compares *absolutus uindicatusque* in Pliny, *Ep.* IV, ix, 1 and VI, xxxi, 3. On this view Cornelia is asking for acquittal rather than declaring her readiness to be tried.]

21–2. assideant fratres, iuxta Minoia sella, et Eumenidum intento turba seuera foro: (?)'let the brothers sit as counsellors with him, the chair of Minos next to his, with the grim Furies (standing guard), and all around attentive to the scene'. If this is right, Rhadamanthus and Minos are 'assessors': see next note; but see also bracketed note below.

assideo is said regularly of friends, colleagues or experts who sit on the tribunal of a magistrate exercising judicial functions and may be consulted before he gives his decision; there is in all this passage a blending of the practices of Roman courts with the picture current in Greek mythology and literature of the three judges in the underworld, Minos and his brother Rhadamanthus and their half-brother Aeacus.

iuxta Minoia sella is (I think) a kind of apposition to *fratres*, Minos being one of them; Minos as senior has his *sella* next to that of the officiating judge; *iuxta* is a regular word in this context, cf. Sall. *Jug.* 65, 2 *ut sellam iuxta poneret*; in Plato, *Gorgias* 524 A and 526 C Minos is described as superintending the work of the other two and deciding the exceptionally difficult cases.

et Eumenidum...turba seuera: the position of *et* as last word of the line is unparalleled but not in itself more difficult to accept than II, xxv, 17 *amor, qui | restat*. With *turba* we have to understand a verb (such as *adsit*) out of *assideant*; for other such ellipses cf. III, v, 41, III, xvii, 37, etc.

intento...foro gives the setting of the whole scene; by *forum* is implied an open space of some extent in which a variety of business is being transacted, so that 'court' would be here a misleading translation.

[If *assideo* can = *assido* = 'take one's seat', or if we read *assidant*, an alternative rendering of line 21 is possible: 'let the brothers (i.e. Aeacus and Rhadamanthus) take their places, with Minos sitting by...'. The picture is then as in Plato, *Gorgias*, 524 A and 526 C, with Aeacus and Rhadamanthus the working judges and Minos superintending in reserve; and there is no thought of a Roman magistrate with 'assessors'.]

23. mole uaces: 'rest from the huge stone (you roll)'.

24. Tantaleus: for this adjective cf. II, xvii, 5 *Tantaleā...ad flumina sorte*; for the two adjectives together cf. II, xxxiv, 35–6 *fallax Maeandria...unda*.

[*Tantaleus* is an emendation; the MSS. have *Tantaleo*.]

26. tacita...sera: apparently the watchdog is chained to the bar (*sera*) set across the door, so that his chain rattles on it when he bounds about in his normal state of activity.

27. poena sororum: in apposition to *infelix...urna*. This is the punishment of the Danaids, who had to work eternally to fill a vessel with holes in it; the *urna* is the water-jar in which the Danaid carries, on her shoulder, the water she draws for this purpose.

29–30. si cui fama...auos: i.e. 'if ever anyone had claim to fame on account of the triumphs of their forebears, that honour is mine; for the land of Africa bears witness of my ancestors, to whom Numantia (also) gave its name'. The highly compressed statement in the pentameter refers to the two Scipios who earned the title Africanus, and to the fact that the younger of them also earned the title Numantinus.

31. altera...Libones: 'and not less noble is that other line (*literally* band) the Libones from whom my mother sprung'.

32. et domus est...suis: 'and each house alike has its own proud record of achievements to uphold its glory'. The *tituli* strictly are the inscriptions under the statues or busts of members of the family, recording their deeds; then the word comes to stand more generally for 'achievements', 'honours', etc.

33. praetexta: the *toga praetexta*, purple-bordered, and worn by well-born children of both sexes, as well as by adults who had held curule magistracies.

facibus maritis: the torches that light the bride to her husband's house; cf. on IV, iii, 13 above.

34. altera uitta: a *uitta* was part of the coiffure of a bride; cf. IV, iii, 16. Apparently, a *uitta* was also worn by unmarried girls, for cf. Val. Flacc. VIII, 6, where Medea about to flee with Jason *ultima uirgineis tum flens dedit oscula uittis*. It is not clear how they differed; but this appears to be the point of *altera* here.

acceptas: perhaps because *capere crines* was the term for adopting the style of hair arrangement proper to a married woman.

36. in lapide hoc: cf. introductory note above; in lines 1, 2 we seem to be actually at the tomb, and it is possible that this whole elegy was inscribed on it.

37. testor: the statement of which she is here asserting the truth begins in line 41 below.

38. sub quorum titulis...tunsa iaces: 'beneath whose glory Africa lies stricken'. The thought behind this is of a monument (or perhaps of a picture, such as were carried in triumphal processions), with a proud inscription, and a figure representing the conquered country. [*tonsa*, the conjecture of renaissance scholars for *tunsa*, may well be right; it would mean 'with shorn head' (in sign of mourning).]

39–40. †et Persen...domos†: the text of this probably corrupt couplet is here printed as it is given in the MS. tradition. The reference, in the hexameter at least, is to the conquest of Perses of Macedon, proud of his supposed descent from Achilles through his grandmother (a daughter of Pyrrhus of Epirus), by the great Aemilius Paullus; who figured among the *maiores* both of Cornelia's husband and of Cornelia herself, since he was true father of the younger P. Cornelius Scipio Africanus. The main difficulties about the text are (*a*) that Cornelia appears to invoke as witness to *her virtue* (not to her forebears' glory, which would be another matter) the beaten enemy of Rome; and (*b*) that *tuas* in the pentameter resists interpretation or correction. Of these, (*a*) might perhaps be resolved by taking *et Persen...quique...* as = *et eum qui Persen...et....* For conjectures and discussion reference must be made to larger editions.

A subsidiary question, concerning the hexameter, is whether we should read with the late MSS. *simulantem*, i.e. 'aping the proud spirit of his ancestor Achilles', or with Lipsius *proauo stimulantem pectus Achille*, i.e. 'whetting his (own) spirit with the thought that Achilles was his ancestor'. The latter of these is suggested by seeming echoes in Silius Italicus (both referring to Perses' father Philip): xv, 291 *proauoque tumebat Achille*, and xiv, 93–5 *materna furori Pyrrhus origo dabat stimulos proauique superbum Aeacidae genus atque aeternus carmine Achilles*. But if Silius (who is anyway very fond of *stimulo, stimulus*, etc.) did read *stimulantem* in our line, we cannot be sure he read it right. The MS. tradition's *Achilli* is a correct Latin genitive of *Achilles*; cf. Quint. *Inst. Or.* I, v, 63.

41. mollisse: an unusual use of the word, presumably meaning (with a reference to the fact that Cornelia's husband was censor in 22 B.C.) 'weakened'; a censor's severity in propounding or enforcing rules of moral conduct would be weakened by moral failings in his own family.

42. uestros: referring to the ancestors to whom she has appealed.

focos: 'house', the hearth standing as symbol of the family.

44. et...pars imitanda...: she too, like her great forebears, was an example to others.

45. nec mea mutata est aetas: i.e. it did not begin well and then deteriorate.

46. utramque facem: the torches of the bridal procession, and the torch that lit the funeral pyre.

47. leges a sanguine ductas: i.e. rules of conduct derived from her inbred virtue, for her as binding as laws in the ordinary sense, and as strict.

48. ne possis: 'so that no fear of judgement could make a woman more virtuous (than I was)'. The ideal second person has the value of our impersonal 'one'. The subjunctive is a potential subjunctive standing in its own right ('one could not be...'), as well as a final subjunctive required by *ne*. We should think a consecutive construction (*ut non...*) more natural, but the distinction between consequence and intention is not always strictly observed, and indeed sometimes in Latin the final form is preferred deliberately as a figure of style where no purpose or intention is present: e.g. in Ov. *A.A.* I, 428, where the man says he has no money and the woman replies that a note of hand will do, *ne didicisse iuuet*, we are being given the poet's comment ('so that you wish you'd never learned to write'), not the woman's motive in making her remark.

49. urna: not this time as in line 19 (see note on line 20), but the voting urn used in trial by jury. The conception has shifted and the poet is now thinking in terms of Roman procedure: cf. note on lines 21–2.

quaelibet austeras...ferat urna tabellas: she does not fear the judgement, though exacting, of any jury in the world.

50. assessu: the 'assessors' this time are not as in line 21, but friends of the defendant who sat by him or her during a Roman trial, and would share the shame of a conviction; cf. Cic. *Planc.* 28 (*principes Macedoniae*) *huic adsident, pro hoc laborant*.

51–3. uel tu...uel cui...: not 'either... or...', but 'you, for instance,... or she for whom'.... For the first *uel* cf. Virg. *Ecl.* III, 50 *audiat haec tantum uel qui uenit ecce Palaemon*.

51–2. quae mouisti...Cybeben, Claudia: when the Magna Mater (Cybĕle or Cybēbe) was brought to Rome in 205 B.C. the ship carrying her went aground in the Tiber. The Claudia here mentioned drew it off, having prayed that this might be proof of her chastity: she had been suspected of loose living. (See Suet. *Tib.* II and Ov. *Fast.* IV, 305 ff.) [Perhaps *Cybēlen* or *Cybellen* should be read here; cf. on IV, vii, 61 above.]

turritae: referring to the mural crown with which Cybele was regularly represented.

rara: 'peerless'.

53–4. uel cui, iusta suos...focos: a Vestal named Aemilia left one of her juniors in charge of the Vestal fire, and it went out. (This was normally taken as evidence that the Vestal responsible had been unchaste.) Aemilia prayed to the goddess to help her if she were innocent, and laid on the hearth a linen garment (or a piece of her linen garment); whereupon the fire blazed up; see Dion. H. II, lxviii and Val. Max. I, i, 7.

iusta: Vesta can be here so called because as a mistress she is fair, and so kind, if firm; cf. phrases such as *iusta et clemens seruitus*.

reposceret: i.e. called her to account for the fire that was in her charge. *reposco* is said of asking for the return of something entrusted to another, and so of calling another to account, or complaining indignantly of a loss.

[*uel cui, iusta suos* is a conjecture for *uel cuius iasos* or *uel cuius rasos* of the MSS. A possibly preferable conjecture is *uel cuius, sacros*.]

57–8. laudor...defensa: i.e. their grief is proof of her virtue.

59–60. ille...uixisse...increpat: 'he complains that one

has died who was a worthy sister of his own daughter'. Cornelia
and Julia were actually half-sisters; see introductory note above.
For *increpo* = 'complain that' cf. III, x, 10 *increpet absumptum
nec sua mater Ityn*. Obviously Caesar would not complain that
she had lived a life worthy of his daughter, so *uixisse* here must
mean 'has died' (i.e. has finished her life), as often.

60. deo: i.e. Augustus; cf. III, iv, 1 *arma deus Caesar...
meditatur.*

61. tamen: i.e. though I died, it was not before I had
accomplished something.

generosos uestis honores: we do not know exactly what is
meant by this. But reading what follows (lines 62, 63 and 67) in
conjunction with Dio Cassius' statement (LV, 2) that Livia (in
9 B.C.) 'was given the status of a mother who had born three
children', we can infer that the reference is to such a status and
to privileges attaching to it. These privileges appear, from the
terms of this line, to have included some kind of dress. *generosos*
(which usually refers to high birth) must here bear a sense indicating abundance of offspring, natural enough from its form,
though not exemplified elsewhere in classical Latin (unless at
Virg. *Aen.* x, 174 *insula...generosa metallis*, where Servius
(Auct.) glosses with πολύγονος). *uestis honores* (poetic plural)
means an honour consisting in a certain kind of dress; the
epithet *generosos* ('transferred' from person to honour) tells how
the honour in question was earned. The effect of the whole line
(including *tamen*) is: 'But I have this comfort. I earned the dress
of honour that marks the mother of many children'.

63. tu...tu: this is the reading of the later MSS., no doubt a
product of emendation; the older MSS. have *te...te*. [If we
prefer to keep *te...te*, we have to understand the accusatives as
due to the sense 'I bore children' which is *implied* in the preceding couplet.]

**65–6. uidimus et fratrem sellam geminasse curulem;
consule quo...:** this reference, parenthetic as it were, to her
brother's consulship comes rather strangely between the mention
of her sons and that of her daughter in a passage (61–74) that is
otherwise wholly concerned with her children. On the other
hand by supplying a further item of consolation it fits with the
feeling of line 61 (cf. *tamen*) and line 63 (cf. *leuamen*), whereas a
new note is struck in the exhortation to the daughter in lines
67–8. Nor is there any other natural place for it in the elegy.

65. sellam geminasse curulem: she saw him attain a second time to the curule chair, i.e. to curule office, presumably by becoming consul, after previously being praetor.

66. consule quo, festo tempore, rapta soror: here *festo* is a far from certain conjecture for *facto* of the MSS. The sentence as printed means that his sister was carried off by death at the (very) time of the celebrations that attended his entering office: cf. Ov. *Pont.* IV, ix, 56 *hic quoque te festum consule tempus agam*. [I have wondered whether to read *paruo tempore* = when he had been consul only a short while. For the phrase cf. Ov. *Met.* VI, 442 and VII, 300 *tempore...paruo*; and for the metrical position cf. Ov. *Fast.* III, 682 and VI, 670 *longo tempore*.]

67. filia, tu specimen censurae nata paternae: i.e. 'you, my daughter, born in your father's censorship, a worthy token of his office...'. *specimen* is an example or sample, or in some contexts a mark of distinction or ornament. What is here spoken of is the birth of the girl, not her virtues, for in 16 B.C. she was only six years old. Her birth marked her father's term of office as censor fittingly, because parenthood in lawful and stable wedlock was something which a censor recommended as a duty to the citizens and ought to exemplify himself.

69. serie: by carrying on the line.

cumba: the boat that carries the shades of the dead across the Styx.

70. aucturis tot mea fata meis: 'when there are so many of mine in whose lives my own life will be prolonged'. For *fata* = 'life' (i.e. allotted span) cf. Ov. *Trist.* V, v, 62 *aequarint Pylios cum tua fata dies*; Sil. *It.* xv, 549 *si patriae uis addere fata*. For *augeo* of extending life cf. Ov. *Fast.* I, 613 *(Iuppiter) nostri ducis augeat annos*.

[*aucturis* and *meis* are emendations, for *uncturis* and *malis* of the MSS. Some go further and change *fata* into *facta*, translating *aucturis mea facta* as 'to magnify my deeds'; but *facta* does not seem appropriate to the domestic virtues of a Roman woman.]

71. haec est feminei merces extrema triumphi: i.e. 'this is the highest reward a woman can win, a woman's triumph'. The genitive *feminei...triumphi* is a genitive of definition, most easily rendered here in English by an apposition. The expression is a very strong one indeed, and it comes as climax to Cornelia's recital of her virtues and achievement. *haec*

163

is explained by the clause introduced by *ubi* in the next line; for the temporal conjunction introducing a substantive clause cf. II, iii, 19, where *Aeolio cum temptat carmina plectro* is parallel to the preceding *quod...formose saltat* and both are subjects of *me cepit* inferred from earlier in the construction; also Sil. It. XIII, 664 *dulce tamen uenit ad Manes, cum gloria uitae durat apud superos nec edunt obliuia laudem*.

72. laudat ubi emeritum libera fama rogum: here the *rogus* (pyre) stands for 'the dead', i.e. the dead person, much as *cinis* does elsewhere. *emeritus* could be either transitive 'having deserved (the praise)', or intransitive 'after a life well lived' (as a soldier is said to be *emeritus* when he has served his time out with honour). The words *laudat...libera fama* have been taken in two quite different senses. (*a*) 'public report, now free of fear or favour, praises her (after she is dead)'. This is the easy and obvious meaning of the words in themselves. In the context, it is less satisfactory. For such commendation is not in any *special* way appropriate to women. Nor is it remarkable enough to justify the extremely strong terms of line 71. Nor is *libera* helpful to the meaning, or even true, for *fama* notoriously is just as outspoken in regard to the living as to the dead; contrast the positive value of the expression *libera fama* in Ov. *Met.* XV, 853 where it is said that though Augustus prefers the merits of Julius Caesar to his own, nevertheless public report, which is free and cannot be commanded, insists that Augustus' achievements are the greater. (*b*) 'renown through (*or* of) her children brings honour to her ashes'. This might indeed seem to a Roman a woman's supreme reward, and so gives precisely the sense required by line 71; but it is not the obvious meaning of the Latin. However, for *laudo* = 'bring honour to' cf. the use of *laudor* in line 57 above, and Mart. XIV, clv *uelleribus primis Apulia, Parma secundis nobilis; Altinum tertia laudat ouis*. For the short form of *libera* as adjective of *liberi* cf. II, xxxi, 4 *femina turba*; IV, iii, 64 *carbasa lina*. For the value required for the adjective ('on account of', etc.) cf. IV, vii, 65 *maternis...catenis* = 'the bonds she endured on her mother's account'; II, xxxii, 21 *famae...pudicae* = 'your name for modesty'. For phrases in Propertius which acquire in their contexts meanings other than those which they would normally bear out of these contexts cf. on IV, iv, 94. For the sentiment (without, in these cases, special reference to the mother) cf. Lucr. VI, 13 *bona gnatorum excellere* *fama*; Quint. *Inst. Or.* III, vii, 18 *afferunt laudem liberi parentibus, urbes conditoribus, leges latoribus*, etc.

73. tibi: with a certain emphasis, for she now turns to address her husband; at line 85 she will address her children. This is all an example of the rhetorical artifice called apostrophe; in conclusion at line 99 she turns again to the court. The rhetorical artifice is adapted by the poet to his own purpose, for of course the pathos of the appeal to husband and children is really intended for the reader, not the imaginary court. See also the introductory note above.

74. haec cura et cineri spirat inusta meo: i.e. this care lives on in me, indelible, even beyond the pyre. *inurere* is used both of branding and of fixing colours by heat; there is a mixture of metaphors here with *spirat*, for which in the sense 'lives on' cf. Hor. *Od.* IV, ix, 10 *spirat adhuc amor uiuuntque...calores*, etc.

79. sine testibus illis: for the ellipse of the verb cf. III, xxi, 33 *seu moriar, fato, non turpi fractus amore*.

80. siccis oscula falle genis: i.e. 'see that no tears on your cheeks betray your grief to their kisses'.

81-2. sat tibi sint noctes, quas de me, Paulle, fatiges: 'for mourning of me let the nights suffice you—then you can mourn without respite—and the dreams in which, often, you seem to see my face (*or* likeness)'. *fatigare* is said as if he importuned the darkness or the hours of night with his lamentations. The *somnia* are said to be *credita in faciem meam* because (*a*) they assume (cf. constructions such as *formantur in...*) her shape, and then (*b*) this shape is believed to be really hers.

84. ut responsurae singula uerba iace: 'speak always as to one who will reply'. For *iacio* = 'utter' cf. II, i, 77 *talia... mutae iace uerba fauillae*, IV, ix, 32 *et iacit ante fores uerba minora deo*. By *singula uerba* is meant of course not every individual *uerbum* but every separate set of *uerba*, i.e. every utterance.

85. seu tamen aduersum mutarit ianua lectum: 'but if a new bed is spread opposite the house-door'. The symbolic *lectus genialis* stood in the *atrium* facing the entrance door of the house; it would be spread anew (or replaced by a new bed; we do not know which) when a widower married again; for *mutare lectum* = 'spread anew' cf. IV, viii, 87 above. *tamen* implies 'despite his affection for me and present grief'.

ianua is subject of *mutarit* either by the form of expression discussed in the note on IV, vi, 25 above, or because of the special sense of *muto* 'change (something belonging to one)' or 'exchange', i.e. 'get a new one'.

86. cauta: 'careful'; she is uneasy and on her guard at first.

sederit: (?) 'takes possession of'.

88. dabit...manus: 'will...surrender'.

uestris moribus: (kind) behaviour, i.e. kindness; cf. line 101 below where *moribus* = 'virtue'. The case may be ablative with *capta*, or dative with *dabit manus*; in effect *moribus* acts as both.

90. libera uerba: here 'unguarded', a sense easily extracted from the common meaning 'frank', 'outspoken', etc.

92. tanti cineres duxerit esse meos: i.e. counts me so dear even in death. *tanti* is genitive of value, cf. IV, iii, 63.

93. sentire: 'realize', 'be aware'; cf. Ov. *A.A.* III, 59 *uenturae memores iam nunc estote senectae.*

94. uacet: *uacare* is commonly used of a space being empty (and so accessible), and its use here with *uia* follows easily from that.

96. prole mea Paullum sic iuuet esse senem: 'thus may Paullus be happy in old age because of my children'. *sic* means 'if you take care of your father (93–4) and are spared to keep him company (95)'. The ablative in *prole mea* may be of cause (cf. II, iv, 21 *uno...uerbo*), or attendant circumstances (cf. III, xxii, 13 *Argoa...columba*), or due to the idea 'take pleasure (in)' that can be extracted from the context.

97. bene habet: 'it is well'; so also *sic habet* = 'it is so'.

lugubria: 'mourning dress' (neut. pl.).

99. causa perorata est: here she resumes (in order to conclude it) her direct address to the court.

testes: perhaps her husband and children, perhaps her ancestors. We must not expect a consistent or realistically plausible picture of the scene. However improbably, her husband and children are addressed as if present at 73 ff. and 87 ff.

100. dum: either 'while' or 'until' the verdict is delivered.

grata: she anticipates that by a favourable verdict the earth, on which she lived, and in whose realm she now is (for the semi-identification of earth with the powers of the underworld cf. I, xix, 16), will be 'grateful for' (i.e. appreciative of) her conduct in life. One might translate '...acknowledges and rewards (the innocence of) my life'.

101. moribus et caelum patuit: 'some for their virtue have been admitted even to heaven'. The qualification 'good' has to be understood here with *moribus*, as has the qualification 'kind' in line 88 above; cf. notes on IV, iii, 19–20 and IV, vii, 10. There is an important emphasis on *et*: some (e.g. Hercules) for their virtue have been given much more than she is asking for herself, hence she asks with confidence.

sim digna: 'may I be (judged) worthy'; for the opinion put as a statement of fact cf. IV, iv, 83.

merendo: 'through merit'.

102. cuius honoratis...aquis: 'that my shade should cross the river by the way of honour'. The conception has shifted (not surprisingly; cf. note on IV, vii, 87) since line 16, for the word *uehantur* can only refer to conveyance by ferry over the infernal river as does *uehit* in IV, vii, 57. In that passage of Elegy vii the good and the bad are conceived as crossing the river by separate ferries (*diuersa...aqua*) leading to their respective destinations. Assuming the same conception here the *honoratae aquae* will correspond to one of these two ways over the river; for the epithet *honoratus* in the sense required cf. Tac. *Ann.* II, 63 *tutam honoratamque sedem*, etc. For *ossa* = 'shade' cf. line 20 above and on IV, v, 4 and IV, vii, 94.

[Many editors prefer the conjecture *auis*, giving the meaning 'that my shade should be conveyed (i.e. across the river) to join my noble forebears (i.e. in the abode of the blest)'. A similar phrase is in fact found in the *Consolatio ad Liuiam*, which echoes this elegy in several places, at line 330 *inter honoratos excipietur auos*; but the author of the *Consolatio* may as well be modifying as reproducing the expression of his predecessor.]